NECRONO...

BOOK TWO

Necronomicon Book Two
Edited by: Andy Black
ISBN 1 871592 38 0
© Andy Black and all contributors 1998, all rights reserved.
First published 1998 by:
Creation Books
Copyright © Creation Books 1998
Necronomicon – a periodical publication.
Design/layout/typesetting:
PCP International, Bradley Davis.
Photos from BFI Stills, Redemption Films; all additional visual material taken from the Jack Hunter Collection.
Cover photo:
Female Vampire, Jesus Franco.
By courtesy of Redemption Films/Jesus Franco.

"Abnormal Ward" by Jack Hunter is taken from *Eros In Hell: Sex, Blood & Madness In Japanese Cinema* (Creation Cinema Collection #9), published by Creation Books, 1998.

Mikita Brottman is the author of *Meat Is Murder!* (Creation Cinema Collection #8), published by Creation Books.

Xavier Mendik is a Lecturer in Media with Cultural Studies at Southampton Institute of Higher Education, whose research specialism is psychoanalysis and European horror cinema. He is currently completing a book on the films of Joe D'Amato and Italian exploitation movies, to be published by Creation Books. "Perverse Bodies, Profane Texts" is part of a longer examination of directors such as Franco through de Sade and psychoanalysis, to be contained in Xavier Mendik and Graeme Harper's book *Violated Bodies*, a forthcoming Creation Books publication.

Bev Zalcock is the author of *Renegade Sisters: Girl Gangs On Film* (Creation Cinema Collection #11), published by Creation Books, 1998.

Julian Hoxter is an independent filmmaker and a Senior Lecturer in Media with Cultural Studies in the Media Arts Faculty of Southampton Institute. He is currently researching into the implications of Kleinian and Post-Kleinian psychoanalysis for the study of film.

Editor's Acknowledgements
As always, almost too many people to mention; but special thanks to all of my contributors, especially Xavier Mendik for help above and beyond the call of duty, Jess Franco and Lina Romay, Beth and Richard at Media Communications, Michael Donovan, James Williamson and Laurie at Creation, and again, the love and support of my wife Caroline and my sons (future Villa strike force perhaps?) Aaron and Alex.

British Library Cataloguing in Publication Data:
A catalogue record for this book is available from the British Library

CONTENTS

CONTENTS

FOREWORD

So, here we go again with *Necronomicon* Book Two and a sense of *déjà vu* as this 'annual' tome appears some *two* years after the first seminal book – oh well, *c'est la vie*. Book One appears to have engendered a strictly divided critical reception comprised simply of those who loved it and those who loathed it. Whatever view you take, in this second volume there can be no argument that the reach *Necronomicon* strives for is as eclectic as ever, combining the arcane with the progressive.

To this end, boundaries are stretched (as well as lingerie!) via Stephanie Watson and Jack Sargeant's revival of one of Russ Meyer's most interesting but neglected films, **Mudhoney**, Matthew Coniam gives deserved attention to Walerian Borowczyk's early *oeuvre*, and tales of nazi sexploitation are frogmarched towards us by Omayra Cruz.

If that isn't enough to satiate jaded appetites, then how about Mikita Brottman's revelatory piece on the correlation between the infamous Manson murders and Roman Polanski's resultant filmic outpouring of emotion, **Macbeth**?

Add to this Jack Hunter's discovery of Eastern promise in the unique Japanese Pink film industry, and Julian Hoxter's groundbreaking introduction of Kleinian theory into the horror genre, in this case Dario Argento's rather abruptly dismissed (critically) **The Stendhal Syndrome**.

I'm also delighted to be able to redress an imbalance from Book One – namely, no mention of the mercurial Jesus Franco. Xavier Mendik's exhaustive work again covers hitherto uncharted territory by discussing the Sadeian influence present within Franco's work, as well as his formative influences such as Orson Welles and Jean-Luc Godard.

The eagle-eyed amongst you will notice how the superior **Seven** and **Nightwatch** have made the transition from the foreword in Book One to warrant fully-fledged articles in Book Two. Well, no clues for Book Three, but the current horror genre revival *is* encouraging, with signs of longevity this time fuelled by the convoluted but captivating **Scream**, which does the impossible by breathing life into the moribund corpse known as the slasher film. In addition, and even more surprising considering the major budgets but missed opportunities of Hollywood's gothic "revival" via Francis Ford Coppola's **Bram Stoker's Dracula** and Kenneth Branagh's **Mary Shelley's Frankenstein**, is the verve and splendour of Sergio Stivaletti's period horror, **Wax Mask**. I was blown away by the convincing performances, loving attention to period detail and an audacious, sci-fi themed denouement which may yet revitalise the Italian (and European) horror industry. (You now know how Book Three is shaping up !)

Given this general air of optimism I'd also like to bang the drum for the new(ish) technologies for viewing films, in laserdisc and DVD. Having only recently become a laser convert I can't recommend the format enough! The opportunity to see classic films in the correct aspect ratios, uncut and with exemplary picture and sound quality is simply too good to be missed. Whether it's Tangerine Dream's rippling synthesisers in **The Keep**, the restored scenes and rich strings of **The Private Life Of Sherlock Holmes** or the snowbound lyricism of **Dance Of The Vampires** – 'disc is here for keeps!

—**Andy Black** (March 1997)

PERVERSE BODIES, PROFANE TEXTS

Processes Of Sadeian "Mixture"
In The Films Of Jesus Franco

Xavier Mendik

"Sexual compulsions are part of the tragic limited fallible condition of man... doomed to endless repetitions that can never satisfy the ideal images of the spirit. There is nothing that reminds man of his precarious metaphysical situation than sex and it is not surprising that 'death' 'dying' and 'little death' should be words for orgasm both in English and in other European languages."[1]

According to Maurice Charney, the connection between sexuality and death evident in a distinct tradition in European philosophy can be traced from the work of the Marquis de Sade to the later theorists such as Freud. In his formulation of the concept of the death drive,[2] Freud retraces the connections between an excess of sexuality and annihilation identified in Sadeian works such as *The One Hundred And Twenty Days Of Sodom* (1785), *Justine* (1791), *Juliette* (1797) and *Philosophy In The Boudoir* (1795).

According to Freud's analysis, the unrepressed tensions which dominate infantile sexuality re-emerge in later life to retard sexual fulfilment and the secure construction of gender identity. This obsession with the traumas of infancy functions through a form of 'compulsive repetition'. This conflates images of sexual pleasure with those of death or impending mutilation which the sufferer continually fears. (Its effect was seen in Freud's patients such as the 'Wolf Man', who found his adult sexuality dominated by repeated and revised scenes of his discovery of a violent act of parental coitus during childhood).[3]

What this close connection between Sade and Freud reveals, is both the construction of human subjectivity through excessive sexual drives as well as the direction of these forms of gratification towards scenarios of annihilation and chaos. In this respect, they provide a useful template to consider the cinematic interests that have marked the phenomenal output of the Spanish fantasy director Jesus Franco. Arguably Franco's interests reflect his self-confessed interest with de Sade and the reformulation of his ideas in both European philosophy and aesthetics.[4]

What the article intends to do is to indicate that the importance of Sade's work extends beyond Franco's literal interpretation of his writings in films such as **Justine** (1968). Rather what it indicates is a systematic combination of images of sexuality, torture and death with an equally chaotic film style that has often bemused his admirers and detractors alike.[5] What I shall argue is that it is not only the uncompromising content of Franco's work which warrants his definition as a Sadeian director, but also the preoccupation with generic deviation and narrative repetition which mark this influence on his film style.

For instance, although Franco's work has varied in content and spanned genres as diverse as horror, pornography, action adventure and historical drama, all share the preoccupation with the sexuality and death that Charney argues defines Sade's interests. The close connection between these physiological states is perfectly defined by two of his most controversial 1970s productions: **The Female Vampire** (1973) and **Doriana Gray** (1975).

Female Vampire

In **The Female Vampire**, Franco's long time partner and filmic collaborator Lina Romay is cast as the vampire Irina Karlstein who seduces a series of male and female partners before killing them at the point of sexual climax. In a marked departure from established cinematic traditions of the vampire, the source of Irina's oral gratifications is the genitals rather than the necks of potential victims. Indeed, the film reiterates its basis in writings such as *The One Hundred And Twenty Days Of Sodom* via its staging of a sado-masochistic stage act which Irene visits. The construction of the sexual act as a site of both punishment and public consumption (evident in this scene and in many other Franco films)[6] confirms Charney's conclusion that in Sade, sexual pleasure is not only equated with annihilation but replaced by principles of pain and oppression.

If the heroine's obsession underscores **The Female Vampire**'s examination of the links between orgasm and death, then this theme is confirmed by the ending of the film. Here, Karlstein commits suicide in remorse at her excessive sexual drives resulting in the accidental death of her lover, played by Franco regular Jack Taylor. Irina's demise once again conflates the sexual with destruction. As she bathes in a pool of blood, her body writhes in the uncontrollable spasm of the death throes. This indicates that both death and the sex act involve a 'kind of epileptic fit or temporary seizure'.[7]

In the later **Doriana Gray**, the connection between orgasm and death is split between two characters (once again played by Romay). While Doriana takes pleasure in seducing her victims before dispatching them with a similar oral sadism to Irina Karlstein, her twin experiences the displeasure that accompanies these death throes. In this respect:

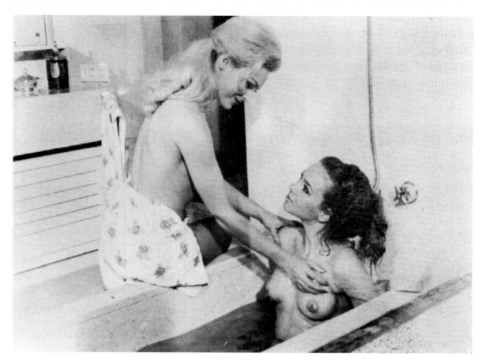

Philosophy In The Boudoir

"Doriana is a film of climaxes. Romay squirms in a fever, seducing everyone with her lust-engorged body. As usual, she's bisexual, who kills with her tongue, bringing her lovers to ecstasy and death."[8]

While Doriana's existence and youth are predicated on these erotic (and ultimately fatalistic) encounters, her twin suffers isolation, as well as a physical decline. As with **The Female Vampire** the eventual fusion of sexual and death drives results in the destruction of both female agents after Doriana literally masturbates herself into annihilation in the film's closing stages.

In her influential book *Creativity And Perversion*, Janine Chasseguet-Smirgel has argued that the interest in sexual annihilation that marks Sade's work is one of many transgressive forms of 'mixture' which dominated the writer's narratives. According to her analysis, works such as *The One Hundred And Twenty Days Of Sodom*, *Justine* and *Philosophy In The Boudoir* are governed by a transgressive drive towards the dissolution of established forms:

"All will be higgledy-piggledy, all will wallow on the flagstones, on the earth, and like animals will interchange, will mix will commit incest adultery and sodomy."[9]

As the above quotation from *The One Hundred And Twenty Days Of Sodom* indicates, Sade's interest is seen not only in collapsing the boundary between orgasm and death, but also other crucial social and psychic boundaries. Chasseguet-Smirgel identifies these

The Awful Dr Orlof

as including the dissolution of the barriers separating man from woman, adult from child, as well as one erotic zone from another. An example of Sade's policy is what she terms as a confusion between 'gender and generations' in his works.

This relocation of sexuality within the familial (as well as the disorder and chaos that inevitably emerges from such encounters) pre-empts some of Freud's comments on the destructive capacities of the infant's sexual urges. It is the dissolution of such boundaries that affect not only the content but also the *structure* of the narrative, which in Sade, shifts to accommodate the bodies altered mode of sexual display.[10]

For instance, his frequent construction of sexuality as a site of public performance and contemplation robs the act not only of intimations of privacy and emotion but translates eroticism into a group activity "in which protagonists build up extremely complex positions which are then unmade and transformed"[11]. Evidence of the processes of transgressive transformation that emerge from increased physiological activity includes Chasseguet-Smirgel's examples of the marriages arranged between children in *The One Hundred And Twenty Days Of Sodom*. While this depiction collapses the division between infants and adults, both this and *Juliette* also use these ceremonies to disturb established gender divisions by dressing men as brides and women as grooms.[12]

Alongside the corruption of those binary oppositions separating sexuality from death, as well as one gender from another, Chasseguet-Smirgel has also identified the theme 'diabolical surgery' in Sade's work. Here, the medical figure utilizes methods of surgery to unite previously disparate body boundaries. In Sade's writings, the role of the transgressive surgeon takes two forms. He is depicted either as a medical figure whose direct intervention on the human form profoundly alters the established boundaries of subjectivity,[13] or as a symbolic figure (such as the libertine) who arranges a series of violent or sexual displays which fuse disparate identities.

In this respect, Chasseguet-Smirgel argues that the Sadeian surgeon places himself in the role of god, who is able to create new forms by transmuting the established human body. This is indicated by one sadistic surgeon who states in *Justine:*

"...these portions of disorganised matter we throw into the crucible of nature, afford her the pleasure of creating anew, under different forms."[14]

Franco's films reiterate the theme of the diabolical surgeon by detailing the activities of medical figures whose activities are conflated with the sexual and the perverse. This was a pattern initiated in the 1961 film **The Awful Dr Orlof**. Here, Howard Vernon is depicted as a perverse medical figure who abducts young women in order to perform skin grafts on the face of his disfigured daughter. Reiterating Sade's conflation of sexuality with violence and death it is interesting that all of Orlof's victims are prostitutes or 'exotic' dancers that he courts at a disreputable club.

The film's basis in the activities of surgeons such as Rodin from *Justine* is indicated in the sadomasochistic paraphernalia that adorns Orlof's location. (These include a torture chamber where the disfigured women whom he has experimented on are chained to a wall and left to die). Orlof is assisted in his activities by a mutant killer aptly named 'Morpho' because his face and physical identity have been irreparably altered by the Doctor's previously unsuccessful experiments.[15]

However, it is not merely **The Awful Dr Orlof**'s violent and literal reconstruction of the self which provides evidence of Sadeian mixture, but the way in which the film presents an uncanny fusion between characters with opposing traits. For instance, Orlof's eventual demise is premised on his sexual fascination with the film's heroine Wanda. After being stalked by the surgeon, she resolves to capture him, much against the wishes of her lover who is leading the police inquiry into his crimes.

Wanda's investigations lead her to the night club where he chooses prostitutes and erotic dancers as future victims. In order to entice Orlof into a confession she transforms her identity from a virtuous ballerina to a provocative inhabitant of the locale. Her sexual transition, in Wanda's own words, allows her to adopt the guise of a 'shameless hussy', indicating the interchangeability of virtue and vice in Sade's view of sexuality. This is reflected in the interrelations between Sade's two most famous women: the sisters Justine and Juliette.

Although the two novels which detail their lives indicate shared childhood experiences, the adult lives of the two sisters are marked by disparate drives towards virtue and vice respectively. However, the fact that Juliette performs all the crimes for which Justine is accused underscores what Angela Carter argues is the reciprocity that exists between the pair. As she notes in *The Sadeian Woman*, Juliette's:

"...vision of the inevitable prosperity of vice, as shown in her triumphant career, and the vision of the inevitable misfortunes of virtue that Justine's life offers... mutually reflect one another like a pair of mirrors."[16]

Tender And Perverse Emanuelle

In its finale, **The Awful Dr Orlof** once again draws this collapsing of identity and sexuality to the theme of orgasm as death. After being captured by Morpho, Wanda discovers that the surgeon's erotic attachment to her is premised on her physical similarity to his (rapidly declining) daughter. It is this transgressive drive towards differing types of physiological 'mixture' which marks not only the **Orlof** film (and the sequels which Franco later produced), but also his versions of other established 'diabolical surgeons' seen in **The Erotic Rites Of Frankenstein** (1972) and **Jack The Ripper** (1976).

Important to figures such as Orlof is not only a medical flair but the will to reproduce God's powers over physiology. They are also seen to possess an ability to verbalise the paradoxes that govern the human condition.[17] It is this duel concern with the medical and creative (thus collapsing another set of dichotomies) that defines the true status of the libertine and the surgeon in both Sade and Franco's work.

Even when depicting figures who are not strictly doctors, Franco's libertines retain an ability to transcend established body barriers through an ability to organise regimes of torture and sexual punishment. For instance, in **Ilsa The Wicked Warden** (*aka* **Greta The Mad Butcher**, 1977) Dianne Thorne reprises her former role of a sadistic camp warden who both mutilates and seduces her female inmates before being ripped to pieces by her former prisoners. As Tohill and Tombs have noted, her links to other Franco libertines is confirmed by not only the direction of her power towards physical violation, but also the construction of her locale around pseudo-scientific principles:

"Ilsa's jail had an assortment of rooms set aside for her sadistic pleasure, some had strung-up, whipped women, others were filled with the human flotsam, the disfigured remnants of her indecent experiments."[18]

The fact that libertines such as Ilsa use power to devise strategies of torture which end in bouts of copulation further confirms the theatrical basis of sexuality in Sade's writings. (While her disposal of these partners following a climax reiterates the close connection between eroticism and death).[19] If one of the logical conclusions of Sade's view of sexuality as a site of both power and spectacle is the depiction of the orgy as 'the most natural form of sexual experience'[20], then it is a feature shared by many of Franco's films.

These works directly depict the orchestration of scenes of mass copulation, as in the organised orgies controlled by libertines such Ilsa or Count Dicken in **The Sadist Of Notre Dame** (1974). Equally, his works often feature locations which exploit eroticism as the site of a public spectacle, as in **Orlof** and the 'Flamingo Club' of **Sadisterotica** (1968). Another related strategy which Franco uses to render sexuality as a site of public contemplation is to use party scenes as a site where communal desires converge on the body of the text's heroine as in **Succubus** (1967) and **Venus In Furs** (1968).

Paradoxically, this public foregrounding of sexuality in Sade produces neither the emotional intensity nor the sexual pleasure associated with the erotic act. This is because for both Sade and later European thinkers such as Freud, sexual excess can never be linked to physical satisfaction or spiritual liberation. Rather, as Maurice Charney has argued, these encounters merely condemn the protagonist to endlessly repeat the conditions of humiliation and punishment that dictate the orgiastic scenario. As he states in the book *Sexual Fictions*:

"Sade's gargantuan sexual imagination is not intended to provoke or inflame desire, rather the vast repetition has a numbing effect. We feel disgust and outrage much more vividly than desire."[21]

Where the effect of these orgiastic and destructive encounters are most marked is in the processes of narrative repetition which dominates both Sade and Franco's work.[22] This is seen in films such as **Lady Porno** (1975) through an obsessive desire to retrace past sexual or violent events. The narrative features Lina Romay as the night club performer Sylvia, whose involvement in a love triangle results in her abduction and forced participation in both orgies and torture. Her involvement in a sadomasochistic relationship with this mysterious couple result in her being subjected to a regime of torture and sexual humiliation by a wooden-legged libertine (played naturally by Franco). Upon waking, Sylvia finds that both her former lovers are dead and is she forced to flee the mansion where the activities are set.

This plot device (revealed as a contrivance in order to blackmail Sylvia into revealing details of her relations with a diplomat) establishes a process of repetition which comes to dominate the rest of the narrative. If Romay's kidnapping and torture features as an absurd trope repeated in the narrative, **Lady Porno** also confirms Timo Airaksinen's belief that sexuality in the Sadeian text also results in an alteration in the narrative's generic mode.[23] While Sylvia's first encounter at the mansion emphasises the degree of punishment that she endures, subsequent abductions to this locale are played much more

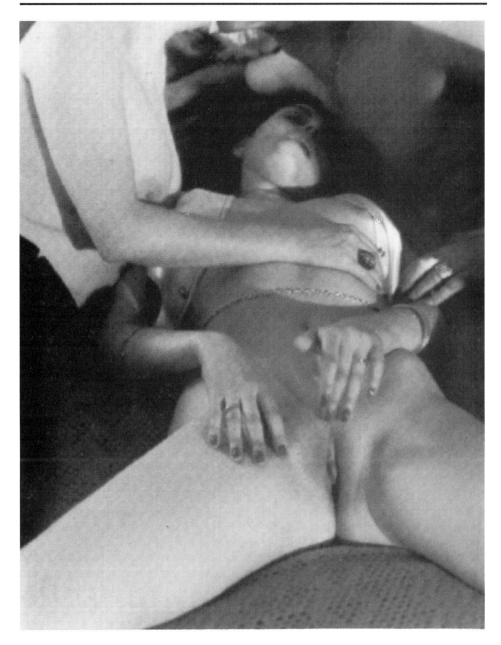

Lady Porno

for comic effect. Examples of this alteration of the generic system through repetition include scenes where a couple's later attempts to ravage Romay are undercut by her repeated giggling at their fumbling. A further example is seen in the 'humorous instance' of her overcoming a female seducer/molester with an unmotivated karate chop.

The shift in the narrative from pornographic titillation, to murder mystery and ultimate comic absurdity, accomplishes another form of Sadeian 'mixture', uniting previously disparate forms. It also functions to openly acknowledge the desires of its audience. This feature is indicated by the inclusion of four distinct sequences where Sylvia addresses the camera and thus the film's audience directly. As with other Franco films such as **The Awful Dr Orlof**, the first example of this takes place in the theatre where Sylvia works. Here, the sexuality of the bodies depicted are displayed in a self-conscious reference to the presence of both fictional and non-diegetic audiences. This self-reflexive strategy remains linked to Sylvia's sexual desires for the rest of the narrative. In three further inserts she addresses the audience and asks them to assess the events depicted while masturbating herself.[24]

While narratives such as **Lady Porno** demonstrate an understanding of the processes of repetition that emerge from an excess of sexuality and suffering, **Venus In Furs** provides a much more complex example of how the issue of orgasm as death affects the structure of Franco's works. The narrative details the impact of a past sexually violent scenario on the alienated musician[25] Jimmy (James Darren), who attempts to uncover his connection to the body of a dead woman found washed up on a beach.

The corpse is revealed to be that of a woman known as Wanda Reid, whom Jimmy recalls as having been killed at a sadomasochistic party at which he was present. Jimmy's subsequent flashback reveals Wanda's oppressors to be three former friends, headed by the sadistic Prince Ahmed (Klaus Kinski). Again on Sadeian lines, Ahmed construct Wanda's sexual humiliation and suffering as the site of a public spectacle. However, Jimmy's implication in the violent transgression that haunts his past is indicated by his voyeuristic obsession with seeing Wanda's body stripped and then mutilated by the guests. Equally, as his voice over to the scene states, he only left the party at this point because of a fear that he was 'as sick as they were'.

The discovery of Wanda's body sets up a pattern of repetition around the depiction of orgasm and death which dominates the remainder of the narrative. This functions by shifting Jimmy across a range of different locations such as Istanbul and Rio, where he encounters a number of doubles of Wanda whom become his lover. Although confused by the fact that he is now the partner of a woman whom he thought had perished, the narrative reveals that Wanda is a spectre who is terrorising those connected with her demise (including Jimmy).

Through this plot device, Franco uses the figure of Wanda to create a series of connections between sexuality and death.[26] For instance, she exacts revenge on her former oppressors by appearing to them individually as a phantasmagoric figure who gestures further seduction only to lead them to their deaths. (Again, her appearance functions as a form of repetition which announces their demise).

An example of this is indicated in her destruction of the lesbian photographer Olga, one of the participants in her original suffering. When Olga encounters Wanda at a party and is seduced by her in front of the guests (reiterating the public as a sphere of sexuality in Franco) she presumes that she was only wounded as a result of her beating at Ahmed's party. This seduction is continued later at Olga's apartment, when Wanda appears, undresses and begins to initiate intercourse with her. It is only at the point of her climax that Olga looks down to discover that her lover is in fact the dead body that she

Venus In Furs

helped mutilate at Ahmed's former gathering.

The links between narrative repetition, orgasm and annihilation are further underscored by Wanda's final encounter with Ahmed. This is a liaison which he admits is premised on his knowledge of her 'from the past', as well as their being 'united through death'. Here Ahmed (dressed in the ceremonial robes of his ancestors) narrates another past event of how an ancient libertine attempted to win the favours of a female slave by collapsing the power distinctions which separated them. This form of social 'mixture' took the reversal of their positions of authority for a limited period, culminating in their engagement in an orgiastic encounter. Importantly, when placed in a position of dominance, the former female slave (depicted once again as Wanda) introduces an element of displeasure into the coupling by forcing the bound Ahmed to watch while she seduces a series of lovers before him. Once again, the finale of this erotic encounter conflates sexuality and death as Wanda fellates her former oppressor to both the point of climax and death. According to Janine Chasseguet-Smirgel, a comprehension of Sade's work allows us a greater understanding of the sexual and destructive urges that Freud argued governed our psychic development. Importantly, the privileging of orgasm as death allows more focus to be placed on the pre-Oedipal drives which negate male control to the wishes of the mother.[27] If these early attractions emerge in later life via a connection between trauma and eroticism, their narrative effect (via a pattern of repetition) is seen in the final shots of **Venus In Furs**.

Here Jimmy, having discovered the actuality of Wanda's death, returns to his retreat in Istanbul. In a recapitulation of the film's opening shot, Franco has him discover a body washed up on the beach. In a marked contrast to the beginning of the narrative, the corpse is revealed to be that of Jimmy himself rather than Wanda. What this finale indicates is that the repetition of this past sexual and violent event do not bring liberation (as Jimmy misguidedly tells a girlfriend). Rather, they condemn the individual to sacrifice sexual pleasure for chaos and destruction. In so doing they confirm the annihilation of the barrier separating eroticism and death as a Sadeian feature that underpins both the content and structure of Franco's films.

I wish to express my sincere thanks to Jesus Franco. His comments on de Sade in relation to his own work provided not only a focus for the interview accompanying this article, but also the article itself.

THE SADEIAN SPEAKS:
AN INTERVIEW WITH JESUS FRANCO

During the last two years, Jesus Franco has re-emerged to claim his title as one of Europe's leading post-war horror and fantasy directors. Several reasons are behind the renewed interest in the Spanish film maker's work, including his recent completion of the films **The Killer Barbys** (1996) and **Tender Flesh, Marie Cookie** and **Beauty And The Beast** aka **Lust For Frankenstein** aka **Legend Of Lady Frankenstein** (all 1997). Alongside Franco's welcome return to horror with these productions, his talents were also celebrated at a number of genre festivals in both Europe and America. Central to these were his and Lina Romay's headlining appearances at the "Chiller Theatre" festival in New York and at London's "Eurofest" (both in the latter part of 1996). These appearances also tied in with a major retrospective examination of Franco's work by Kevin Collins. This innovative paper took the form of an exclusive and exhaustive interview (contained in a special edition of *European Trash Cinema*).

As well as producing this elaborate examination of the director's work, Kevin Collins was also gracious enough to organise a number of interviews between myself and Jess Franco for the second *Necronomicon* book. The interview that is contained here is extracted from a longer series of dialogues which I conducted in both New York and London. What it represents is an overview of Franco's own opinions on his cinematic career as well as an examination of his influences.

Xavier Mendik: There has been renewed interest in your work recently in Britain, following the release of books such as *Immoral Tales*. How do you feel about this?

Jesus Franco: I am very happy about this because I am a film maker, I have been working in film all my life. But I was never waiting for any critical acclaim. I just wanted to have some popular success. My work has always been for the public, I don't think that cinema should be the reserve of intellectuals, it should be a form of entertainment for everybody. I have noticed that in France recently there has also been a lot of interest in my work, particularly from young people. They seem to be interested in how I have put these films together. And for this interest in both countries, I am very grateful, as I really did not expect it.

XM: You say that your films are popular films but they all seem to have an intellectual project running through them.

JF: That's true because I have an intellectual formation, I do make films for everyone but they have an intellectual side to them.

XM: Have you found it difficult trying to put forward these ideas in a popular format?

JF: Yes, but it is the formula that I have always used, and hopefully it has been working for a long time. Jean-Luc Godard told me once that he made the film **Le Mépris** with Bridget Bardot and Fritz Lang. He had to do a number of shots in which Bridget was completely naked. I asked him why did you have to do this and he replied that after the film was finished it was felt that it wasn't commercial enough. So he added these shots in order to give it a more popular feel. At that point in his career he was interested in putting his energies into films that had both intellectual and popular appeal. I have tried to follow that, I have tried to blend my beliefs into a film, but do so in a very popular way.

XM: Godard's work is very stylized, was he influential on your work?

Le Mépris

JF: I think **Le Mépris** was influential when I saw it, not only as I say because he shot the film with an awareness of both art and the popular. The early cinema of Godard had a lot of influence for me mainly in the way of editing a film. In particular the way he used jump cuts, cutting into a shot in his first films was very influential. He used to jokingly refer to this process as a beautiful method of cutting film, but I'm sure, that was the truth of the matter. The real joke is that I used to see these early films in the small cinemas and on very old prints because I was a very poor man at the time, and so there were even more jump cuts! But this did not matter, what was fantastic about those early films is that they showed that you did not have to move logically from one scene to another in order to create an effect.

XM: Many of the films you produced during the late 1960s do seem to cross over the art cinema divide. I'm thinking here of films such as **Venus In Furs** and **Succubus**, which quotes Godard as part of its history of cinema.

JF: Yes, but the Godard quoted in **Succubus** is not the Godard of the late 60s. I say this because although I do like many of Godard's films, they fall into specific phases of his career. The period of **Succubus** coincides with a period of Godard during the late 1960s which I am not at all fond of. That is the period following the release of **Weekend**, when Godard was involved in many different political groups. It was a period when his films were not so involved with the popular, they were more concerned with the political. I don't think this was wholly successful, he is no longer involved in such groups and is making better films again. Often to be politically engaged means that it is very difficult to make a good film. Cinema must be free, it cannot afford to be engaged in politics

Succubus

which will hold it back.

XM: OK, but Godard trades on the fact that he is considered an *auteur*, do you feel you feel that you fall into this category? You use the same actors and actresses such as Lina, Howard Vernon, and Antonio Mayans. You also use the same sort of shot set-ups from one production to another.

JF: I have to consider myself as an *auteur*. I have had some critics, who have said that I have made some bad films, but my reply is that the person who writes the script, directs the film, edits and even sometimes composes the music for the film is an *auteur*. [Laughs] He may be a bad *auteur*, but he is still an *auteur*.

XM: As with art cinema directors such as Godard you seem much more concerned with style than content. For instance you have often been criticised for your use of zoom shots, yet films such as **Female Vampire** and **Doriana Gray** use this method to explore different areas of on-screen space.

JF: Yes, I am very glad that you have brought this up, because I never thought that anyone would finally understand this! This is why I use this method, but again it is to be used in a popular work.

XM: Films such as **Succubus, Venus In Furs** and **The Sadist Of Notre Dame** make use of non-diegetic inserts and discrepancies between the temporal ordering of shots to confuse the viewer. In particular, I am thinking of your delayed introduction of the master shot in the party scene of **Succubus**, which makes it difficult to isolate where the characters are in relation to each other. Again, these are features one finds in art cinema.

JF: You know, one critic in Barcelona said that Jess Franco is the least commercial of all the commercial directors and his main invention is of the "B-movie for art cinemas", for both art and commercial audiences. I thought his words were very nice. As a matter of fact, I always try to be commercial, I want to be commercial, I want to arrive to everybody. Yet sometimes I can't do this and in those times I just follow my soul and my feelings and some people say what I produce is artistic. This is good, but I like it to be commercial. Hitchcock said that "I'm a vacant film for 5,000 friends and 50 million people at least", so I would like to be like him and make a film that everybody likes.

XM: Your fascination with the work of Orson Welles has been well documented and would seem to have begun before you worked with him on **Chimes At Midnight**. He was a director with a distinctly European film style with his emphasis on features such as long takes, was this one of the things that interested you in his films?

JF: The influence of Orson Welles on my cinema started a long time before I met or worked with him. It started when I saw **Citizen Kane**, I said "Oh my God, this is great cinema, this is something I wish to follow". Then I saw **The Magnificent Ambersons**, which was a confirmation of everything I thought about him. In fact all the films of Orson, even when he didn't like the final result, I thought had great elements to it. For instance, he was very critical of **Touch Of Evil**, probably because he didn't do the final cut so he saw it as a different film. But I told him that he was wrong, that if he looked at it again he would see something different in it. So in the case of Orson Welles, I was under his influence, since I saw **Citizen Kane** when I was kind of fourteen. Then, the other guy who was an enormous influence both on my life and work was Robert Siodmak, followed by Nicholas Ray. But Nicholas Ray was a lot less of an influence than the others because his cinema was much more erratic, often I would have to see a film of his three or four times to really love it. He used to shoot films in a very odd way, like **Johnny Guitar**. He was completely mad as a film maker, but a wonderful man.

XM: So it's clear that commercial American cinema was more of an influence than art cinema.

JF: Yes, particularly by these directors. Do you want to know something? Nicholas Ray, Joseph Losey and Orson Welles were from the same small town in the American mid-West. All three were born in a town which had 3,000 people, which is amazing. Also, Joseph Losey and Nicholas Ray were very close friends in this town, and both of them admired Orson a great deal. [Laughs] However, Orson did not admire the work of the other two at all. In particular he did not like the work of Joseph Losey at all, he said he couldn't stand it, he thought it was boring! This was because... it was true! One thing about Orson was that he never lied and I have to agree with his opinion.

XM: What about Nicholas Ray?

JF: Well Nicholas Ray was a nice person, kind of a nice quiet fellow, you know, very clever and calm.

XM: What was he like to work with?

JF: Erratic, though more methodical than Welles! I remember that when Orson arrived to shoot a scene he never knew what to do, never! He would arrive on set looking very sombre, and the crew would ask him "where is the first shot?" He would look at them for a while and reply "No questions!" He used to do this repeatedly, he would arrive on set smoking a cigar and walk around while people looked at him for direction. Often he would do this for around half an hour before setting up a shot. One day I finally said to him "You know, I understand why you say no questions, because there are no answers!"

XM: How did he take this?

JF: Very well, he would start to roar with laughter. Orson was a man who enjoyed life and...

XM: Enjoyed cinema?

JF: Cinema, he loved it. You know, in the time people believed that he wasn't shooting, he was clearly shooting, every day! Everywhere he went, he took his 16mm camera, and would shoot anything that caught his eye; it could be a French castle or some picture he had discovered around Madrid, whatever. He was always working. He was always working, making cinema, he lived for it. One of the things I'm very happy about is that when I arrived to buy what he shot for the production of **Don Quixote** I also bought 50,000 metres of negative on 16mm, shot by Orson in those times when critics thought he wasn't working. One day I would like to make a serial of Spain which uses this material. He thought about Spain in the same way that Eisenstein thought about Mexico. He decided that he could do a resumé of the human condition, shooting it in the different areas of Spain.

XM: So Welles is obviously a key figure here. I was thinking about Welles and also your time in France, you said your time in France was a key period where you learnt about cinema. I wondered how much did the theory of film go along with that, I mean your cinema seems to fit into a type of cinema that Bazin praised in terms of say Rossellini or Welles, this idea of film is a stepping stone to explore the wider mysteries of life. Do you think your time in France helped you understand not only film but the theory of film?

JF: Well I think so, but theory can also become a prison when making films. My way of filming depends more on what we can call inspiration, I follow feelings. I need to have feelings about a subject which provides the inspiration in order to shoot it properly. I know that my work is very irregular, but this is because some days there is a lack of vision, without any inspiration. My way of shooting film is like being a jazz musician, some days they have no inspiration and they play just the things they know they have to play. On these days they play their instrument just like a machine. But on other days, when you have this inspiration you can do other things, greater things either as a musician or a film maker.

XM: Critics of your work have often pointed to what they see as its varied quality. How do you feel about this?

JF: I know I'm unequal, but constantly I prefer to be unequal rather than boring. The whole of film need not display these talents. I think a film maker whose work has four or five moments of beautiful cinema, each saying different things becomes interesting immediately. For instance, I loved the first films of Budd Boetticher. These were very low-budget films but they contained some moments which were fantastic. This is the point where people realise that the director is *not* stupid, not banal at all but very good, quite extraordinary. Certain directors have the power to use certain scenes in this way, and I think I am of this kind.

XM: Moving away from your influences in France and people such as Welles, de Sade is also an obvious influence on your works. His ideas seem to extend beyond the obvious example of your version of **Justine**.

JF: I think Sade's influence speaks more of my literary formation and my views on the role of the intellect. This is because I have been making a joke during our dialogue, by insisting

Justine

my work be seen as popular. I am not anti-intellectual and would like to show once in my life that I *am* an intellectual. However, in principle I hate the word intellectual and I hate the intellectual cinema because it is false intellect. What many people call intellectual cinema is shit, it is not "deep". It is made by people that try to show how clever they are and yet they aren't. For Sade, intellect is bound up with the vulgar and the ability to entertain. The two should not be divided.

XM: Recent work on de Sade has emphasised his interest in surgery as a way of intervening on the human body. There seems to be a strand in your work which follows this. For instance the figure of the surgeon is present from early films such as **The Awful Dr Orlof** and **The Diabolical Dr Z** to more recent works such as **Faceless**.

JF: This comes from both Sade and Gothic horror cinema which I love. Both present this figure in a very modern way. Even those Gothic films which feature the supernatural were filmed in a very modern way, such as **Nosferatu**. They depict the unexpected, nothing remains the same.

XM: What about Sade's view of women, has it affected your depiction of figures such as Irina Karlstein or Doriana Gray?

JF: Yes, in a way. What Sade does is depict women who have power, I think these films do the same.

XM: Sade's narratives were very complex, often containing many different stories and scenes. You seem to have adopted the importance of the role of the storyteller that one finds in his works. In early works such as **The Awful Dr Orlof** the storytellers are multiple in their recounting of Orlof's activities. In later films such as **Lady Porno** you even stage much of the action towards the camera, with Lina addressing the audience directly.

JF: Yes, this is so. With that film, I intended it to be theatrical, in the same way that Sade's work is theatrical. I think of the cinema as a show and the show must be good as a show. I don't accept the confusion between cinema and philosophy, or cinema and social or political meanings. This does relate to Sade, who was in his own way very interested in the role of the comic rather than the intellect.

XM: Yes, a film like **Lady Porno** uses repetition and comedy in depicting Lina's repeated abductions.

JF: Yes, these are encounters which become absurd in the same way that Sade is absurd and comical. It's like if you went to the circus and the clowns started to talk about Mallarmé you would realise the confusion between intellect and entertainment. I don't want to go to the circus to hear Mallarmé's poems you know. I want to go to see fun and to see the fantastic acts, to be amused by the clowns. In that way I think I am very close to the mainstream American cinema because even Orson Welles wanted to be commercial. He told me that once he met a lot of the new generation of Spanish directors and as I said before he never lied. He said to them, "Frankly I don't like your films. I don't like them because I accept that the people must consider the problems of their actual society and they have to explain the story which is concentrated in the social situation of the country. All of that is very good, but how does it affect your ability to produce a good show? Well, you start the film and show the poor woman who comes back home, very tired, because she has been working very hard. Even though she is tired she has to prepare dinner for her husband who also works because of their poverty. Then the husband arrives and they discuss their work and the social situation... and then someone must knock on the door and produce some action". This is what Orson would demand. He told them that if you materialised this couple's condition into an hour and a half long production, with no other unexpected event, then all that you produce is a boring film! I hate this kind of film, because it lacks entertainment. It is okay to produce your explanation about society and the social life of the people but something unexpected must happen. I think Welles was correct here. It does not mean that you are not interested in intellectual ideas, but you also realise that film is a medium of entertainment, of story-telling.

XM: In a way this does relate to de Sade, his narratives twist and turn and constantly introduce the unexpected.

JF: Yes, this is something that Sade understood very much, he was firstly a showman. To be a good showman is very difficult and very important to the performance of a story. This ability to introduce the comic, the unexpected into a story continues today not only in cinema, but in the work of "clowns" such as Rowan Atkinson. He is a comic creator, and in his own way as creative as a good cinema director, what is the difference? There are actors, writers who also are able to produce this fantastic effect. You must understand that we have talked here a lot about cinema, but the creativity that I am interested in often goes on outside the cinema. This is important, many people are *only* interested in the activities of the cinema director! I wouldn't claim to be any more important than them.

XM: This is an interesting point, and links in with a question that I wished to ask you about the cameo roles you often have in your own films. Often these are very... odd characters that you portray! For instance, you played a mute killer in **Virgin Among The Living Dead**, a sexual abuser in **Barbed Wire Dolls** and, most notoriously, Vogel the perverted priest of **The Sadist Of Notre Dame**. These roles seem almost to be a critical reaction against the notion of the director as genius (rather than showman) which still dominates much of the writing around cinema.

Sadist Of Notre Dame

JF: Yes, yes, if I depict such characters with problems it is because I want to show the reality of the director's role. We must not forget that in terms of artistic expression, the cinema is a recent medium, and its range of possibilities has never been fully explored. The cinema is still very old-fashioned when compared to other arts such as theatre and music which have much more freedom now. In their own ways these arts are forging ahead and presenting new expressions and creating fantastic things. Yet what is happening to cinema? Its progression is far slower, the stories have not really changed since the beginning of the century. To give you an example, imagine that I was a script writer and wished to adapt a novel like James Joyce's *Ulysses*. If I adapted the second book and sent it to a producer, no one would accept it. Yet this is one of the greatest books ever written, but it would be too radical to be produced through cinema. So I still think that cinema is very old-fashioned, and if there are intellectuals in this field I would like to see them use the medium in a much more creative and modern way. This goes back to my point about the false intellect that some directors employ when directing film. They often claim that they are producing some new, deep insight into life, but all that is there is the same story with the same progression and the same ending. Very little has changed since the beginning of the century. I would like to see cinema become as creative as something like theatre, we must reconsider what it means to be a film maker.

Tender Flesh

XM: Since the mid-1970s a great many of your films have focused on Lina Romay, what do you think she adds to your cinema?

JF: Well as you know, she is much more than an actress to me.

XM: So, another source of inspiration?

JF: Yes, but much more because she is a collaborator with me. Actually, she is the editor of my films, she works with me in the preparation, when she can, when she is not acting. She is also my assistant director, so she is a brilliant collaborator.

XM: After a long absence, you have recently made a welcome return to horror cinema with the film **The Killer Barbys**. As we talk, **Tender Flesh** is also in post-production. Do you hope these films will push awareness of your work into the mainstream?

JF: I would hope so, in the past a lot of work has been held up because of the attitude of producers.

XM: In what ways?

JF: Because, as with some directors they lack vision. They refuse to see the creative potential of cinema, they want a reason or explanation for everything. When one works in a genre such as horror this is not always possible. I remember a conversation that I had with one of them about the horror film and he was asking "why does this man become a werewolf?" I had to reply that "I don't know, it could be the full moon, a curse, I don't know or care". But that is not enough for them, you have to give them an explanation. Even a stupid explanation is better to them than none at all! I think that one of the main problems that cinema has in fulfilling its potential is the attitude of producers, they are some of the most un-civil and ignorant people ever to have existed.

XM: So you feel in a way that you've obviously never really crossed over into the mainstream, because of your insistence on making the kind of films that baffle producers and distributors.

JF: Yes, yes I have became an outsider, yet, personally I am very happy with this. It is very simple to me, as long as I can continue do the films with limited cost, limited budget I'll never have a problem. It's kind of funny because although I am an outsider, I have a following of people all around the world who like my films. These are my customers, these are the people I work for. These people are in Britain, some are in France, some in Italy and others in the United States. They are only a small audience, but their support is good enough for me because I am making films which are not very expensive and so I will be paid almost immediately, so I can do another film if I want.

I would like to offer my sincerest thanks to both Jesus Franco and Lina Romay for agreeing to the series of interviews, and offering their kindness, patience and enthusiasm throughout. I also wish to extend my thanks to Kevin Collins of 'One Shot Productions' without whom the interview (and the article which emerged from it) would not have been possible.

NOTES
1. Maurice Charney, *Sexual Fiction*. London: Methuen & Co, 1981, p33.
2. Outlined in his important paper "Beyond The Pleasure Principle". (In Freud's *On Metapsychology*; Harmondsworth: Penguin, 1984).
3. For a fuller account of this case study see "From The History Of An Infantile Neurosis" in Freud's *Case Histories II*; Harmondsworth: Penguin, 1981.
4. Sade's influences (both directly and through movements such as surrealism) on Franco are most clearly examined in Kevin Collins' exhaustive interview with the director contained in Craig Ledbetter (ed) *European Trash Cinema (Special Edition #1)*, October 1996.
5. For instance, see Cathal Tohill's article "The Franco Files", Cathal Tohill in Allan Bryce (ed) *The Dark Side #31*, April 1993. Here, Tohill defined Franco's style as featuring "the same derailed desire to mix eroticism, melodrama, crazed humour, horror and a fertile love of humour" (p21).
6. One important example of this is the sado-masochistic stage routine performed by the sexually confused heroine Lorna (Janine Reynaud) in **Succubus** (1967).
7. Maurice Charney, p38.
8. Cathal Tohill and Pete Tombs, *Immoral Tales: Sex And Horror Cinema In Europe 1956–1984*; London: Primitive Press, 1994, p119.
9. Sade, *The One Hundred And Twenty Days Of Sodom*, p56 (cited in Janine Chasseguet-Smirgel, *Creativity And Perversion*; London: Free Association Books, 1992).
10. Chasseguet-Smirgel's conclusion that sexuality is used as a tool to subvert established power structures in Sade is pertinent. She notes that this inversion is seen in his *Philosophy In The Boudoir*, which with its subtitle "Teachers Of Immorality – Dialogues For The Education Of Young Ladies" subverts the notion of the educator as guardian of the moral welfare of the children in their charge. Indeed, it is not merely that youth is introduced to vice via contact with these older instructors, but as *The One Hundred And Twenty Days Of Sodom* indicates, they also suffer punishment and violation as part of this initiation. Franco's cinema often follows this Sadeian root by depicting female characters who suffer sadism at the hands of mentors. Examples of this type of narrative include **Love Letters Of A Portuguese Nun** (1978), which features William Berger as a head priest who castigates young women for their inability to resist temptations of the flesh only then to molest them when they are sent to his convent for repentance. More controversially, this strategy is also seen in the series of 'Women In Prison' films that Franco began to make with producer Erwin C. Dietrich during the mid 1970s.
11. Ibid., p 2–3.

12. This last example is a point more fully explored by Angela Carter in *The Sadeian Woman*; (London: Virago, 1990).

13. Chasseguet-Smirgel gives the example of the sadistic surgeon Rodin from *Justine* who places himself in the position of God by creating new physical forms through direct medical intervention. As she notes, the operation he performs on his daughter involves the removal of her womb, effectively deleting fertility as a key feature which separates masculine from feminine.

14. Ibid, p4.

15. This inclusion of the mutant as Orlof's assistant itself provides a point of textual mixture of fusion between the two. Although Orlof's character is depicted as a rational counterfoil to Morpho's brutality the two are continually conflated by both the police and public assisting in the enquiry. An example of this is seen in the scene where an artist's impression of both men causes consternation in the crowd, who believe they have seen the same man attempting to abduct women in the city.

16. Angela Carter, p79.

17. The connection is confirmed by Orlof's assumption of the role of a libertine (whose function Sade saw as to contemplate the nature of love, morality and ethics) when depicted in the bar. In one scene he uses his attempts to seduce a prostitute with references to her good looks to launch into a monologue on the inevitable link between beauty and decay.

18. Cathal Tohill & Pete Tombs, *Immoral Tales: Sex And Horror Cinema In Europe 1956–1984*, p115.

19. Equally, the film's most controversial scene, which involves the forced consumption of faeces by a prisoner, reiterates Chasseguet-Smirgel's emphasis on pre-Oedipal states such as anality in Sade.

20. Charney, p33.

21. Ibid., p53.

22. An example of this process of repetition through copulation is given in *Juliette*. Here, a narrative sub-plot surrounding the heroine's capture by various male aggressors (such as a cannibal and a brigand chief) is repeated to ensure Juliette's freedom through her participation in further orgies. Importantly, during these encounters, Juliette is aided by female characters such as Clairwell, confirming Angela Carter's view that Sade's heroines are constructed through a subversion of male power.

23. In his book *The Philosophy Of The Marquis De Sade*; London: Routledge, 1995. The importance of Airaksinen's work is the emphasis he places on the narrative alteration that Sade's orgasm as death trait provokes.

24. The preoccupation of Franco's heroines towards acts of auto-eroticism once again confirms the contradiction around identity and sexuality in Sade's writings. Although characters such as Sylvia function as the classic Sadeian 'whore', their pleasure extends far beyond the mere servicing of the male characters that these works depict. Rather, they show an ambivalence towards male sexual power recalling some of the dominant women that populate narratives such as *Juliette*. For instance, Angela Carter has noted the heroine's gravitation towards characters such as the nymphomaniac Madame de Clairwell, whose sexual pleasure is premised on masturbation and the use of vibrators. In so doing, Carter argues that this character combines an excess of sexual desire with a rejection of the male in preference for the 'disembodied' phallus. Arguably, Sylvia's mocking attitude towards her two male lovers is indicated in her continued evasion of their attempted seductions. Irina Karlstein of **The Female Vampire** also maintains an ambivalent relationship to male potency. Although the phallus is her favoured object of achieving the orgasm as death trope that Franco's films detail, her own sexual pleasure is premised on masturbation, which the film reveals as separate to her interactions with male lovers.

25. The fact that the narrative depicts Jimmy as a jazz musician is important. Not only does it reflect Franco's much noted interest in this musical genre, but it also indicates this type of composition to be a form which is open to the 'mixing' of different styles. It is interesting to note that Chasseguet-Smirgel refers to certain types of free form music as being open to deviation from established tonal structures.

26. As Franco discusses in his interview with Kevin Collins in *European Trash Cinema*, certain named characters reoccur across his texts. Beyond the obvious example of Dr Orlof, characters such as Morpho have also appeared as barbaric henchmen in films such as **Sadisterotica**. From a Sadeian perspective this degree of overlap indicates that repetition is occurring both within *and* between Franco films.

27. According to Maurice Charney, the importance of the mother's body to the child's sexual drives are evidenced by a speech given by Clément, one of the libertines from *Justine*: *"It is in the mother's womb that there are fashioned the organs which must render us susceptible of such-and-such a fantasy; the first objects which we encounter, the first conversations we overhear determine the pattern; once tastes are formed nothing in the world can destroy them."* (Cited in *Sexual Fictions*, p51.)

ABNORMAL WARD

The Forbidden Visions of Hisayasu Sato

Jack Hunter

"I want to make a film which has the influence to drive its audience mad, to make them commit murder."

—Hisayasu Sato

To this day – probably more so than ever before – the world of adult films remains the most opportune, if not the only, arena in which young Japanese film-makers can hone their craft whilst exploring their own personal visions and obsessions. In the last decade the pink *nouvelle vague* cinema has produced such experimental, innovative directors as Kazuhiro Sano, Toshiki Satoh, Takahisa Zeze and, most interestingly of all, Hisayasu Sato.[1]

In some ways, Hisayasu Sato is reminiscent of a modern-day Koji Wakamatsu[2]; not just in his prolific output of movies (around 50 in just over a decade), but also in the controversial, provocative content of those works with their marriage of porno sub-culture to *avant-garde* expression. Working with regulars like writer Shiro Yumeno and actress Kiyomi Ito, Sato has produced a body of films – averaging in length to around 60 minutes – which are dedicated to exposing the dark void at the heart of contemporary existence. They brim with mute hysteria and deal with a violence of the soul that often erupts into the outside world. Films like **Gimme Shelter** (1986), **Lustmord** (1987), **Re-Wind** (1988), **Love Obsession** (1989), **Slush, Naked City, Look Into Me** (1990), **Doll, Wave,** (1991), **Close Dance, Dirty Blue** (1992), **Negation, Kyrie Elesion, Angel In The Dark** (1993), **Sick People, Love – Zero = No Limit** (1994), and **Night Of The Anatomical Doll** (1996); films peopled by maniac rapists who explode their rage against women's bodies, who reside in darkened basements, mortuaries, container trucks, lightless tanks, porno cinemas. Women in schoolgirl sailor uniforms separated from reality by phobias, paranoia, suicidal impulses, narcolepsy, the melancholy of the exposed embryo; inhabiting a virtual world of white noise, blue screen, destructive desires and fatal madness. In **Hanrahonban: Joshidaiseiboko-hen (Raping Female University Students,** 1989), a computer salesman turns rapist by night, attacking only women who live in white buildings; in **Hitozuma Collector (Married Woman Collector,** 1985), a taxi driver is a gasmask-wearing rapist who victimizes his female passengers; and in **Chikandensha: Iyarashi Koi (Train Of Perversion: Dirty Actions** *aka* **Birthday,** 1994), a sociopathic pervert declares his utter divorce from reality. In **Boko: Climax (The Rape: Climax,** 1986), the estranged female protagonist was born in a white cell without knowing her parents, while the heroine of **Hentaibyoto SM Shinryoshitsu (Abnormal Ward: Consultation Room Of Sadism And Masochism,** 1989) was separated from her identical twin by the scalpel of a strange doctor; and in **Seifukushikei: Nejirikome! (Private Torture Of Uniforms: Thrust It In!** *aka* **Just An Illusion,** 1990), a dissociated woman is pathologically unable to remove her school uniform. In **Hentaibyoto Hakuizeme (Abnormal Ward: The Torture Of White Dresses** *aka* **Love Letter In Sand,** 1988), a nurse cannot touch the button of her elevator without repeatedly disinfecting it; she becomes attached to a young girl who was raped on a rainy day, to the point where she inherits the girl's experience and, when it rains, beats men to death at random with a

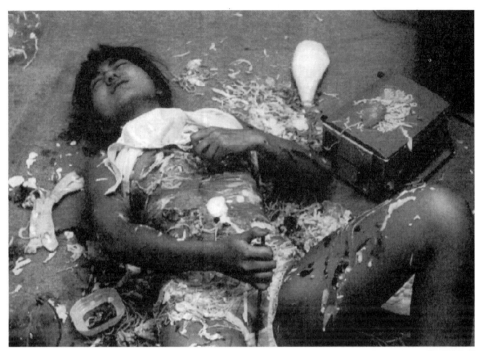

Lustmord

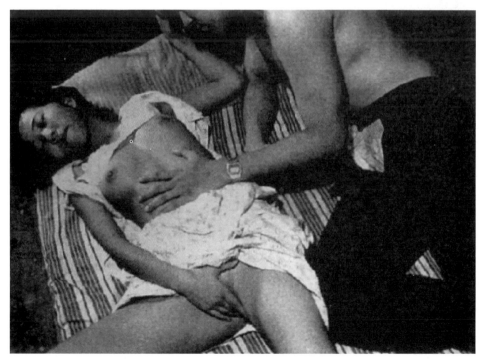

Married Woman Collector

metallic bat. Though she has no memory of her actions, every night upon returning home she screams hysterically into a hole made in the middle of sand in a water tank.

Two typical Sato films are **Tosatsu Report: Insha! (Hidden Filming Report: Sneak Shots!** *aka* **Turtle Vision**, 1991) and **Uwakizuma Chijokuzeme (Unfaithful Wife: Sexual Torture** *aka* **Aria For Gazes** *aka* **The Bedroom**, 1992)[3]. **Turtle Vision** opens with a sequence of secretly-shot, voyeuristic video images. Eiji (played by Koichi Imaizumi), a young cameraman, makes his living by filming these tapes and selling them to the porn industry. He is a solitary person who lives alone in a dark loft and has no outside contacts save for those he sells his tapes to. One night, while filming, he discovers a prostitute in a schoolgirl's sailor uniform (Rei Takagi) working the backstreets of Okubo, and secretly follows her with his camera. The girl leads a middle-aged man to a deserted building site, where she lets him grope her body as he likes. Suddenly, she pulls out a concealed knife and stabs her client viciously in the eyes. The man collapses and writhes in agony, blood pouring from his eye-sockets. Fascinated, Eiji decides to pursue this weird girl wherever she goes.

We learn that her name is Saki; she lives a bizarre double life as a cheerful high school student by day, disturbed prostitute by night. Saki lives in a flat with her elder sister, Maki. Maki seems equally strange; she never leaves home, sitting all day with drawn shutters, wearing dark sunglasses. She never speaks and her face remains blank, inscrutable, even when Saki tells her about her day at school. One night, as they sleep side by side, Maki is tormented by an unknown nightmare; Saki awakes abruptly, dresses in her sailor uniform and heads off into the night. Once again she lures a man to a lonely spot then mutilates his eyes.

One night, after a similar attack on a client, Maki appears to fall down unconscious. Eiji, who has been filming, aids her and finds she is in a somnambulistic state; she can later remember nothing of her actions. Eiji takes her to a psychiatrist who probes her subconscious, eventually locating the imprint of a trauma which Saki has apparently inherited from her sister Maki, as if by psychic infection. The trauma is revealed to have occurred when Maki was a high school student. Her boyfriend at the time was filming her one day with his video camera, when a group of thugs disguised in stocking masks appeared and attacked them. The boyfriend was knocked unconscious, and Maki was viciously gang-raped in a prolonged assault. Halfway through her ordeal her boyfriend came around, but was too scared to help her, averting his gaze; then, inexplicably, he picked up his camera and began compulsively to film the brutal rape. Maki, who by now was resigned to her fate, turned hysterical upon seeing the camera, endlessly screaming "No, no!!". This was the root of her eye-trauma, and the story also has shocking repercussions for Eiji: he realises *he* was the boyfriend! And thus his own fetish, his voyeurism, was born; seeing himself powerless to help Maki, he became detached from the exterior world, his only way of communicating with it now being through a video lens.

Having come to turns with the past, Eiji returns to the scene of the crime. Maki, dressed in her sailor uniform, awaits him on the highschool roof. They embrace, then ritualistically slice open each other's eyes; both die in cathartic streams of blood. Saki, left alone, still bears the traumatic imprint. Soon after, we see her wandering the streets; caught in the cyclopean gaze of a video camera she erupts, slashing at the camera's lens with her knife. Fade to white noise.

Turtle Vision

In **Turtle Vision**, Sato presents one of his main themes: the persistence of madness – as a ghostly imprint on the minds of others – even after its source has been destroyed. Two people, fatally detached from the world by trauma, are able to mutually terminate their psychosis in a bloody tryst, yet this insanity lives on in the scream of one close to them. Finally, as Saki's knife swipes at the video lens, it is the voyeuristic eyes of the film's audience that are also in danger of mutilation. Sato's films often end with a switch to white noise and the signal "Game Over", reinforcing the virtual nature not only of the cinematic experience, but of our relationship to "reality" and the exterior world itself. Perhaps traumatised by his images, the audience emerge warily from the dark of the porno cinema as their eyes are stabbed by the blinding white light of day.

The Bedroom opens with a shot of a video camera lens being spray-painted black. Thus commences another libidinal psychodrama in which the identities of two sisters are intertwined, leading to murder and madness. This time the film centres around a sect of alienated young people who use/abuse a narcotic called Halcion and frequent The Bedroom, a dark cell lit only by a huge video screen of silent static. Here, girls take sleeping pills and lie naked on a bed while various men photograph, grope, explore and penetrate their comatose bodies. Kyoko is one such girl, whose younger sister Maya has just been found dead, wrapped from head to foot in cling-film, next to an empty bottle of Halcion. Kyoko's husband, Esaka, is devoid of love for her and can only communicate by abusive sex; Kyoko is now involved in an affair with Kei, her sister's former boyfriend. They make love blindfolded, under ultra-violet light. Kyoko keeps a compulsive video diary of her life, which is punctuated by bizarre hallucinations/flashbacks and a growing phobia

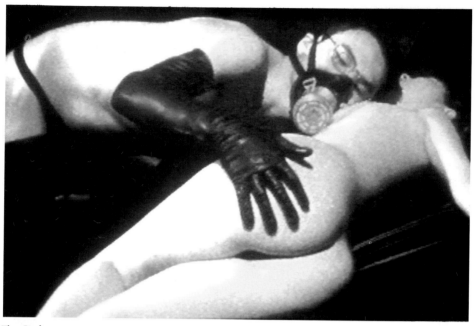

The Bedroom

of surveillance cameras, presumably the result of Halcion use. (She likens the drug to a feeling "like Spring was put to an end by death" – presaging the rainy season – its very name evoking *haru-shi-on*, the Japanese characters for Spring, death, sound.)

Kyoko starts using the Bedroom without taking the sleeping pills, staying conscious – but never opening her eyes – while men in gasmasks and latex probe her nude body. On one visit, she and her friend discover a dead girl in the Bedroom, killed by an overdose of Halcion. She also discovers that her lover Kei is a long-term Halcion user. Kyoko's hallucinations start to include herself being videoed, naked, by her mother. Her relationship with Kei descends into video delirium. She stares into the watching lens as they fuck, anamorphic close-ups of her nipples and Kei's tongue flashing on-screen; she films her own genitals as she masturbates, and the TV relays each detail to Kei; they film each other, closer and closer, until the lenses of their cameras clash in a cold kiss. On Kyoko's next visit to the Bedroom, she opens her eyes for the first time as she is fondled, and is horrified to see that the man is Kei, wearing the dark glasses of a blind man and apparently in a narcoleptic trance state.

Meanwhile, another girl is found dead in the Bedroom, her metallic-painted body viciously striped with knife-tracks. Kyoko asks Mr Takano, the master of the Bedroom seen only via a distorted image in the video screen, whether he is responsible for her murder (ever the provocateur, Sato gave the role of Mr Takano to cannibal killer Issei Sagawa[4]). When she returns to Kei's flat, she finds him comatose next to a near-empty bottle of Halcion. Finding a video he has made, she watches it. It shows a terrified girl being chased, about to be raped, from the camera-user's point-of-view; Kyoko realises that Kei must be the killer. She revives him, he drowsily calls her Maya. She stabs him in the neck, cuts open her own hand. As Kei lies dying on the floor, she stuffs the rest of the Halcion

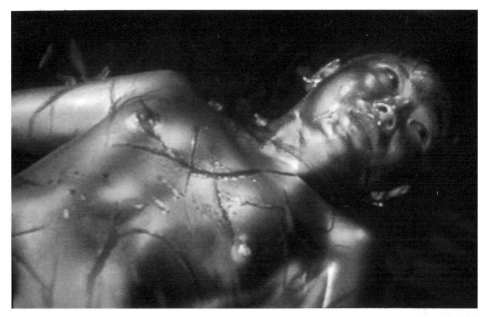

The Bedroom

into his mouth. "Me or my sister – which one did you love?".

As Kyoko tries to push Kei's body into the fridge, Mr Takano arrives. He claims that she is his wife, and shows her surveillance recordings of her visits to the Bedroom which reveal that *she* is the killer. She is in fact the younger sister Maya – it is Kyoko who has died, overdosed on Halcion; her death has traumatised Maya, confusing her identity, driving her to take more and more pills, to become paranoid of gazes. "That day, the world entered the rainy season. Everything that is surrounded by the capsule of endless falling water is dissolving. The earth... the cities... me..."

The film terminates with a bizarre coda, Kyoko's suicide by cling-film viewed in reverse, as the disembodied voice of Takano welcomes her back from the dead. END scrolls upscreen. With **The Bedroom**, Sato has produced another stylish composition of complex intercuts, flashbacks, recurring images, traumas, violence, hallucinations and perverse eroticism. Once more it is the camera's persistent gaze which punctuates the lives of his protagonists, as they struggle under the melancholy of subliminal manias and blurred identity, submerging the viewer by degree into the director's addictive, tactile pessimism.

Perhaps the most extreme and bewildering of Sato's recent films is **Nyogyaku: Naked Blood (Woman Abuse: Naked Blood**, 1996), in which the director on one hand takes a noticeable step away from sex cinema towards a more mystical plane, yet on the other encompasses along the way some of the most gruelling and graphic scenes of mutilation ever committed to film. As in **The Bedroom**, the premise of **Naked Blood** hinges on the invention of a new psychotropic drug. Eiji, a seventeen-year-old student, has developed a stimulant named Myson, a "pure anaesthesia" which by promoting the mass secretion of endorphins can literally turn pain into pleasure. At the same time his mother, a doctor, is conducting research into a new form of contraceptive medicine. Eiji

Naked Blood

secretly injects Myson into the contraceptive drips, and the three young girls taking part in an experiment to test the birth control drug are unwittingly dosed with his revolutionary pain-killer. Eiji videotapes the experiment from an adjoining rooftop; one of the girls, Mikami, sees and watches him.

We later learn that all three girls have their own eccentricity; one is obsessed with eating, another is a narcissist, and Mikami herself suffered such a trauma on the occasion of her first period that ever since that day she has been unable to sleep. Mikami lives in a stark white, antiseptic apartment which also contains a giant, silver cactus which she talks to. She also links to it "telepathically" via VR headsets wired to the plant and to her black leather sleep simulation chair. In this way Mikami experiences how the cactus feels and dreams of desert landscapes; but she is also plagued by vivid menstrual nightmares which place her in overlit arcades, her whole body and school uniform drenched in catamenial blood, the only escape a swimming-pool which forever clouds with crimson.

Watching videotapes of his mother's experiment, Eiji becomes obsessed with Mikami as she stares into his lens; he starts to follow her around, filming her, until she confronts him. She takes Eiji to the botanical gardens, a place which she hates despite its beauty, since due to her hypersensitive hearing she is virtually deafened by the "screaming of the flowers" and the indecipherable chatter of insects. This, Mikami confides, makes her suicidal. They adjourn to the tranquillity of her apartment (the "dormant" cactus, she explains, is the only silent plant), where Eiji tries the VR headset and soon "sees" an oceanic dreamscape.

The film now intercuts between the other two girls who took part in the experiment, and Eiji's mother. One girl, the narcissist, examines her body in the mirror.

Plucking a stray hair from her armpit, she is surprised that this normally painful act feels somehow pleasurable. She then pierces her ears with needles, beginning to revel in the sensation. Meanwhile the other girl, the glutton, cuts her thumb while preparing *tempura*, and sucks on it with greedy pleasure. She is soon compelled to thrust her batter-coated hand into hot oil, feeling no pain, and then starts to chew on her own cooked fingers in auto-cannibalistic ecstasy. The Myson is taking effect...

Eiji's mother is watching old Super-8 films of herself and her late husband. A beach scene, she is pregnant with Eiji. Her husband sees a "flash of light" on the horizon, wades out into the sea to investigate and suddenly, in the blink of an eye, is gone forever. We later learn that he was a scientist researching into immortality, by means of the transmogrification of mortal mass into light.

Cut to the narcissist, who by now has punctured nearly her entire body with safety-pins, bodkins and even the thick, sharpened awl which we now see her driving in and out of her forearm. Her entire skin is blood-drenched and hanging with silverware, her compulsive pleasure at this self-perforation almost orgasmic. Cut back to the glutton, for what is surely the most bizarre and gut-wrenching sequence of self-mutilation ever shown in a commercial film. She is naked, sitting on the kitchen table, and slowly, deliberately, eating herself with a knife and fork. Starting with the erogenous zones, she cuts off her own vaginal lips and devours them, raw and bloody; next comes her nipple, sliced clean off, and then she plunges the fork into her own eyeball, extricates it roots and all, and chews it deliriously while her empty socket weeps cataracts of crimson[5].

The next time we see the narcissist she is dead, a six-inch awl stuck through her forehead into her brain, victim of the ultimate piercing. Likewise the glutton, who lies lifeless on her kitchen table in a veritable ocean of blood. Eiji's mother, learning of their deaths, is understandably distraught; she analyses her contraceptive drug and discovers traces of Myson. Eiji admits his deceit and rushes away. The doctor calls Mikami to the hospital, and finds alarming levels of endorphins in her bloodstream. We next see Mikami leaving the hospital to join Eiji, who has cycled to her apartment. Cut to Eiji's mother, who now lies immobile, barely alive, on a bed in the experiment room; her abdomen has been cut wide open, the skin and sinew peeled back to expose her pulsating viscera.

Eiji injects himself with the remaining Myson, and he and Mikami don the VR headsets. "The dream will live inside us forever." They fuck in virtual space, naked bodies entwined over psychedelic backdrops of purple cacti, overlit clinical wards, vast oceanic/ maternal spaces[6]. In flashback we see Mikami visiting and dispatching her two colleagues: plunging the awl into the narcissist's head, repeatedly stabbing the glutton with a butcher knife till her blood sprays out in fountains. Next she is seen vivisecting Eiji's mother with a scalpel, opening up her belly, tearing apart the skin and stomach walls. Eiji is filming from the next rooftop.

Mikami and Eiji cease copulating, remove the VR sets. Mikami pulls out a retractable blade and slashes Eiji's throat, repeating the act with savage violence till his blood spurts in geysers. As he expires, we cut to the hospital where his mother has a dying vision of her late husband. He climbs head first into her gaping abdomen, disappearing completely inside her, and pulls closed the flaps of flesh and muscle behind him. She dies, her body dissolves into light. Cut back to Mikami's apartment – her cactus has flowered. Fade to white screen. A brief coda shows Mikami several years later, a nomad accompanied by the young son she conceived with Eiji (also named Eiji and already weaned onto his first video camera), on a mission to defoliate the planet of all plant life

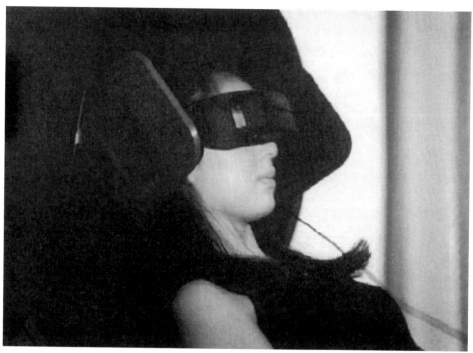

Naked Blood

except the cactus. "The dream will never be over."

Mixing shock gore effects with cybersex, medical fetishism, video mediation, narcoleptic delusion and Nietzschean notions of eternal return, **Naked Blood** may well be the ultimate fusion of the visceral, the psychopathological and the metaphysical, a film whose nearest analogue in Western cinema would be the work of David Cronenberg[7]. Hisayasu Sato's *oeuvre* is fast becoming equally, if not more, disturbing than Cronenberg's, and although his films lack the latter's technical polish – primarily as a result of budgetary limitations – his future directions threaten to lead the viewer into uncompromising, hitherto uncharted realms of venereal psychosis and virtual delirium.

NOTES

1. Born 1959 in Shizuoka City, Hisayasu Sato graduated from Tokyo College of Industrial Arts to become an assistant director at Shishi Productions. After working for various directors he made his solo debut in 1985 with **Totsugeki! Rorita Mitsuryo (Charge! Lolita Poaching)**. For this and two other films he directed the same year, he won the prize for Best New Director at the pink film industry's annual Zoom-Up Festival. Since then he has produced around 50 adult films.

2. Koji Wakamatsu was the *enfant terrible* of 1960s Japanese porn cinema, a primitive genius producing non-stop works of pop *avant-garde* sex and violence such as **The Embryo Hunts In Secret, Violated Angels, Narcissus Of Lust, Violent Virgin** and **The Angelic Orgasm**. For further details, see *Eros In Hell: Sex, Blood & Madness In Japanese Cinema* (Creation Books, 1998).

3. **Aria For Gazes** has now been sub-titled and released in England by Screen Edge Video under the title **The Bedroom**.

4. In 1981 Issei Sagawa, the son of a wealthy Japanese businessman, was 32 and putting the finishing touches to his doctoral thesis in Paris. Sagawa, "a clever and delicate young man", became obsessed with a fellow postgraduate student, a 25-year-old Dutch woman named Renée Hartevelt. On June 11th 1981, Sagawa invited Hartevelt around to his apartment for dinner and a discussion about literature. After the discussion, Sagawa asked Hartevelt if she would have sex with him. After she declined, he requested that she read a poem into a tape recorder for him to work on his pronunciation. While she was doing so, Sagawa went to get his .22 calibre rifle and shot Hartevelt in the back of her head. He then had sex with her body, slept with it and ate portions of it raw. Two days later, he stuffed the remains of the body into a pair of suitcases which he dumped in the Bois de Boulogne, where they were soon discovered by the police.

When they raided Sagawa's small Paris apartment, police officers found pieces of red meat carefully wrapped in plastic bags, which were taken to the police laboratory. Forensic evidence established beyond any doubt that this was human flesh, cut from Hartevelt's arms, thighs and hips. Other pieces of human flesh in the refrigerator were eventually identified as coming from the victim's lips. These pieces matched the strange mutilations found on Renée Hartevelt's dismembered corpse.

Arrested and tried, Sagawa was found to be insane and committed to a French mental hospital. In May 1984 his father's company, Kurita Water Industries, signed an important business deal with the French chemical conglomerate Elf-Aquitaine, and, not accidentally, at the same time, Sagawa was transferred to a mental hospital in Japan. In August 1985 he was released from care, even though many doctors – including the hospital's deputy superintendent – considered Sagawa to be an untreatable psychotic.

Other notable Japanese killers of the modern era have included Tsutomu Miyazaki, an impotent paedophile "vampire" who in 1989 mutilated and murdered four schoolgirls and wrote odes to the body parts he kept in jars beneath the floorboards. Miyazaki was an avid collector of videos – he had around 6,000 of them – including such splatter/gore films as the notorious **Guinea Pig 2**. As a result, sale of certain videos in Japan was at last restricted to those aged over 18.

5. In its prolonged and detailed presentation of these horrendous autophagous acts, **Naked Blood** goes as far as other Japanese films such as **Guinea Pig** or **Atrocity**, and possibly even equals the violent excesses of notorious Italian exploitation horrors **Cannibal Ferox** and **Cannibal Holocaust**.

6. The ocean, swimming-pools, pools of blood, are a recurring maternal motif in the film. Eiji's mother even describes Myson (my son) as being "the colour of the sea".

7. Cronenberg's films need no introduction. **Naked Blood** might be most closely compared to **Videodrome**, while the themes of Sato's other films echo both the sibling traumas of **Dead Ringers** and the sex/technology interface most cogently expressed in **Crash**.

STRANGE IMAGES OF DEATH

Manson, Macbeth, Polanski

Mikita Brottman

"I have supp'd full with horrors:
Direness, familiar to my slaughterous thoughts,
Cannot once start me."
(William Shakespeare, *Macbeth*, V.v. 13–15)

Mid-July, 1969. Roman Polanski, eagerly awaiting the arrival of his first child, is dining with producer Michael Klinger at the Polish Club in Kensington. Polanski reveals to Klinger that his life has rarely been so happy. Things finally seem to be coming together for him, emotionally.

Polanski's wife Sharon, more than eight months pregnant, is impatient to leave for L.A. to prepare the couple's new home for the birth of her baby. The airlines will not permit her to fly, so Roman arranges for her to sail home on board the QE2 in the company of her new puppy, Prudence. Polanski himself, too restless for an ocean journey, promises to join her in L.A. in a few days. As he says good-bye to Sharon on board ship, a grotesque thought flashes through his mind: "you'll never see her again". The premonition implants itself indelibly on his consciousness. He leaves Sharon on the ship and walks back to his car trying to shake off the morbid feeling, promising himself to call his friend, *Playboy* impresario Victor Lownes, to dine at the Playboy Club, to meet up with some girls....

6pm, Friday August 8th, 1969. Polanski's friend and compatriot Voytek Frykowski drops in to the Beverly Hills Wilshire Hotel to see his friend, the artist Vitold Kaczanowski, who's laying the carpet in the Hotel's Art Gallery in preparation for the opening of his new exhibition. Voytek invites Vitold and his girlfriend, Christine Larene, out to dinner that night with himself, his girlfriend Gibby Folger, Sharon Tate and Jay Sebring, then back to Sharon and Roman's place on Cielo Drive for drugs. But Vitold needs to finish preparing the gallery, and declines the invitation.

Voytek shows off his new pink, flower-patterned trousers.

"If you want to be a fag, go ahead", laughs Vitold, "but the fags are going to be after you".

Voytek tells Vitold that he's on the ninth day of a continuous mescaline trip.

8.45pm. Jay Sebring arrives at Cielo Drive at Sharon's invitation. Jay, Sharon, Voytek, Sharon and Gibby go to dinner at El Coyote restaurant, the return home to the Polanskis' house on Cielo Drive.

11.30pm. Gibby retires to a bedroom at Cielo Drive. Jay and Sharon go to Sharon's room for a chat. Voytek crashes out on the couch in the living room, which is draped with an enormous American flag.

12.08am. The house on Cielo Drive is assailed by a person or persons unknown. Sharon and her unborn son are stabbed to death, along with Jay Sebring, Voytek Frykowski, Abigail Folger and a young man named Steven Parent, who is visiting the house's caretaker, William Garretson.

Meanwhile, in London, Polanski dines out at the Playboy Club with Victor Lownes, then returns home to his mews house in Eaton Place with a girl Lownes describes as a "bimbo". Neither Lownes nor Polanski recall her name.

Cut to January 1970. Less than six months later, Polanski begins filming that most inauspicious of Shakespeare's plays, *Macbeth*.

*****

1957. The Polish Film Academy, Lodz. The young Roman Polanski is showing his first film – a three-minute, voyeuristic horror short entitled **The Crime**, or **Murder**. A shadowy, knife-wielding figure visible only from the chest down, creeping through the darkness, discovers the open door of a room where a man lies sleeping, and stabs him several times before leaving. The film has no dialogue, merely a dark setting and a bleak act of murder.

Polanski's subsequent films, including **Knife In The Water** (1962), **Repulsion** (1965), **Cul-de-Sac** (1966), **The Fearless Vampire Killers** (1967) and **Rosemary's Baby** (1968) all feature protracted scenes of macabre violence and mayhem. By 1969, many critics begin to feel that it is about time the promising young director moves on to some subject other than sex, murder and violence. But if his earlier films appear compulsively brutal, Polanski seems to have saved his fullest efforts for **Macbeth** (1971).

At least, the critics seem to think so. William Shaw points out that "murder, disfigurement and dismemberment are presented with scrupulous attention to detail. ...Polanski's use of violence certainly makes unmistakable and palpable the full horror of Macbeth's deeds"[1]. Wendy Rogers Harper is shocked at the way in which Polanski "reddens the celluloid, graphically and brutally depicting those incidents which Shakespeare only reports: Macbeth hewing enemy soldiers, Duncan hanging the Thane of Cawdor, Macbeth repeatedly stabbing Duncan, Macbeth's henchmen murdering Banquo or raping and destroying Macbeth's household, Macduff decapitating Macbeth. Crumpled bodies and blood-spattered messengers litter the screen"[2]. Normand Berlin is horrified by the film's litany of "mutilated bodies, hacked limbs, throats cut, heads lopped off, bloody faces – a parade of horrors", warning his readers that "Polanski does not relent in his visual presentation of the horror"[3].

Nudity, madness, quirky sexual relationships, varying degrees of neurotic compulsion... nobody is surprised to recognize these elements in a film typical of Polanski's morbid imagination. What makes people shift around uncomfortably in their seats is the amount of violence the film contains. This discomfort is couched in various guises. Nigel Andrews in *Sight And Sound* criticises "the film's general intention to de-mystify"[4]. Kenneth Rothwell claims to be unhappy with the film's barren landscape of desolate nihilism[5]. But this, of course, isn't the real problem. What really makes people feel uneasy is the fact that Polanski has chosen to make such a violent adaptation of an exceptionally harrowing story so soon after the recent terrifying tragedy in his personal

Rosemary's Baby

life. The honest and thoughtful critics, like Paul Zimmerman in *Newsweek*, say so straight out:

"The parallels between the Manson murders and the mad, bloody acts of these beautiful, damned Macbeths kept pressing themselves upon the viewer, as though Shakespeare's play has provided Polanski with some strange opportunity to act out his own complicated feelings about mystic ties, blood, evil and revenge. ...All that is good here seems but a pretext for close-ups of knives drawing geysers of blood from the flesh of men, women and children. No chance to revel in gore is passed up... [the film is] a rationalization of a psychic compulsion ...[a] work of art – in the grand manner of Buchenwald, Lidice and, yes, the Manson murders."[6]

Time magazine points out that "Polanski is most at home dealing with black magic... His affection for the supernatural is so unrestrained that many of the movie's straight scenes have an almost cursory air"[7]. In *Women's Wear Daily*, critic Gail Rock observes that the violence Polanski presents us with outdoes even that of Manson and his Family. "[The film] is an assault on the audience", she complains, "that seems to me to divert us from the intellectual thrust of Macbeth and turn us into voyeurs at a killing spree that makes Manson and his friends pale in comparison"[8]. It is somewhat ironic, in this light, that journalists writing in *Time* and *Newsweek* described the horrors of the Manson murders by comparing them to Polanski's films. According to *Time*, the killings are "as grisly as anything depicted in Polanski's film explorations of the dark and melancholy corners of the human character", and *Newsweek* concludes that the crimes outdo even Polanski[9].

Roger Ebert, syndicated critic of the *Chicago Sun-Times*, is also honest in describing his feelings about the film: "It is impossible to watch a film directed by Roman Polanski and not react on more than one level to images such as a baby being "untimely ripped from his mother's womb". Polanski's characters all resemble Manson... they are anti-intellectual, witless and driven by deep, shameful wells of lust and violence[10]." Most uneasy of all, however, is Pauline Kael, writing in the *New Yorker*: "In the Manson murders, there was an eerie element that the public responded to. Even though we know that Roman Polanski had nothing whatever to do with causing the murder of his wife and unborn child and friends, the massacre seemed a vision realized from his nightmare movies. And there was an element of guilt and embarrassment in this connection we made. ...[Polanski] didn't quite understand... through either a strange form of naïveté or a divided consciousness... that this connection was inevitable... [but] one sees the Manson murders in this **Macbeth** because the director has put them there[11]."

Polanski, understandably, is shifty and defensive about such allegations. In an interview with Bernard Weinraub in *The New York Times Magazine* in 1971, he argues that his film is violent because "...the play is violent. And life is violent too... if you don't show [violence] realistically, then that's immoral and harmful. If you don't upset people, then that's obscenity"[12]. And in an interview with Sydney Edwards of the *London Evening Standard*, Polanski tries to divert public attention away from the Manson murders and towards earlier events in his life. "If anything," he says of the assault on Macduff's castle in **Macbeth**, "the scenes were prompted by something I went through a long time ago in Poland ...when two young Nazi officers walked into our apartment ...and I saw them drag a woman down the stairs by her hair from the fifth floor. The attitude of the murderers in **Macbeth** is the attitude of those two Nazis"[13]. Later, however, in his autobiography, Polanski claims that it is his father, not himself, who witnesses the incident ("[he] had seen a woman being dragged downstairs by the hair. We sat and waited, the room lit only by the glow from the stove. Idly I licked my finger and drew a swastika on the wall. My father angrily wiped it off")[14]. There is no doubt that the young Polanski, hiding out like a rat in the war-torn ghettos of Krakow, plays witness to unspeakable atrocities, including his mother and grandmother being dragged off by the Nazis on to an Auschwitz transport carriage. Those close to Polanski, however, see statements like the one he makes in the *London Evening Standard* interview as deliberately evasive. Many of his friends and colleagues feel that he has chosen **Macbeth** as a kind of spectacular response to media pressure and to show everyone he has not lost control. Martin Shaw, who plays Banquo in the film, comes to believe that the filming of **Macbeth** is Polanski's own special way of coming to terms with an immense grief ("...everybody has their own way of expressing or expiating something awful that has happened, and I suppose that was his"[15]). In fact, Polanski's collaborator on the film, Kenneth Tynan, becomes increasingly concerned as filming progresses that Polanski is turning **Macbeth** into a macabre re-run of the recent tragic events in his life. Tynan confesses to feeling uneasy about the project, but agrees to abide by Polanski's ground-rule that the murders won't be discussed on set. Tynan eventually comes to the conclusion that Polanski believes that the power of evil is real, is a definite force. The director's alleged paranoia is well-known, but many who know him believe the horrors of the Manson murders have pushed him over the edge into paranoid psychosis. "They said... that I did not need a psychoanalyst because I am perfectly balanced," claims Polanski, "which grieved me very much, for I always took myself for a madman"[16].

Macbeth

The most timid and tentative of critics analyze the film without reference to Polanski's personal life and circumstances, finding it more legitimate, more consistent and certainly a lot more tasteful to analyze the violence in **Macbeth** as an independent assemblage of signs and images, irrespective of any synchronicitous connections with the director's biography or personal life. But nobody can appreciate the full dramatic impact of Polanski's film without knowing what happened on that terrifying evening in Bel Air in August 1969. Whether he chooses this narrative as a deliberate way of coming to terms with the horrors of that hot August night, or whether other, stranger factors are at play, it's clear that Polanski is drawn to the story – at least initially – for reasons that are intensely personal. In fact, in the context of certain revelations that have recently come to light about Polanski's early life and the details of the Manson trial, the tangled web of connections between Polanski, the Manson murders and Shakespeare's *Macbeth* becomes increasingly frightening and mysterious.

*****

"...safe in a ditch he bides,
With twenty trenched gashes on his head,
The least a death to nature..."
(III, iv, 25–7)

Macbeth

A knife sinks into human flesh, drawing out a thick pulse of blood. *Macbeth* is a story that stinks of "bloody execution". The opening sequence of Polanski's film is one in which "battle-axes, knives, spears, swords and maces sever, puncture, crush, crunch and crack"[17]. Shakespeare makes no bones about it: Polanski shows it like it is. Duncan (Nicholas Selby) is covered in "gash'd stabs", his flesh punctured over and over again by Macbeth's fatal dagger until his skin is "lac'd with his golden blood". His two minions are put to death with no less violence, stabbed with their own daggers, "unmannerly breach'd with gore". Banquo, hunting in the forest, is knocked off his horse by a flying arrow and gets an axe in the back, a knife in the throat, and "twenty mortal murthers on his crown" before returning, "blood-bolter'd", to shake his "gory locks" at the unquiet King (Jon Finch). Macduff's castle is laid to waste, his wife, children and servants besieged in their own home while their master is away, and slaughtered by a sudden hail of vicious stab wounds. And in the final, climactic battle, both Macduff (Terence Baylor) and Macbeth's last desperate retainers are butchered by enemy knives before the final death-blow, which slices cleanly through Macbeth's spinal cord – a sequence best described by Normand Berlin:

"...as Macbeth climbs stairs to get to Macduff, Macduff's large and furious stroke severs Macbeth's head from his body. Polanski's camera follows the head as it leaves the body and rolls on the floor... and then the camera cuts to the body, sans head, which balances for a second on the steps before it sways backward, crashing down the steps. A horrible,

sordid, realistic sequence. Shakespeare has Macduff return to the stage with Macbeth's head on a pole; Polanski shows us how it got there."[18]

Viciously physical acts of stabbing – but all of them evoked by Shakespeare, whose imagery is spliced through with countless allusions to piercing knives, probing swords and twisting daggers bursting through human flesh, from Macbeth's own "air-drawn dagger", its blade and dudgeon splattered with "gouts of blood", to his desperate plea that his "keen knife see not the wound it makes". In his final piece of "bloody business", Macduff alleges that his "voice" is in his "sword". Malcolm (Stephen Chase) fears that "there's daggers in men's smiles: the near in blood, the nearer bloody ... This murtherous shaft that's shot Hath not let lighted", and Macbeth compliments his personal hit-men on being "the best o'th'cut-throats". And most strikingly of all, Scotland is described as a woman under assault by knife, and "each new day a gash Is added to her wounds".

After their shocking discovery of the body of Steven Parent, slumped over the wheel of his car with three bullet wounds in his chest and one in his face, L.A.P.D officers entering the compound at Cielo Drive on the morning of August 9th are confronted with what looks like a group of shop-window mannequins that have been dipped in red paint then tossed haphazardly on the grass, their limbs pointing stiffly in various directions. As the officers get closer, they begin to realize that these are the bodies of real human beings, all stabbed to death viciously, displaying a total of 169 puncture wounds between them. On the grass in front of the house sprawls the body of Voytek Frykowski, who appears to have put up a vicious struggle, killed by 51 stab wounds and 2 gunshot wounds to the torso, causing extensive haemorrhaging. His head has been smashed 13 times with a blunt instrument, later revealed to be the gun handle. Further out, towards the pool, lies the body of Voytek's girlfriend Gibby Folger, her white nightdress stained with blood, who has been chased out of the house and across the grass before being caught and stabbed 28 times in the heart and elsewhere, also causing extensive haemorrhaging. In the front room, beside the fireplace, sprawls the body of Sharon's friend Jay Sebring, his body covered in dried blood, dead from exsanguination from various stab wounds. And there, on the floor, on the other side of the sofa, lies the body of Sharon, over 8 months pregnant, clad only in panties and a bra, killed by 16 massive stab wounds to the chest and back which penetrate the heart, lungs and liver causing an enormous haemorrhage. There is blood everywhere. In each case, the cause of death is exsanguination. The victims, quite literally, have bled to death. Each body has been stabbed between 7 and 30 times, as well as shot. Many of the minor stab wounds are in and of themselves fatal – "the least a death to nature".

An early shot in Polanski's **Macbeth** shows us the Thane of Cawdor stretched out and tied to a rack on the ground. The camera then cuts to what Kenneth Rothwell describes as "a Breughel-like nightmare"[19] involving a massive scaffold from which several hanged men already dangle, with appropriate gurgling sounds dominating the soundtrack. Condemned prisoners, panting and sweating, line up to await their own executions, as long ropes are tossed gracefully over the tall scaffold. One reluctant prisoner, struggling with the executioners who are attempting to place a noose around his neck, is violently beaten into submission. When Cawdor is executed, he's forced off a castle parapet to die brutally at the end of a chain tied round his neck.

Macbeth

Vicious executions resonate in equally vivid images of hanging and strangulation. One of the items the witches bury in the sand is a hangman's noose from a gibbet. The well-rope used to draw water on the night of Duncan's murder ends in a thick, noose-like hook. No sooner has the blood been washed from the hands of the murders than we witness other hands pulling impatiently on a bell-rope. The same image is used to announce the uncanny removal of Burnam Wood to Dunsinane. Banquo is knocked off his horse by a trap consisting of a looped noose tied around a taut sapling. One of Macduff's children is left dead in a haycart, a noose fastened tightly round his throat. The Thane of Cawdor, his neck broken, swings in circles on the end of a chain. At the same moment, Macbeth is being honoured by the presentation of Cawdor's own chain-mail coat of arms, which the King hangs proudly around his neck.

But Shakespeare's play contains only two actual references to hanging. The first comes when Macbeth, moments after the first murder, looks down aghast at his bloodied "hangman's hands". The second comes when he threatens a messenger. "If thou speakst false," he claims, "Upon the next tree shalt thou hang alive Till famine cling thee". Both images are vivid, but both are metaphoric. Polanski gives us the real thing.

August 9th, 1969 – the night after the slaughter at Cielo Drive. Nine or ten miles away, in a suburban house in the quiet residential suburb of Los Feliz, two blood-covered bodies lie dead on the floor. Both bodies have nooses round their necks. They are Leno and Rosemary LaBianca, selected for slaughter at random by Charlie and his Family, creepy-crawling round the suburbs in the middle of the night, itching for some action.

Leno is lying on the living room floor. The noose around his neck, knotted so tightly he appears to have been throttled by it, is tied to a massive lamp. His hands are tied behind his back with a leather thong.

Rosemary lies upstairs in the bedroom, on the floor next to the bed she shares with her husband. Her hands are not tied but, like her husband, she has a pillowcase over her head and a lamp cord wrapped round her neck. The cord is tied to one of a pair of bedroom lamps, both of which have overturned. The tautness of the cord, plus a second pool of blood about two feet from Rosemary's body, suggests that perhaps she's tried to crawl along the bedroom floor to get to the phone, pulling the lamps over while doing so.

Ropes are also found round the necks of two of the victims at Cielo Drive – Sharon Tate and Jay Sebring. Before the party leave the Spahn ranch, Charlie reminds Tex to bring a long rope with him, and it is this rope that he flings over one of the exposed beams in the sitting room at Cielo Drive, forming a kind of makeshift double scaffold, at the same time linking together the bodies of Sharon and Jay. And although for reasons of discretion he decides not to include it in his autopsy report, Dr. Thomas Noguchi, the famous Beverly Hills "coroner to the stars", mentions during the trial that one of the bodies has some unusual marks on it. The body is Sharon's. The marks are rope-burns on her left cheek. Noguchi believes, after studying these abrasions quite carefully, that Sharon has been hung. He hastens to point out that hanging definitely wasn't the cause of her death, and in fact she'd probably been suspended for less than a minute, in all. But he's quite sure that the abrasions on Sharon's cheek are rope-burns.

Perhaps it is these rope-burns that draw Polanski to the image of hanging when he comes to adapt Macbeth. Perhaps he cannot rid his mind of the picture of Sharon, almost nine months pregnant, choking and swinging helplessly from the rafters of their new home. Perhaps it is this image which fuels his obsession with thoughts of hanging and strangulation in his next film. Or perhaps this obsession is fed by another image – the image of Sharon sharing the last moments of her life with her ex-lover Jay Sebring, tied to him on the end of the same rope, in death as in life. When police question Polanski about Sharon's relationship with Jay, he lets slip that the celebrity hairdresser was a sadist and something of a rope fetishist who had quite a few kinky "hang-ups" (Polanski's words), including bondage and faux-strangulation. "I started liking Jay very much," confesses Polanski during one of his many interrogations by the L.A.P.D. "Oh, I know he had his hang-ups. He liked to whip-tie girls. Sharon told me that he tied her to the bed once... very funny, but very sad"[20].

*****

"By the pricking of my thumbs,
Something wicked this way comes"
(IV, I, 44–45)

Shakespeare's Macbeth: a play whose history is plagued by accidents, bad luck, macabre rumours and frightening circumstances; a story which tells of the Devil working through his earthly minions. "The instruments of darkness" win Macbeth over through their "supernatural soliciting", showing us how the Devil really can "speak true", can "win us with honest trifles, to betray us In deepest consequence". The play is full of witchcraft

Polanski, Tate: The Fearless Vampire Killers

and demons, of "black Hecate's summons", of "Night's black agents" and sights "which might appall the Devil". Macduff swears that "Not in the legions of horrid Hell can come a Devil more damn'd In evils, to top Macbeth", and Malcolm, the future King of Scotland, claims that he is a man "who would not betray The Devil to his fellow".

Demons are nothing new to Polanski. The two films he makes right before Macbeth are both full of evil. In making **The Fearless Vampire Killers** (1967), Polanski and his collaborator Gerard Brach hole up in various of the world's libraries to research the occult folklore surrounding vampirism.

Demons are nothing new to Sharon, either. While Polanski is researching occult folklore for background to **The Fearless Vampire Killers**, Sharon is in London working on a horror film of her own, **The Eye Of The Devil** (aka **13**, 1967) with David Niven, Deborah Kerr, Donald Pleasance and David Hemmings. The film tells a cryptic tale of black magic and devil-worship, and a hooded cult which practices ritual sacrifice. Sharon has just a small part in the movie. She plays a girl who is a practising witch.

And demons have never been anything new to Charlie. Some people even consider him to be a demon himself. Some people call him "The Demon of Death Valley". Other people call him a deity, Jesus Christ, God or The Devil. Bruce Davis, a leading Family member, calls him "an instrument of the evil supernatural". Sharon's mother calls him a "butcher" – a word that is also used, and also by a relative of one of his victims – to describe Macbeth. After the fatal last battle, Macduff refers to his overthrown enemy as "This dead butcher".

In the days following the Tate/LaBianca murders, there is an enormous amount of press speculation about the ritualistic nature of the killings. Some people say that

Sharon Tate

Sharon is found nude, her unborn child ripped out of her womb, that one or both of her breasts had been slashed off; and that there is a swastika carved into her stomach and the bloody handle of a paring knife found next to her leg, its blade broken off. Other people say that some of the victims have been sexually mutilated. Some say that the towel Sadie Atkins has thrown over Jay's head is a white or black hood, that he has been sexually mutilated, found wearing only the torn remnants of a pair of boxer shorts, his body also bearing swastikas carved into the flesh.

But some things we know to be true. We know, for example, that Voytek Frykowski, sprawled out on the sofa, is brutally awoken, like the sleeping Duncan, to come face to face with his own killer.

"What kind of game is this?", asks the dazed Voytek. But this is no game.

"I am the Devil", Tex tells him calmly. "I'm here to do the Devil's business".

Another true fact: right now, Tex Watson, from his prison quarters in Obispo, California, is the pastor of a mail-order Christian ministry.

*****

"What are these,
So wither'd and so wild in their attire,
That look not like th'inhabitants o'th' earth,
And yet are on't?"
(I, iii, 39-42)

Caliban: the monstrous offspring of the Devil's copulation with a witch in *The Tempest*. Caliban Films: the production company formed by Polanski to pay for his production of Macbeth.

Three witches, one young and pretty and the other two older, gnarled and mutilated, mutter a series of curses as they drop their morbid charms into a ditch: a severed hand, a vial of blood, a greasy hangman's noose. When Macbeth visits their cave to learn more of them, it is filled with a coven of nude witches, some young, but mostly old. This, according to Normand Berlin, is an especially skilful touch on Polanski's part: "Nudity in a young woman (whether witch or Lady Macbeth) is pleasing to the eye; nudity in old hags, with breasts hanging and shape distorted, is offensive, grotesque, disgusting. That young and old are together forces us to acknowledge that the young will become old, fair turning to foul; that the cave is crowded makes us realize that the world contains many witches – both ideas reinforcing the all-encompassing quality of the witches suggested in Polanski's first sequence. The grotesqueness of their bodies is matched by the wildness of their looks."[21] In his article "Golgotha Triumphant", Kenneth Rothwell agrees that this is one of the most dramatic and effecting sequences in Polanski's adaptation: "Overtones of the Manson murders and **Rosemary's Baby** again intrude, as a gaggle of naked crones, hags, Struldbrugs, geriatric horrors of every description, convene in a cave to concoct a witches' broth of brain-numbing revoltingness. ...Against a backdrop of flashes showing a foetus being removed from a womb, ...Macbeth reaches out, accepts, and then quaffs this loathsome brew."[22]

The opening scene with the witches is shot in a remote spot in the mountains of Snowdonia. To get to the location, the actresses playing the witches have to be driven two miles along ancient Roman roads in a Land Rover, then carried through howling

Macbeth

winds and pouring rain to a battered building where Polanski and the rest of the crew are waiting. Shooting in these terrible conditions is almost impossible. Polanski's instructions are virtually inaudible, visibility is poor and the actors are put off by the gale-force winds. One camera man is blown off a boom and into a crevice in the rock face, narrowly escaping death.

Polanski's witches' cave is reached through a small, tunnelled dugout in the side of a cliff, disguised by a thick growth of sage and bracken. Into this dugout the "secret, black and midnight hags" disappear, seemingly to vanish, then appear again suddenly, one witch popping out to flash her bloomers at Macbeth contemptuously before scuttling back down into the bowels of the earth.

Learning that Hugh Hefner's birthday is coming up, Polanski decides to surprise his benefactor with a sign of gratitude for Hefner's generous financing of the film's already over-run budget. Polanski makes him a gift on celluloid – footage of a group of ghastly, naked witches singing "Happy Birthday Dear Hef", which Polanski posts to the financier back at the Playboy mansion in Los Angeles.

The world contains many witches. In the Summer of 1970, L.A.P.D. officers Powell and Pursell are searching the desolate hills of California's Death Valley for Manson Family lookout posts. Powell comes across a very well-disguised dugout, its tin roof hidden by brush and dirt, on the side of a hill south of the Barker ranch[23]. The officers have almost walked right past it when they suddenly spot a bedraggled female emerge from the brush, squat, and urinate, then disappear back into the bushes. Powell covers the entrance with his rifle while Pursell climbs on top of the dugout, chooses a heavy-looking rock and drops it down hard on the tin roof. The hills echo with the sudden sound it makes. Three dusty and barefoot young women rush out of the cave and are arrested immediately. Among them are Tate/LaBianca murderers Patricia (Katie) Krenwinkel and Leslie (Ouisch) Van Houten.

Later on, while they're searching the outskirts of the Barker ranch – one of the Family's most secret outposts – officers Powell and Pursell stumble across a group of seven silent females, all nude or partially so, hiding behind various clumps of sagebrush[24]. The officers question the women, but receive no useful information from them.

The world contains many witches. During Charlie's trial, Family member Linda Kasabian, bravely turned witness for the prosecution, confesses she still feels as though she's being controlled by Charlie's personal vibrations, and there are times even now when she actually believes herself to be a witch. When she was living at the Spahn Ranch, she was quite convinced of it. But then, the Spahn Ranch is a very strange place. Searching through some of the ranch's outbuildings, prosecutor Bugliosi suddenly hears some odd, muffled sounds coming from a doghouse. When he leans down and looks inside, he sees two dogs and behind them, crouched in the corner, a toothless, white-haired old woman of about 80. He later checks with one of the ranch hands to see if the strange guest needs any help, but he says that she's happy where she is.[25]

There are witches in Polanski's life, too. The day before her murder, Sharon presides over her own little gathering of three. Her two best friends, Joanna Pettet and Barbara Lewis, arrive at Cielo Drive at about 12.30 for a leisurely gossip and chat. The maid, Winnie, fixes lunch for the three girls in the kitchen while they sit outside by the pool, where it's cooler. The conversation is all gossip and small talk, women's talk. Sharon, her swollen belly uncomfortable in the heat, is wearing just her bikini; she's been floating in her rubber tire to take some of the weight off her feet and back. They chat about the baby, due any day now. Winnie brings out lunch and they eat outside, by the pool. At the far end of the house, the decorator has just arrived to start painting the end room that's going to make the most perfect nursery.

Roman hasn't returned to L.A. as soon as he promised. Instead, he's been hanging around in London, working on his script for *Day Of The Dolphins* and partying vigorously. Sharon, waiting impatiently for him to come home, has kept herself busy buying baby clothes and books about child care, getting ready for the baby's birth. Joanna and Barbara are surprised to hear that Roman's still away in London with Sharon so heavily pregnant. Sharon's really angry with him. She's been planning a big party for his 36th birthday, on the 18th, and she's already enroled him in a course for expectant fathers. Now, this morning, he phones her at about 11am and tells her that he might not be back even then. She can't understand why he feels he has to stay away for so long. After all, it's not as though he can't work on his script at home – what does he have to hang around in London for....? Joanna and Barbara can only sympathize. The last few weeks of pregnancy are the worst – everybody knows that. It's bad enough Sharon having to cope being so heavily pregnant on her own, but she's also ended up playing hostess to Roman's friends as well. It's not Gibby that's a problem, it's her junkie boyfriend Voytek, who Sharon's really starting to dislike, and if it wasn't for Jay coming over to help her out she doesn't know how she'd manage. It seems really selfish of Roman.... Joanna and Barbara agree. How can he expect to treat her like this? If he's going to be a father, he's going to have to start taking his responsibilities a lot more seriously, and not be so obsessive about his work..... The gossip session goes on well into the hot afternoon. Winnie comes out to collect the lunch dishes and takes them into the kitchen to wash, then gets on with a bit of light housework. When she's finished, she goes outside and tells Sharon that she's going to leave. Since it's so hot, Sharon invites her to stay overnight at the house, but she has to get home.

Round about 3 o'clock, Sharon kisses her friends good-bye. After they leave, she feels anxious and restless. She calls her friend Jacqueline Susann, who she met on the set of **Valley Of The Dolls**, and asks her to come over for cocktails early in the evening. Jacqueline tells Sharon that she can't really come over since the critic Rex Reed is staying with her. Sharon invites her to bring him along, but in the end Jacqueline and Rex decide to go straight to dinner.

Meanwhile, in London, Polanski's having lunch with his doctor friend Tony Greenburgh and the producer Simon Hessera. Conversation is rather subdued. The three friends have just learned about the sudden death of a friend of theirs, Danielle – the ex-girlfriend of Polanski's set designer, Richard Sylbert. Danielle was a beautiful French girl in her early twenties, and the news comes as something of a shock. "Makes you wonder who'll be next", says Polanski.

Sharon climbs back into the pool and floats around in her rubber tire to cool down in the afternoon heat. She closes her eyes and dozes off for a while. She has less than ten hours left to live.

One of Sharon's lunch companions, Joanna Pettet, is no stranger to murder. Not too long before she and Sharon got so close, she'd had another best friend, a girl called Janice Wylie. What happened to Janice was a horrible thing. It was in the Summer of 1963 that it happened – another terribly hot Summer. Janice was living in New York that year, sharing her apartment with a friend of theirs, Emily Hoffert. In the middle of the night, somebody had broken into the girls' apartment and murdered them both. The killings had later come to be known as "The Career Girls Murder Case". They never caught the man who did it.

*****

"Your castle is surpris'd; your wife, and babes,
Savagely slaughter'd"
(IV, iii, 204–5)

Hosts and hostesses; friends and visitors; porters and gatekeepers; mothers and babies; family murders and Family murders.... both *Macbeth* and the Tate murders tell stories about guests murdered in the very home they have been invited to visit. In *Macbeth*, Duncan is murdered by the same host under whose roof he has been gratefully invited to stay, an aspect of the crime that particularly disturbs its perpetrator ("his host... Should against his murtherer shut the door", he muses anxiously, "Not bear the knife myself"). The discovery of the murdered body of Duncan is initiated by the drunken gatekeeper who acts, appropriately enough, like the keeper of Hell's gate, since the murder of the king has transformed Macbeth's castle, whose pleasant seat and good, fresh air Duncan had specifically commented on, into a living hell.

Bel Air. On a hot night in August, a young driver rolls down his car window to be shot directly in the head by Tex Watson. The first victim at Cielo Drive is Steven Parent, an 18-year-old youth who has no connection whatsoever with the Polanski residence. He's never even set foot inside the house. He's just visiting his friend, Bill Garretson, to see if he's interested in buying a radio. Garretson, who acts as gatekeeper and caretaker to the property, is living in a small cottage on the grounds. After Steve has left, Bill spends the rest of the night drinking beer and listening to his stereo. Unable to believe that he's heard nothing unusual on that night of all nights, homicide detectives arrest Garretson as the initial suspect in the case. He's given a lie-detector test, and subsequently released.

Act III of *Macbeth* presents us with a violent assault on Macduff's wife and family. Right before her home is besieged, Lady Macduff is complaining to Ross that her husband should feel it appropriate to be absent from his home and family at such a dangerous time. She asks herself how he could have abandoned "wife and child (Those precious motives, those strong knots of love) Without leave-taking?", especially at such a terrible time, when "Each new morn, New widows howl, new orphans cry; new sorrows strike heaven on the face". Moments later her castle is attacked and laid waste by Macbeth's men; she is raped and murdered in her own castle hall. The next wife to die is Macbeth's own, who is killed by throwing herself from the castle parapet. Macbeth, regarding his wife's mangled body, neither embraces her one last time, nor orders his servants to remove her body from sight. It is an indication of the extremes to which Macbeth's "bloody business" has taken him that the Queen's body is left lying in a crumpled heap in the castle courtyard, where it remains until the end of the film.

The killers of Macduff's family are instructed by Macbeth – who, like Manson, generally relies on his followers to commit his murders on his behalf – to "give to th'edge o'th'sword His wife, his babes, and all unfortunate souls That trace him in his line". Polanski gives us Macduff's small son being stabbed in the back and bleeding to death, and naked, blood-covered children being slaughtered one by one. Smearing mock-blood on the face of a child actress for this scene, Polanski asks the girl her name.

"Sharon", she replies.

The connections with the events at Cielo Drive are clear, and are recognized by Kenneth Tynan when he and Polanski come to write the scene. "I had not been looking forward to it," wrote Tynan later, "and a difficult moment arrived when I questioned the amount of blood that would be shed by a small boy stabbed in the back. Polanski replied bleakly 'you didn't see my house last summer. I know about bleeding'".[26] And because of their obvious resonance for the director, there is tension on the set when Macduff's poignant words on the killing of his wife and children have to be delivered. As Macduff, actor Terence Baylor differs with Polanski on a fine point of interpretation.

"No," says Polanski when he doesn't want to argue the point any more. "You'll do it this way. *I know*".

There is an echo here not only of the murder of Banquo and attempted murder of Fleance, but also of other images of children and violence in the play – most notably, children born into violence, or born violently. After drinking the witches' foul brew, Polanski's Macbeth experiences a series of hallucinations culminating in the rending open of a stab wound and a living child being pulled out of the bloody gash. In the final moments of the play, Macbeth comes to understand that the fiends have been juggling with him yet again, as he learns the news that "Macduff was from his mother's womb

Sadie, Tex

Untimely ripp'd".

Tex Watson thrusts his knife into Sharon's chest and she stops screaming and slumps to the floor. Sadie, knife in hand, pounces upon Sharon's body, slippery with blood. Holding the heavily pregnant woman in her arms, she dips the corner of a towel in her wounds and scrawls a word on the wall in blood: PIG. Sharon is still alive, making strange guttural noises. Sadie wants to cut out the baby and take it back as a prize for Charlie. Even if it's dead, he could still use it for a ritual. But Tex suddenly announces that it's time to leave. And Tex is speaking on behalf of Charlie.

Monday, August 11th, 1969. Police pathologist Dr. Thomas Noguchi declares to the gathered press that Mrs. Polanski was in the eighth month of her pregnancy; that her child was a perfectly formed boy; and that had the baby been removed by post-mortem Cesarean within the first twenty minutes after his mother's death, his life probably could have been saved. But by the time the bodies were discovered, it was too late.

Wednesday, August 13th, 1969. The body of Sharon Tate Polanski is buried at Holy Cross Cemetery, along with that of her "perfectly formed" unborn son, whom Roman has named Richard Paul – after his father, Ryszard Polanski, and Sharon's father, Colonel Paul Tate. Although the coffin is closed, Sharon is buried in a Pucci mini-dress selected from her closet by Roman's friend Victor Lownes. After the service, the guests attend a funeral brunch at the home of Hollywood producer Robert Evans. Guests include such celebrities as Warren Beatty, Yul Brynner, Peter Sellers and John Phillips.

The same day, Jay Sebring is buried at Forest Lawn Cemetery after a funeral attended by a host of celebrity clients, business associates and friends. Gibby Folger is buried by her parents at a private Catholic service in San Francisco. Steven Parent is buried quietly, by family and friends, and Frykowski's body is flown back to Poland.

Paris, 1957. Polanski is visiting France for the first time since the end of the war, to be reunited with his sister Annette and her new husband, Marian. Having waited sixteen years to find the right moment, Annette reveals to her brother that when the body of their mother was recovered from Auschwitz, she was found to be six months pregnant.

Paris, 1993. Thirty-four years later, Polanski is back in Paris. His 26-year-old French wife, Emmanuelle Seigner, has just given birth to Polanski's first living child, a baby girl. Her name: Morgan. Is Polanski aware of the name's long association with witches and witchcraft? Or is it Emmanuelle's choice – a pretty, up-to-date, international name?

The world has many witches.

*****

"Lamentings heard i'th'air; strange screams of death,
And prophesying with accents terrible
Of dire combustion, and confus'd events
New hatch'd to th'woeful time"
(II, iii, 55–58)

"You could feel something in the air, you know. You could feel something in the air."
(Spahn ranch hand Juan Flynn)

The night of Duncan's murder in Macbeth is an unquiet one – a night of strange noises, terrible storms, uncanny incidents, ominous sights. Screams are heard on the wind; sleep is broken by thunder and lightening; Macbeth's horses break out of their stable and, to the amazement of onlookers, set about eating one another. This restless night is a harbinger of Scotland's impending chaos: "sighs, and groans, and shrieks that rent the air Are made, not mark'd" and "violent sorrow seems A modern ecstasy". It is almost as though Macbeth's greatest fear had come true, that his "horrid deed" is being blown "in every eye, That tears shall drown the wind".

August 8th, 1969. In the woodland about three quarters of a mile directly south and downhill from Cielo Drive, camp counsellor Tim Ireland is poking at the embers of a campfire. He's volunteered to stay up through the night to supervise an overnight camp-out. The kids are all in their tents by now, most of them asleep after a hard day's hiking. Tim's already picked up the remains of the litter and candy wrappers from the cookout. There's no noise at all except the muted chirp of the cicadas and the occasional hoot of an owl. At about 12.30am, Tim goes for a brief walk into the forest, just to check everything's OK round about. Suddenly, the quiet is broken by a chilling cry – a solitary male voice screaming "Oh God, no, please don't! Oh God, no, don't, don't, don't...". The

Charlie

screaming seems to be coming downwind from a long distance away to the north or northeast. It lasts from ten to fifteen seconds, then stops in an abrupt silence almost as chilling as the cry itself. Tim looks at his watch. It's 12.40. Since there are no further cries, he decides not to investigate and wanders back to the camp where the kids lie in their tents, sleeping.[27] About two weeks after the night of August 8th, a girl called Barbara Hoyt is walking towards the creek that lies at the back of the Spahn Ranch, looking for somebody to drive her into town. Barbara's been living with Charlie and the Family, on and off, since April, and she's pretty much getting to know the way things work around the ranch. If you need a ride into town, the first thing you've got to do is search out one of the ranch hands, who look after all the cars and trucks around the place. Suddenly, Barbara hears a series of high-pitched screams coming from somewhere down the creek. She's sure she recognizes the voice as belonging to Shorty Shea, one of the ranch hands. Barbara turns round and heads back to the ranch in a hurry. She doesn't tell anybody about what she's heard, but after that day she never sees Shorty around the place again.

The next day, sitting on the porch with some of the other girls, she overhears Charlie telling one of the Hell's Angels that hang out at the ranch that Shorty's committed suicide, "with a little help from us".

At the trial, it is revealed that Shorty Shea had been hit over the head with a lead pipe, stabbed multiple times, decapitated and cut up into nine separate pieces.

"Give to our tables meat, sleep to our nights,
Free from our feasts and banquets bloody knives"
(III, vi, 34–5)

As a youth wandering the derelict streets of wartime Krakow, Polanski is attacked by a man who beats him on the head with a rock and leaves him for dead. The man is later discovered to be a multiple murderer. When Polanski comes to consciousness, he is aware of a stream of liquid trickling down his face. In his confused state, Roman believes this liquid to be water. When he tries to wipe it away, however, he discovers it to be blood.

In every film he makes after this incident, the blending of blood with water becomes a significant motif for Polanski, generally used to suggest the fragility of the human pretence to self-sufficiency.[28] In his early film **Two Men And A Wardrobe** (1958), a young man is beaten to death by an attacker who hammers his victim on the head with a rock then forces his head underwater in order for the camera to focus down on the mingling of blood in the sea, thereby re-enacting the director's earlier fear and fantasy of water and blood on the face.[29]

Similarly, in **Macbeth**, Polanski takes great pains to realize visually "the concatenation of images – especially of darkness and blood – which the poetry conjures up in the mind's eye".[30] These sets of imagistic vignettes include the famous sequence in which Macbeth and his wife anxiously attempt to wash the blood off their hands immediately following their murder of Duncan and his guards, as well as the scene in which the sleepwalking Lady Macbeth is mortified by her own neurotic hallucinations of indelible bloodstains polluting her hands. At another point, in the scene where Macbeth visits the weird sisters in their cave, Polanski presents us with a mesmerizing sequence in which Macbeth, staring into a pool of bloodstained water, is horrified by a prophetic vision of his own, decapitated head. Wherever possible, Polanski explicitly demonstrates the violence which is described in the text, following Polish critic Jan Kott's interpretation

Macbeth

of *Macbeth*. "Blood in *Macbeth*," writes Kott in *Shakespeare Our Contemporary*, "is not just a metaphor. It leaves stains on hands and faces, on daggers and swords ... A production of *Macbeth* not evoking a picture of the world flooded with blood, would inevitably be false".

Driving away from the scene of their terrible crime, Tex, Sadie, Katie and Linda change out of their clothes in the car, climbing out of their black creepy-crawly clothes, now dirtied with blood, and changing into the spare clothes Charlie told them to pack in the back of the car. Tex dumps the bloodied bundle over the edge of a hillside, but there's still a hell of a lot of blood around, all over their hands and faces, so after driving for some distance further, Tex pulls over outside somebody's house where there's a hose lying on the lawn for the sprinkler system. Sadie goes over and turns the guy's tap on and they take turns pointing the hose at one another and washing the blood off their hands and out of their hair. But the water's cold and Sadie keeps playing around, splashing and screaming, and in the end she wakes up the guy whose house it is, and he comes out in his pyjamas and turns off the hose starts bawling at them to get off his property.

    This homeowner, awoken by the noise in the early hours of the morning, later plays an important part in identifying the Family's vehicle and its passengers during the trial.

During the scenes in **Macbeth** that are shot on set in Shepperton Studios, Polanski and Tynan, consciously copying Kozintsev's *Hamlet*, decide to use domestic animals to suggest the authentic feel of the period. Ever the perfectionist, Polanski attempts to direct and choreograph the movements of chickens, doves and dogs. He often has a great deal of difficulty getting the animals to behave exactly as he wants them to. These difficulties are amplified by the bear-baiting sequence. The first bear they manage to acquire is far too gentle, cringing at the sight of the dogs; the second is far too vicious. Walking past its cage one day, a crew member is pawed by the bear who attempts to haul him inside the cage. Eventually, the part is played by an intrepid stunt-man in a bear-suit.

On the bare heath, the youngest of Polanski's witches pulls along a large goat on a lead. The courtyard of Macbeth's castle is full of chickens and pigs, one of which is chosen for the slaughter when news of Duncan's impending visit is heralded by a messenger to Dunsinane.

Pigs, goats and chickens are, of course, all creatures with Satanic associations, all regularly used for sacrificial purposes. "Piggies" is what the Family call the police, blacks, and all members of the establishment. At Cielo Drive on the night of August 8th, Sadie scrawls the word "PIG" on the wall in Sharon's blood, before she is entirely dead.

Among the many items the police take into custody from Cielo Drive is a videotape that Polanski made of his houseguests hosting a dinner party. Gibby is there, and Voytek; Jay Sebring is there; Sharon and Roman are there. The film records an easy-going, laid-back meal livened up by a series of jokes, anecdotes and gossip, but there's a more sober moment where Gibby tells a story about one time when Voytek, stoned on drugs, is looking into the fireplace and suddenly spots a strange shape in the flames. He rushes for a camera, hoping he can capture it. The image, remembers Gibby, is that of a blazing pig's head.[31]

Amongst other things, *Macbeth* is a play about the horrors of warfare. Polanski takes particular care to emphasize the screams and cries of battle, the anguish of betrayal, and the agonies of the mutilated bodies lying helpless on the battlefield. Charlie, obsessed with his delusion that warfare is imminent in Death Valley, models himself as the self-styled military commander of a Dune Buggy Attack Battalion. As protection, he gathers together his own personal troupe of Hell's Angels, lured by promises of easy sex with the girls on the ranch, to protect himself against the threat of attack by the Black Panthers.

In Los Feliz, at the LaBianca murder site, someone writes a word on the wall, scrawled with a towel dipped in Leno LaBianca's blood. The word is "RISE". And, in addition to a number of stab wounds in his abdomen, someone has carved a word into Leno's naked flesh. The word is "WAR".

Macbeth contains a number of vivid images of the sight, sound and texture of knife against bone. In his final battle, Macbeth vows to "fight, till from my bones my flesh be hack'd". Polanski rends the murder of Duncan in explicit detail: "Macbeth plunges his dagger again and again into Duncan's body; the effort is great, Polanski forcing us to hear knife hitting bone".[32]

During the Manson trial, coroner Thomas Noguchi testifies that many of the knife wounds at the Tate murder scene actually penetrated the bones. Linda Kasabian, speaking on behalf of the prosecution, testifies that in the car on the way home from the murders, Katie was complaining that her hand hurt from the knife striking against bones. And during Polanski's video of the houseguests' dinner party at Cielo Drive, the microphone is placed in the middle of the table next to the roast. As Gibby carves the meat, the only noise picked up by the mike is the sound – amazingly loud, over and over again – of knife grating against bone[33]

"....nothing is, but what is not"
(I, iii, 142)

"No sense makes sense."
(Charles Manson)

Macbeth's "bloody business" comes to pass when the "instruments of Darkness" indulge and exploit his "vaulting ambition" with their juggling, equivocal, ambiguous prophecies. Their predictions are full of relativism, double-meanings, linguistic anomalies and dualities. Their battles are both "lost and won", their deeds come "without a name". Their resonant incantation ("fair is foul and foul is fair") is no sooner uttered than it is echoed on the lips of Macbeth himself ("So foul and fair a day I have not seen"), and then on those of Banquo ("Good sir, why do you start, and seem to fear Things that sound so fair?"). The witches' predictions for Banquo are starkly equivocal. According to these minions of Satan, Banquo is destined to be "Lesser than Macbeth, and greater: Not so happy, yet much happier".

And it is not long before the balanced rhythms and alliterative tones of these nonce-rhymes find their way into Macbeth's own harried meditations. "What thou wouldst highly, That wouldst thou holily", he muses to himself; "Wouldst not play false, And yet wouldst wrongly win", a fact which does not escape him for long: "false face must hide what the false heart doth know", he concludes, cryptically. Knowing that his own pride and ambition will interpret their "supernatural soliciting" as "earnest of success", the instruments of darkness find in Macbeth the perfect recipient of their unholy deceptions, struggling to twist their cryptic charms to his own auspicious predictions until, in the last moments of the play, he finally comes face to face with the full extent of their fiendish manoeuvres:

"....be these juggling fiends no more believed
That palter with us in a double sense;
That keep the word of promise to our ear,
And break it to our hope"
(V, iix, 19-23)

But Macbeth should have been ready. As Banquo warns him in Act I:

"...oftentimes, to win us to our harm,
The instruments of Darkness tell us truths;
Win us with honest trifles, to betray's
In deepest consequence..."
(I, iii, 122-125)

In one of the breaks during the trial, Bugliosi notices that Linda Kasabian, his star prosecution witness, is looking anxious and uneasy. Charlie's giving her the evil eye. Bugliosi asks Linda what she thinks about Charlie now. She's still in love with him, Linda tells her lawyer. "Some things he said were the truth," she observes thoughtfully. "Only now I realize he could take a truth and make a lie out of it".[34] Anyone who's ever heard any of Charlie's lyrics, poetry or philosophy will recognize in his strange, rhythmic mantras overtones of the juggling equivocations of the witches in *Macbeth*. The uncanny credo of Manson Family life is formed by Charlie's apocalyptic prophecies, which are themselves inflected by an unnerving combination of influences, from the *Book Of Revelations* and the lyrics of the Beatles' *White Album* to the drug jargon of Haight-Ashbury. Later on, in Death Valley, Charlie teaches his children to speak in his own tongue, using words like "slippies", "piggies", "creepy-crawlies" and "helter-skelter". "I am not of your world," Charlie tells his children. "When I was a child I was an orphan and too ugly to be adopted. Now I am too beautiful to be set free".[35] "The truth is now," declares Charlie to his crowd of followers, from the steps of the porch. "The truth is right here; the truth is this minute, this minute we exist. Yesterday – you cannot prove yesterday happened today, it would take you all day and then it would be tomorrow, and you can't prove last week happened. You can't prove anything except to yourself. My reality is my reality, and I stand within myself on my reality."[36] "You can do no wrong, no bad," declares Charlie in another of his sermons. "Everything is good. Whatever you do is what you are supposed to do; you are following your own karma." To Charlie's way of thinking, there is no death. "Death is only a change," says Charlie. "Death is a fear that is born in man's head and can be taken out of man's head, and then it will no longer exist..."[37] "Words go in circles," says Charlie. "You can say everything the same," he says, "but it is always different. ...Because with my words... your thoughts are dying. What you thought was true is dying. What you thought was real is dying. Because you all know, and I know you know, and you know that I know you know. So let's make that a circle."[38] "There is no crime, there is no sin," he claims. "Death is beautiful." Talking to Charlie is "like the Devil buying your soul"[39], and according to Sadie's testimony at the trial, Charlie is God, Christ and the Devil all rolled into one.

"Do you think Charlie is an evil person?" Bugliosi asks Sadie, standing in the dock. She pauses and narrows her eyes for a moment before giving her reply. "In your standards of evil, looking at him through your eyes, I would say yes," she says. "Looking at him through my eyes," she adds, chillingly, "he is as good as he is evil; he is as evil as he is good."

"Unnatural deeds
Do breed unnatural troubles"
(V, I, 68–69)

Like Shakespeare's other tragic heroes, Macbeth endures an anguish imposed by outside influences struggling to exploit the weaknesses of his own character. Uniquely amongst Shakespeare's tragedies, however, *Macbeth* is a play in which our sympathies for the hero are gradually eroded by the effects of his own violent personality. Unlike our sympathies for Lear, Hamlet or Othello, our sympathy for Macbeth diminishes as he estranges himself from wife, friends, liegemen and servants. In Act I, on the battlefield, he is commended by Banquo for being "nothing afeard of what thyself didst make, Strange images of

Macbeth

death", but by Act V these words have come to resonate with less propitious meanings. The "bloody instructions" which Macbeth has taught himself soon begin to "return To plague th'inventor", and whilst his own material success is acknowledged, it is also universally acknowledged that he has "play'd most foully for't". He is suspected by the English troops of pandering to the forces of evil, of making a pact with the Devil (in the form, some critics have suggested, of his mysterious henchman Seyton). By the time his destruction is imminent, by the time he begins to feel "his secret murthers sticking on his hands", all sympathy for the noble thane he once was has been lost, along with his once-loyal retinue.

Macbeth is a play in which the natural progress of history is distorted. Instead of following the ebb and flow of social and political forces, the path of history is transformed into a regressive maelstrom, eternally reproducing horror and corruption. The play unfolds within a nightmare world where evil magic replaces logic and rationality, where all men can do to influence their fate is attempt to avoid the horror. Historical change is inevitable, but the change in Macbeth is that of a psychological regression, worsening what was already horrific to begin with. The most obvious illustration of this downward spiralling in Polanski's film is the fact that it both opens and closes with scenes involving the witches. As the film opens, they meet on the beach to enact their prognosticative rites; as it closes, these rites have worked their dark spell twice over as Duncan's younger son Donalbain arrives at their cave during a violent thunderstorm.

Polanski's own interpretation of the play seems heavily influenced by the work of Polish critic Jan Kott. "Unlike Shakespeare's historical plays," writes Kott, "Macbeth does not show history as the Grand Mechanism. It shows it as nightmare. History, shown as a mechanism, fascinates by its very terror and inevitability. Whereas nightmare paralyses and terrifies". According to Kott, Macbeth's progress represents his gradual realization of this terror. "He can accept himself at last," writes Kott, "because he has realized that every choice is absurd".

In moments of unbearable personal tragedy, some people may find solace in religion. In Polanski's case, the opposite happens. "Any religious faith I had was shattered by Sharon's murder," he claims. "It reinforced my faith in the absurd."[40]

Material success, as everybody knows, tends to breed suspicion and resentment. In the case of Macbeth, this suspicion is justified; in many other cases it is not. At first, when nobody is arrested for the Tate murders, unhappy rumours began to circulate that Polanski himself might, in some way or another, be implicated in the horrible crimes, which might help to explain why he is so reluctant to return to L.A., despite Sharon's repeated requests.

Then news of Gibby and Voytek's autopsy reports is leaked to the press. Apparently, at the time of her death, Gibby has 2.4 milligrams of methylenediox-amphetamine (MDA) in her system, and Voytek has 0.6 milligrams in his. News is also leaked regarding the delicate issue of sleeping arrangements at Cielo Drive. Whilst Gibby and Voytek, a long-established couple, were sleeping in separate rooms, Sharon and Jay were sharing Sharon's bedroom. Roman claims that the dent in the mattress beside that left by Sharon's body is made by the pillows, which she always hugs instead of her husband when he's away. Roman's scenario suggests that his wife is alone that night, but subsequent testimony by the killers indicates that Sharon and Jay are sharing the same bed.

Polanski himself, in turn, fed by the frantic paranoia in the wake of the murders, begins to whisper some names of his own to the homicide detectives. At first, Roman is convinced that someone in his circle is responsible for the murders, and starts to conduct his own investigation. The main clue he focuses on initially is the word "PIG" scrawled on the wall of his house in Sharon's blood. When producer William Castle visits Polanski at Paramount to offer his condolences, the first thing Roman does is to hand him a piece of paper and ask him to print out the word "PIG".

Victor Lownes, for his part, is particularly suspicious of Roman's friend, the author Jerzy Kosinski. Kosinski's behaviour following the murders seems unreasonable to Lownes. First, Kosinski plans to arrange Voytek's funeral. Then it turns out that Voytek's family have been planning the funeral all along – something that Kosinski must surely have known. He then claims in a press interview that he was due at Cielo Drive on the night of the 8th August, but his luggage was sent to New York by mistake and he never made it to L.A., thereby saving himself from the slaughter. But nobody knew anything about Kosinski being expected at Cielo Drive that night, and Witold Kaczanowski – who was invited over that night – dismisses Kosinski as merely seeking publicity, in a sick kind of way. And then there is Kosinski's *Steps*, a book full of violent imagery, preoccupied with the notion of achieving a kind of freedom through an act of pointless murder.

Sunday 22nd August, 1969. Victor Lownes writes a letter to the L.A. Homicide Division suggesting that they question Kosinski, asking "Is it just remotely possible that the author of such weird material might himself be a very weird person indeed?".[41] Kosinski is eventually cleared of any connections with the Tate/LaBianca murders. He later publishes a novel, *Blind Date*, in which the slaughter at Cielo Drive is meticulously fantasized, using an arsenal of fictive techniques. His reputation as a writer is greatly enhanced by the later publication of *The Painted Bird*, a classic in Holocaust literature. In 1990, Kosinski commits suicide by putting a plastic bag over his head.

This paranoia is itself fed by a strong undercurrent of rumour painting a vivid picture of drugs, orgies, black magic rituals, witchcraft and kinky sex at Cielo Drive. Both *Time* and *Newsweek* make much of "theories on sex, drugs and witchcraft cults... fed by the fact that Sharon and Polanski circulated in one of the film world's more offbeat crowds". They "habitually picked up odd and unsavoury people indiscriminately, and invited them home to parties". According to *Time*, "how much of a role drugs played in their world is hard to discern", but of course "Polanski is noted for his macabre movies". The article goes on to claim that "there also appeared to be a dark side to the other victims". Voytek is "a hanger-on with sinister connections to which even the tolerant Polanski objected". Gibby Folger becomes an "aimless heiress".

The rumours are greatly distorted and elaborated, but there is sufficient truth in each of them for the news magazines and gossip columns to "bind them together in a horrific package of fanciful and exaggerated claims which built into a vivid portrayal of unadulterated vice"[42], whose bleak lesson is "what goes around, comes around". Polanski's friend Dennis Hopper, himself a leading member of the L.A. counterculture, says as much himself. "The people at the Tate house were killed because they were into bad shit," claims Hopper. "The people at the Tate house were victims of themselves."[43]

And even after the full, horrifying story of the Manson murders has come to light, Sharon and her friends are still not granted their innocence, nor are they forgiven for making us come face to face with the horrors of that hot night in August. In his closing speech at the trial, Charlie's attorney Irving Kanarak declares of Sharon and her houseguests, that "but for the fact that at least some of these people were engaged in a narcotic episode of some type, these events would not have taken place".[44] Most people somehow feel, despite all evidence to the contrary, that it is Polanski himself who has "played most foully for't". There are those who imply that the Tate murders are somehow connected to Polanski's own interest in sex, violence, horror and domination which, "being taught, return To plague th'inventor". There are those in Hollywood who whisper that the Manson murders are somehow, in some way, a kind of inevitable retribution for Polanski's playboy lifestyle, or at least a spin-off of the sordid stories told in many of his films. Macduff's exclamation in *Macbeth* on learning the news of his family's murder might be an equally fitting apologia, if Hollywood gossip is anything to go by, for the murder of Sharon and her friends on Cielo Drive:

"Did Heaven look on,
And would not take her part?...Naught that I am,
Not for their own demerits, but for mine,
Fell slaughter on their souls..."
(IV, iii, 225–227)

Sharon's body lies, blood-splattered, by the living-room sofa, draped with its Stars-and-Stripes flag. She is badly mutilated, but neither of her breasts have been cut off, her unborn child resides intact in her womb, and there is no swastika carved on her stomach. Roman and Sharon, Voytek and Gibby, Jay and Steve Parent – none of them are involved in black magic; none of them are particularly interested in kinky sex; none of them are heavily involved in drug dealing. But there is enough in each strand of the story to start whispers, to fuel rumours, to back up implications, and to finally create the general impression, however shadowy, that these young people have brought down this disaster on their own heads. And if the victims themselves can't be held fully accountable for the tragedy that has befallen them, then the responsibility lies with Polanski himself, for spending most of his turbulent life "nothing afeard" of what he himself has dared to create: "strange images of death".

NOTES

1.   Shaw, William P., 1986. "Violence And Vision In Polanski's Macbeth And Brooks' Lear", *Literature/Film Quarterly* xiv:4, 211.
2.   Rogers Harper, Wendy, 1986. "Polanski vs. Welles On Macbeth: Character Or Fate?" *Literature/Film Quarterly* xiv:4, 203.
3.   Berlin, Normand, 1973. "Macbeth: Polanski And Shakespeare", *Literature/Film Quarterly* l:4, 290–298.
4.   Andrews, Nigel, 1972. "Macbeth" (review), *Sight & Sound* 41:108.
5.   Rothwell, Kenneth, 1973. "Roman Polanski's Macbeth":71–75.
6.   Zimmerman, Paul, 1974. "Blood And Water", *Newsweek*, July 1st 1974, p.94.
7.   "Macbeth By Daylight" (interview), *Time*, January 25th 1971.
8.   Rock, Gail, *Women's Wear Daily*. cit in Leaming, Barbara, 1982. *Polanski: The Filmmaker As Voyeur*. Hamish Hamilton: New York.
9.   See Leaming, 1982:72.
10.   Ebert, Roger. *Chicago Sun-Times*. cit in Parker, 1993. *Polanski*. London: Gollancz, p. 189.
11.   Kael, Pauline. *The New Yorker*, January 1972:7.
12.   See Weinraub, Bernard, 1971. "A Visit With Roman Polanski". *New York Times Magazine*, December 12th 1971:72.
13.   Sydney Edwards, *London Evening Standard*, cit. in Parker, 1993:90.
14.   Polanski, Roman, 1984. *Roman By Polanski*, London: Heinemann, p. 264.
15.   Martin Shaw, cit in Parker 1993:181.
16.   See Michael Delahaye & Jean-Andre Fischi, "Interview With Roman Polanski", *Cahiers du Cinémain English*, February 1966. Reprinted in Polanski, Roman, *Three Film Scripts*. London: Lorrimer, 1975.
17.   Shaw, William. 1986:211.
18.   Berlin, Normand. 1973:297.
19.   Rothwell, 1973:72.
20.   cit. in Parker 1993:106.
21.   Berlin, 1973:294-6.
22.   Rothwell, 1973:74.
23.   See Bugliosi, Vincent (with Curt Gentry), 1974. *Helter Skelter – The Shocking Story Of The Manson Murders*. London: Arrow Books, p.170.
24.   See Bugliosi 1974:169.
25.   See Bugliosi, 1974:163.
26.   See Parker 1993:178.
27.   See Bugliosi 1974:4.
28.   See Leach, James. 1978. "Notes On Polanski's Cinema Of Cruelty", *Wide Angle* 2:1, 34.
29.   See Parker, 1993:47.
30.   Mullin, Michael, 1973. "Macbeth On Film", *Literature/Film Quarterly* 1:4, 335.
31.   See Bugliosi 1974:88.

32. Berlin 1973:283.
33. See Bugliosi 1974:88.
34. See Bugliosi 1974:370.
35. See Rubin, Jerry, 1971. *We Are Everywhere*. New York: Harper & Row, p.39.
36. See Parker, 1993:69–70.
37. See Bugliosi 1974:301.
38. See Parker 1993:71–73.
39. See Bugliosi 1974:319.
40. See Polanski, 1984:392.
41. See Leaming, 1982:71.
42. See Parker, 1993:155.
43. See Parker 1994:157.
44. See Bugliosi 1974:607.

COMIC-BOOK KARMA

From "Baba Yaga" To "Cemetery Man"

Andy Black

"Dellamorte Dellamore is not a horror film... horror is just an excuse for opening the doors of fantasy, at least for me."
—Michele Soavi, director of **Dellamorte Dellamore** (*aka* **Cemetery Man**)

"There's something different about Baba Yaga. It's as if she came from another world."
—Valentina, character in **Baba Yaga**

Whenever that peculiar hybrid, the comic-book/horror sub-genre is mentioned, critical gaze usually confines itself to such obvious entries as the William Gaines' EC comics-inspired films such as Freddie Francis' **Tales From The Crypt** (1972) and **Vault Of Horror** (1973), or George A. Romero's **Creepshow** series; or to characters morphed from the printed page such as Wes Craven's **Swamp Thing** (1982), and more high-profile entries like the **Batman** series, **The Crow** (1994), and **Judge Dredd** (1995).

Whilst this strain of purely American comic-book horror and fantasy is generally full of one-dimensional characters and juvenile situations – admittedly with some stylish locations/sets and well-realised *milieux* – the Europeans have tended to produce decidedly more erotic and challenging films derived from graphic material.

Perhaps the seminal comic character in all of this is Jean-Claude Forest's *Barbarella* (first appearing in 1962) – memorably portrayed by Jane Fonda in her (then) husband, director Roger Vadim's 1968 film adaptation, which did full justice to the aesthetic importance and intellectual strands prevalent in the form, so deservedly elevating it to the vertiginous heights bestowed upon it by the critical debates which raged upon its release.

Dominant, forceful, liberated characters such as Forest's *Barbarella* were seen as breaking new ground, offering imagination and originality, coupled with no small measure of sexuality. This formed a potent cocktail, epitomised by other equally alluring sirens such as Guido Crepax's raven-haired *Belinda*, first published in 1960.

Crepax also ventured further into this territory with the highly successful *Valentina* – transformed into a TV/film series in Italy during the 1980s – whilst other luminaries such as Philippe Druillet and Paul Curelier continued to push back the boundaries of taste and style.

And, just as the Germans had their *krimi* series of detective novels and the Italians the *giallo*, so too was the term *fumetti* coined for this particular brand of comic capers – or *fumetti per adulti* for the more risqué titles! Of these, the first was the *Diabolik* series, which was to have a profound influence on both **Baba Yaga** director Corrado Farina and **Cemetery Man**'s guiding hand Michele Soavi – partly through the printed page, and more overtly via the camera lens of Mario Bava's 1967 film visualisation.

Other comic incarnations such as Magnus and Bunker's *Kriminal* series materialised, as did the *fumetti neri* (black) style, whilst the publication of the

Mario Bava's Diabolik

sex-orientated *Isabella* in 1966 (filmed by Bruno Corbucci in 1969) proved the catalyst for an explosion during the '70s and '80s of more graphic and sexually explicit material.

The filmic mantle was more willingly taken up by Jesus Franco with his **Lucky The Inscrutable** (1967) acting as a homage to the comic-book form, whilst the ghost of Crepax's *Valentina* pervades the mesmerising **Necronomicon** (*aka* **Succubus**, 1967).

Farina's version of **Baba Yaga** (1973) has also undoubtedly exerted some influence over Soavi, and we also have the likes of **Gwendoline** (1984) and **Valentina** (1989), plus Soavi's ironic naming of the mayor's daughter in **Cemetery Man** as Valentina. That said, it is interesting to compare the approach by both directors to their comic-inspired material – given the different sources and a hiatus of 20 years between the two films.

As previously mentioned, Farina's **Baba Yaga** (*aka* **Devil's Witch**) is culled from the sado-fetishistic comic strips of Guido Crepax – there's a scene where Valentina (Isabelle De Funes) and Arno (Luigi Montefiori, of **Absurd** [Joe D'Amato, 1981] fame) flick through some comic-book erotica before then performing their own live-action interpretation! And although some of the fashions and dialogue have obviously dated, the S/M imagery – thigh-high boots, mini skirts and so forth – has if anything reached pre-eminence today, as fetish fashions have become assimilated into the mainstream. As evidence, we have the current trend for stilettoes as a must-have fashion accessory, sexy advertising and the explosion of high quality fetish publications such as *Secret*, *Skin 2* and *Marquis*. The film's best asset for such attire is found in the alluring form of the usually dour Ely Galleani as Annette, resplendent in her stunning S/M outfit.

Dylan Dog

Soavi's **Cemetery Man** (1994) on the other hand eschews some (but not all) of the sexual imagery of **Baba Yaga** in favour of a more fantastical, horror setting, itself inspired by the popular Italian *fumetti* character Dylan Dog, created by Tiziano Sclavi.

If you want to encapsulate the single over-riding influence in both of these films however, the word "temptation" would appear to be the most appropriate. Soavi's main character, cemetery caretaker Francesco Dellamorte (Rupert Everett) volunteers upon seeing the voluptuous She (Anna Falchi) that she is "the most beautiful woman I have ever seen", whilst in Farina's film the nubile Valentina is the object of the mysterious Baba Yaga's (Carrol Baker) affections, with Baba Yaga being "madly in love with her" (Valentina), as one character observes. Likewise and perversely, Valentina is drawn to her elder admirer as if drawn by some mystical force, unable to resist temptation.

Both Dellamorte and Valentina are intoxicated by the black-clad figures of She – a grieving widow – and the beguiling Baba Yaga respectively, which reinforces the witch-like spell by which both characters hold their victims captive. Baba Yaga even takes some lipstick from Valentina, explaining that she "needs a personal object" of hers, continuing even more mysteriously that "there are forces which control our actions and our feelings".

The prevalent themes of witchcraft, sorcery and mysticism inform both films to a high degree; in Soavi's, witness the zombies or "returners" who are resurrected from Dellamorte's cemetery (including She), the elegiac tone accentuated as former *Playboy* centrefold Falchi's morbid fascination with the cemetery ossuary knows no bounds; "I have never seen anything so exciting," she drools, surrounded by walls of skulls, gushing that "I couldn't ask for anything more, it's like a dream". The necrophilic atmosphere concludes with She kissing Dellamorte passionately – though only having wrapped his head in a red shroud – climaxing (literally) in their lovemaking upon her late husband's grave – and yes, the earth does move! Unfortunately, it is the irate husband "returning" as he witnesses the carnal chaos before him, ravenously biting a chunk out of his wife (to compensate for not eating something else perhaps!).

Cemetery Man

Of Baba Yaga, well, her complexion is bone-white, with deep black eyes and pale lips – very much a "returner" herself in appearance – her marble-like face mirroring that of the malevolent doll in bondage attire which Baba Yaga keeps as a plaything (or familiar?). Her sorcery is further glimpsed as we see the developed film from a camera she has touched – the fashion model in the shots now transformed into an S/M icon with spikes bursting through her body.

There's also an intriguing parallel to be drawn between Soavi's love of secret passageways and labyrinth tunnels – as seen in the esoteric construction of the cathedral in **The Church** (1989) and the hidden chambers of the woodland cabin in **The Sect** (1991) – and Baba Yaga's surreal mansion house, which bizarrely features a large, foreboding pit in the lounge!

"I have an old house... you might find it interesting, Valentina," Baba Yaga ventures enticingly. Upon its subsequent appearance, we can glean that it is certainly arcane, and very dark as Valentina finds out to her cost – dropping a roll of film down into the pit. Baba Yaga dismisses the intriguing "feature" as just being "an old part of the house – don't worry".

Valentina conjectures on the hole that "It doesn't just lead down to her basement – there's no end to it". But Valentina's companion Arno rejects the importance she places on the abyss: "Soon you'll be telling me that it's the pearly gates of Hell and you're Baba Yaga's custodian witch of it... witches don't exist." He continues unabated that "If it's anything, it's the world we're living in."

Although not particularly sympathetic, Arno does possess a certain potency in cutting straight to the chase: "You meet an old lesbian and a friend of yours gets a headache, and suddenly it's witches and sorcery."

Baba Yaga

The finale, as lightning flashes coarse through the creepy, dimly-lit house, serves as a reminder to the echoes of German Expressionism which stalk the frames – including the appearance of **The Golem** (1920) playing on a TV set in the scene – whilst the image of the nebulous Baba Yaga, silhouetted against an all-white photo screen, instantly recalls Crepax's own line-drawn graphic pages.

With Baba Yaga quite clearly representing death or the Grim Reaper and the sultry Valentina, very much "love", there is a symmetry with Soavi's portrayal of "death" and of "love" in **Cemetery Man** – as stated in the film's Italian title **Dellamorte Dellamore** translated.

There's a startling materialisation from Soavi when a burning phone book reassembles into a Grim Reaper spectre: "Stop killing the dead – they're mine!" he admonishes the zombie-killing Dellamorte, then offers his own advice: "If you want to stop the dead returning to life then start killing the living."

Only for Soavi the term "love" becomes combined with "life" as we see the returning She appear as an "angel" – complete with white shroud dress and wild foliage hair – her passion for Dellamorte rather too all-consuming as she bites a chunk from his shoulder. Here, She encapsulates the full cycle of life, love, death and rebirth.

It is left to the often forlorn figure of Dellamorte to signify the existence of life and love – chiding that "Life goes on" at the very beginning of the film, after he has just shot down another "returner".

Cemetery Man

Cemetery Man

The ensuing dramatic tracking shot – past Dellamorte and beyond the door and leading into the rows of graves in the cemetery outside – immediately establishes that Dellamorte lives in a world of "death"; even his aforementioned sexual sparring with She takes place either in the ossuary or on a gravestone. As Dellamorte knowingly remarks later: "Hell, at a certain point in life you realise that you know more dead people than are living."

As Soavi himself has commented, the whole remit of the zombie genre he flirts with here has been deliberately turned around: "The main character is not scared of zombies because killing them is a normal job to him. What is more scary, is living. Instead of being a horror film about being scared of death, it's more a film about being scared of life."

To this (literal) end Soavi concludes the film fittingly with Dellamorte and his loyal assistant Gnaghi (Francois Hadj-Lazaro) existentially poised upon an isolated precipice.

As they survey the dramatic but desolate scene before them, Dellamorte comments: "I should've known. The rest of the world doesn't exist." "Could you take me home please?" the previously mute Gnaghi asks, as snow begins to fall, obliterating their figures as the snowflakes layer the landscape.

It is very much a case of **Cemetery Man** capturing the pessimistic mood of its own decade, reflecting the somewhat nihilistic forces of our own times. Perhaps because of this, that master of realistic, prosaic dramas, Martin Scorsese, declared **Cemetery Man** to be the best film of its year.

It is as if all the events played out within **Cemetery Man** now have no significance to the two characters; their lives will carry on, unchanged by time and almost oblivious to external forces, or so it seems.

Baba Yaga

There's a rather more circular denouement to Farina's **Baba Yaga**, as Valentina and Arno return to the old house where the previous night Arno had destroyed the eerie doll – and seemingly Baba Yaga as well – only to now find the house deserted, and apparently so for many years previous.

This merely confirms the oneiric, timeless quality of the film, reaffirmed in Baba Yaga's comment as she caresses Valentina's camera lens which is shooting a model: "That's the eye – the eye that freezes reality," she purrs profoundly.

The "reality" is momentarily blurred however, in the bizarre dream sequences which punctuate the film – the erotic charge as Valentina, draped only in bra and panties, parades in front of a German officer in a night-time wasteland before being summarily frog-marched away by stormtroopers under a glaring spotlight, or the *outré* sight of Baba Yaga relaxing in a chair perched on a cliff-edge and enjoying the "fantasy" of Valentina dressed only in a peaked cap and sporting a rifle as she slowly walks into the foaming sea.

Of all the images in both films, this is perhaps the most apt to conclude with, as we have become immersed in the fantasy of the events being realised upon the screen, compelled by the poetry of the compositions – be they gothic cemeteries or arcane dwellings – and forever intrigued by the diverse and often mysterious characters on show, captivated by their emotional and psychological motivations.

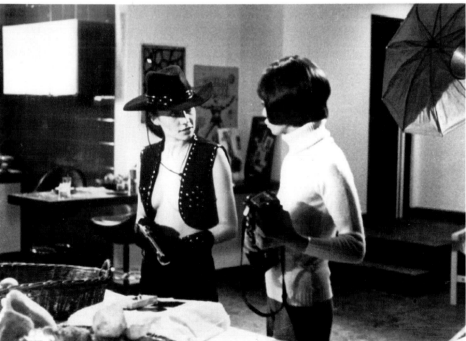

Baba Yaga

Baba Yaga

DC or EC comics these ain't – but animated and provocative they are. We may not discover all of Baba Yaga's beloved cosmic secrets, or comprehend all of the complexities of Dellamorte's life's quest – but then surely to reveal all would dissipate the intrinsic mystery and fantasy of these striking, enigmatic films.

ANGEL GAMES

The Early Films Of Walerian Borowczyk

Matthew Coniam

The National Film Theatre, London, 1975. Polish director Walerian Borowczyk's new film **La Bête/The Beast** is to be shown at the London Film Festival, after work in progress had been previewed to considerable controversy a few years before. The screening is massively oversubscribed, and outside the building, black-market tickets are selling at several times their value.

The National Film Theatre, London, 1997. The cinema is to show a programme of the same director's early animated and short films. I ring the box-office two hours before the performance is due to begin: "Excuse me, I'm afraid I've left it a bit late, but I'm ringing to see if you have any seats left for the Borowczyk films tonight."

"I'll just check... Yes we do."

"Should I reserve one or have you got quite a few?"

"We have quite a few."

"What, so if I just turn up, I'll have no trouble getting in?"

"Erm, no. No trouble at all."

Really, I shouldn't have been surprised that Borowczyk is no longer big news on the art-house circuit. He is two directors; the innovative animator whose considerable critical following deserted him when he switched from experimentation to eroticism, and the maker of bizarre, atmospheric sex films whose fans view his early work as a barely-tolerable prelude to the features. David Thomson's overview of his career in *A Biographical Dictionary Of Film* ends with his first features **Goto** (1968) and **Blanche** (1971), the point, more or less, where Cathal Tohill and Pete Tomb's *Immoral Tales* begins. For this latter book, and for Colin Davis who profiled the director in *Shock Xpress 2*, the shorts are something to be briefly mentioned along with essential biographical information. Similarly, it is enough for Thomson to simply record; "As far as can be ascertained, the more recent Borowczyk has settled for sex and exploitation."

And yet, when one watches a representative selection of these early works it becomes clearer than ever that there is only one Borowczyk, and the outrageous fantasy of **La Bête**, the picturesque voyeurism of **L'Interno Di Un Convento/Behind Convent Walls** (1977) and the Sadean excess of **Le Cas Etrange De Dr Jekyll Et Miss Osbourne/Blood Of Dr Jekyll** (1981) are merely the flip side of the same inventive, frequently savage imagination that conceived the duelling dwarves of **Gavotte** (1967) and the murderous married couple of **Le Concert De Monsieur Et Madame Kabal** (1963). The most fascinating and helpful aspect of his filmography, in fact, is its linearity – there is a clear and consistent sense of progression – and from his earliest 15 second shorts to his final feature **Ceremonie D'Amour/Rites of Love/Tout Disparaitra/Everything Must Go** (1988) each film builds upon and draws from those that preceded it.

Borowczyk first got noticed with a series of short, deliberately simple animations made in his native Poland. For someone who has expressed considerable distaste for the concept of collaboration, Borowczyk frequently shares the director credit in these films. **Les Astronautes** (1959) was made with the help of the noted documentarist Chris Marker, several others saw Borowczyk working in association with Jan Lenica (who would

Goto

also move to France and make, among others, **Monsieur Tête** and **Labyrinth**.)

The first of the joint Borowczyk-Lenica films, **Byl Sobie Raz/Il Etait Une Fois/Once Upon A Time** (1957), aims for a child-like primitivism; its titles are roughly-lettered in crayon, the backdrop at all times clearly a sheet of rough paper. But it is deceptive, beginning with the bland, jerky animation of characterless shapes, but slowly working up to the use of cut-outs, photographs and even snatches of borrowed live-action film, depicting a jazz band and a clean-cut male voice choir. The film's use of cut-out figures from newspapers, magazines and paintings will instantly remind modern audiences of Terry Gilliam's animations from *Monty Python's Flying Circus* and *Do Not Adjust Your Set*; like Gilliam's cut-outs they are only semi-animated, and so never "come alive" as cartoon characters, yet clearly have become something more alive than photographs.

But the breakthrough for the duo was **Dom/House** (1957) which, though seemingly unremarkable today, caused a massive impact on the international scene at the time. Though conceptually as simplistic a montage as **Byl Sobie Raz**, **Dom** is technically several points ahead. There is a freer, more fluid use of photographic animation and an excellent, brief bit of stop-motion, as well as a more aesthetic sense of image composition and considered use of music. The film marks the "performing" debut of Borowczyk's wife, Ligia Branice (usually referred to by her married name, and sometimes simply as Ligia), who appears in a series of portrait photographs rudimentarily animated to give the impression of her raising and lowering her head. This rather lovely sequence (it is red-tinted) is the pivot around which the film seems to revolve, as if it is Ligia imagining the

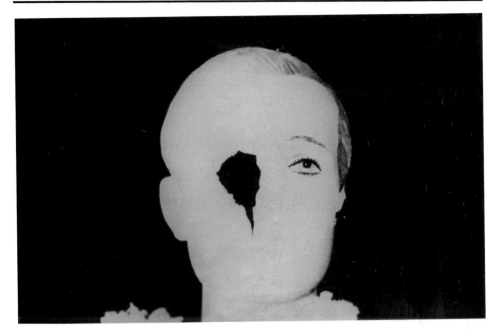

Dom

sequences which compose the film. This slim sense of structure nonetheless marks it as a more considered piece than the earlier works.

A number of Borowczyk's recurring obsessions make their debuts here. There is the lingering interest in everyday objects, the fascination with antiquarian curiosities, especially Victorian group portraits (another constant in Gilliam's work, incidentally) and even the snail that watches the Beast ravishing Sirpa Lane puts in a brief cartoon appearance. The two best scenes anticipate the object-manipulations of Jan Svankmajer, who pretty much picked up where Borowczyk left off with regards to the fine art of making inanimate objects seem invested with separate personalities. In stop-motion, we see a girl's wig come to life, crawling along a table like the Creeping Terror, it pounces upon a ball of newspaper and eats it, chases an orange and then breaks a glass. Later, Ligia sets a male wig block on a pedestal and begins to caress and passionately kiss it, until in stop-motion it begins to crumble grotesquely. The macabre potential of dolls and doll-faces, especially in stages of dismemberment, would become a staple, a cliché even, of Borowczyk's work, as well as Svankmajer's and indeed just about all *avant-garde* animation to come.

By the time of **Les Astronautes** (1959) Borowczyk had made another important step towards his break into features; for the first time one of his shorts had a consistent, if simple and frequently bizarre, plot. **Les Astronautes** tells of an eccentric inventor and his pet owl who build a rocket in their attic and fly into space for a number of adventures, before crashing back to earth, dying, and going to heaven.

The film asks "What is animation?", and defies the viewer to categorise it as either animation or live action. At first glance, the question seems absurd; the film is just a series of photographs manipulated so as to achieve animation of the simplest kind. But

Les Jeux Des Anges

then again, these photographs are not cut-outs or found images, they have been specifically taken for the film and show actors, named in the opening credits, assuming poses pertaining to the details of the story. These photographs may be sufficiently few in number to create the jerking effect of cut-out animation, but don't forget that all live action film is a sophisticated illusion using identical technology; a series of still photographs presented at a speed sufficient to cheat the eye into perceiving movement. Thus **Les Astronautes** is both animation and a kind of primitive live-action at one and the same time.

It also hints – albeit in an extremely brief and innocuous fashion – at the voyeuristic eroticism that would soon consume Borowczyk, when the astronauts' ascent is temporarily diverted by the sight of Ligia undressing by the window of a multi-storey apartment block.

By now Borowczyk had achieved some celebrity, and found himself in the peculiar position of having his new work eagerly anticipated by a growing army of cineastes and devotees. He responded with what is surely his masterpiece. **Renaissance** (1963) is a ten-minute animation of breathtaking technique and effect, in which a simple but brilliant idea is visualised with such perfection as to cross the boundary between conventional cinematic excellence and bona-fide work of art stature.

Renaissance opens to a scene of total destruction; a room in which nothing is intact. The wall is charred and black, with strips of wallpaper hanging from it, and the ground is littered with wreckage of all kinds; wood, metal, china. Slowly, using reversed film, the room begins to reassemble itself one item at a time. The wallpaper reforms and returns to the wall, a table is assembled from the piles of broken wood, a chunk of twisted metal becomes a trumpet which, when fully restored, begins playing. A wicker hamper, two books, a doll and a china plate all find their original forms from amidst heaps of rubble. Finally, the room reclaims its final object; a hand-grenade. As the trumpet plays merrily, the hand-grenade pulls its own pin, and the scene returns to chaos.

Another intriguing aspect of Borowczyk's work around this time is its apparent playfulness, its simultaneous adoption and deconstruction of formalist strategies whereby the films enslave themselves to rigid structures that they then almost immediately abandon. This degree of parodic referentiality, if that is what it is, would be hardly worthy of comment in a film made today, but is highly unusual for its time. **L'Encyclopedie De Grand-Maman En 13 Volumes** (1963), for example, is a title that may well bring Peter Greenaway to mind, both for his films-as-libraries **Prospero's Books** and **The Pillow Book**, as well as the games-playing of films like **The Falls** and the excellent **Drowning By Numbers**, which builds an absurdist narrative around the numbers one to a hundred. Borowczyk's film begins with the letters of the alphabet, and sets the convention that each section of the film will begin with a letter in correct sequence. But the film abruptly gives up after "C", and ends three letters and one volume in. (Incidentally, this is the most Gilliamesque of all Borowczyk's films, depicting cut-out car and balloon races in which Victorian gentlemen speed along streets and down flights of steps). Similarly, as its title suggests, **Diptyque** (1967) is presented as a film in two halves, yet the two episodes are as unrelated to each other as is conceivable, not merely in terms of their nominal subject, but in every conceptual, aesthetic and technical sense as well. Part one is a monochrome, hand-held mock-documentary depicting a farmer and his dog tilling a field and driving off in a van, the footage is grainy, shaky and crudely assembled. Part two is static, studio-shot, richly coloured and lushly photographed – a series of tableaux depicting ornate vases, cut flowers and cute kittens, all set to a soundtrack of classical music and opera.

Borowczyk's final animations were cartoons adopting a consistent visual style. This could indicate a deepening realisation on the director's part of his own style and strengths, or a growing disinterest in the form and an urge to branch into more straightforward narratives.

The films themselves cater to both arguments. **Le Concert De Monsieur Et Mrs Kabal**, one of his least interesting shorts, was rejigged to make his uninspired debut feature **Le Théâtre De Monsieur Et Madame Kabal** (1967). But the short **Jeux Des Anges/Angels' Games** (1964), an exercise in animated watercolour, was superb and remarkable, depicting the internal machinations of a totalitarian factory where angels have their wings sawn off.

Despite their occasional excellence, I am inclined to think that these last shorts reflect a Borowczyk itching to try something different, as shown by his experiments with pure, if not especially *active*, live-action in the shorts **Rosalie** (1966), **Diptyque** and **Gavotte** (1967). The latter, which could be dismissed as a mere triviality were it not for the extreme artificiality of its set-up (requiring a great deal of effort in terms of casting, costume and set-dressing, and tending to suggest therefore a labour of love), is a static, single-shot absurdist comedy depicting a bored regency dwarf. After picking at some food and trying to read some books which he immediately throws away he attempts to sleep on an ornate chest. When another dwarf steals his cushion a fight ensues, and the film ends with the first dwarf overpowering the second and dumping him inside the chest.

Gavotte is a joke, a diversion, but **Rosalie** is one of Borowczyk's most brilliant works, a vivid filmed monologue inspired by a Guy de Maupassant story. An opening caption briefs us as to the circumstances of the story; Rosalie, a servant-girl made

Rosalie

pregnant out of wedlock by a soldier, has twins in secret, smothers them and buries them in the garden. The film opens to the sound of a woman's sobbing and a slow pan along the bench upon which a series of objects have been neatly arranged and numbered; a bloodstained pillow, a shovel covered in earth, an antique sewing-kit, and a parcel wrapped in newspaper that is clearly a dead baby. The pan ends upon a witness box, in which we see that it is Rosalie who has been crying. The rest of the film takes the form of a single shot of Rosalie's face (played by Ligia, and shot in a monochrome so harsh that only her hair and individual features are clearly discernable), interspersed with quick, brief cuts to the objects and, repeatedly, to a framed portrait of Rosalie's seducer. Rosalie recounts the details of her pathetic story, and the film ends on another caption, informing us simply that she was acquitted.

There is one tiny but brilliant piece of animation as Rosalie describes knitting jackets for the impending child and we see these garments, as if in recognition of their own futility, unpicking themselves back into a ball of wool. It is a brief, haunting re-use

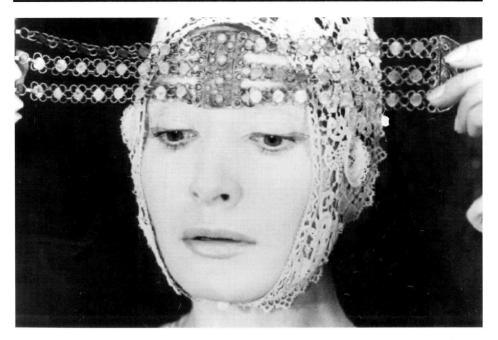

Blanche

of the reverse-film techniques of **Renaissance,** here given an even greater potency by their narrative justification. A first for Borowczyk, that, and a significant one, and it is also significant to note that the film's greatest assets are its spare, moving script and its mesmerising central performance. (Not bad for an animator and visualist.) In time Ligia would be replaced as Borowczyk's regular heroine by the more overtly fetishized Mariana Pierro, but her performance in **Rosalie,** even more than in **Blanche,** consolidates her position as by far the most important human presence in the director's *oeuvre.*

Between them, **Rosalie, Diptyque** and **Gavotte** point out another intriguing paradox. Of all three films, only the first half of **Diptyque** in any sense "uses" the camera to present location or an even movement, whereas the animations were unfettered in their depiction of all worlds, inner and outer, their restlessness and their range.

Borowczyk had stumbled upon the problem Spike Milligan identified as the difference between radio and TV comedy; the latter will always be contained imaginatively by the walls of the studio, whereas in the former you can do anything and go anywhere. As an "extra dimension" reality is ambiguous, often restricting rather than liberating the imagination. Working without the luxury of large budgets, crews and resources, Borowczyk had to curtail, or at least adapt, his vision in these first live-actions. The simplicity of **Diptyque** and the absurdity of **Gavotte** were solutions of a sort, but **Rosalie** is the greater success simply because it is braver. Completely rethinking his approach to film, Borowczyk consciously sought to use, rather than attempt to side-step, the limitations imposed upon him. A single camera, a single actress and a single set combine to produce a film that resonates with power, a masterpiece of minimalism from a master of extravagance and excess.

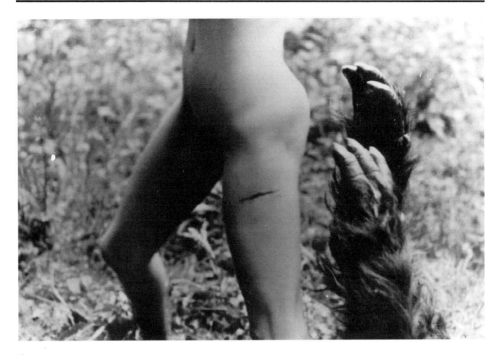

The Beast

As Borowczyk moved into features, the difficulties identified by these shorts would only in part be alleviated. Though he would of course work on locations with professional crews, huge budgets were never his to squander and his imagination would always be his most useful tool. So, if there is a case for arguing that the later Borowczyk is an artist in decline, it has nothing to do with squeamish debates over nudity, sex or the representation of women.

There is the lingering feeling, even before his relegation to the likes of **Emmanuelle 5,** that the director has lost some of his old energy and passion, and – especially – his penchant for the surprising and the *outré*. **La Bête** is a good case in point here. When it premiered at the London Film Festival it was in the form of a short – **La Veritable Histoire De La Bête De Gevaudin** – amazing, surprising, vintage Borowczyk. Originally intended as one section of his episodic **Contes Immoraux (Immoral Tales,** 1974) but restructured as a feature, it is surprising to see how stodgily-plotted Borowczyk felt obliged to make it, creating a kind of intrigue-laden familial saga replete with endless dialogue sequences. The original film becomes a fantasy-flashback, carefully "explained" by the surrounding narrative.

It may be that which makes the difference, certainly I have no quarrel with the subject matter of the later features, all aspects of which had been fully rehearsed in the shorts if you look for them. The best of the later films (and despite my reservations I would include **La Bête** in their number) are those which most remind the viewer of the flickering, temporal, unstable world of the shorts, a world that is uniquely Borowczyk's. The features are a mixed bag, but they are riveting because the viewer knows that Borowczyk could open the door to that world at any given moment, and the fun is

Immoral Tales

finding out when he will go and for how long. When he does, there is not a filmmaker in the world to match him.

TITS, ASS & SWASTIKAS

Three Steps Toward A Fatal Film Theory

Omayra Cruz

"I urge you: learn how to look at 'bad' films, they are so often sublime."
—Ado Kyrou, Le Surrealism Au Cinéma

"Exploitation films are the only ones that come close to the dreaded word 'art'. I still wonder why film students babble on about Orson Welles or Howard Hawks when they ignore the greatest masters in film history: Russ Meyer and Hershell Gordon Lewis. Even the worst films by these two directors are infinitely more interesting than 'Citizen Kane'."
—John Waters, Kitsch In Sync

Aside from simply antagonising the sensibilities of film theorists, I propose that Kyrou and Waters in the above quotes are suggesting something about the manner in which film studies are conducted, and that promoting the dregs of cinematic practice contributes to film theory in general. Although their flippant levelling of art and exploitation strikes me as somewhat dubious, I support the gist of their claim: crudely speaking, film studies is plagued by a figurative history of kings. Open most text on cinema history and you will find reference to high art and classic Hollywood-type productions. Critical acclaim is unfailingly bestowed on these films so that the history of film comes to resemble those grammar school texts which plot time according to dynasties. Contemporary historiography has carved spaces for "popular" histories. I expect nothing less from film historians, yet since so few have kept up, I have taken matters into my own hands. In order to help carry out a part of this redemption, I turn to exploitation cinema.

In spite of their commercial success, low-budget exploitation films receive very little critical attention. Attempts to give them cultural respectability, have concentrated on specific areas which can be reclaimed according to traditional critical canons of authorship and genre.[1] But this espousal of certain exploitation directors, which rests on the assumption that individual genius somehow overcomes basically uncongenial materials, does not take exploitation seriously on its own lewd grounds.

Dragging exploitation up from the depths to which respectable film studies have cast them could of course be approached from a variety of perspectives. Yet rather than address exploitation's relationship to viewers according to sociology or psychology, I have chosen to explore what I consider the driving force of exploitation filmmaking; its unabashed commodity status. This allows me to produce a space for this often derided, nearly forgotten corpus of film, on its own constitutive grounds. European exploitation, one of the most abhorred forms of exploitation cinema as compared to other large industries such as the United States, South America and Asia; highlights the ligature between exploitation cinema and economics by attributing to the geographic home of art the capitalist rapacity of exploitative endeavours. Yet even a comprehensive study of European exploitation proves too large a task. As such, I focus on certain aspects of European, particularly Italian, exploitation that act as disruptive supplement to legitimate cinematic practice and the film theory which circumscribes it.

EXPLOITATION: AN ECONOMIC IMPERATIVE

Exploitation does not revolve around simply classified (and dismissed) subjects. A quick glance at the breadth of topics that such films address easily enfeebles classification. So rather than attempting to categorise exploitation films according to content thematics, I propose we understand exploitation as filmmaking methodology distinguishable by reference to economic determinants. Exploitation is generally accepted as a derogatory term; capitalist selfishness flourishes at the expense of the proletariat. Applied to film, it retains this sense and acquires a second, an economic imperative dominated by: "very low budgets, tight production schedules, low-paid, inexperienced personnel, minimal production values and 'sensational' selling campaigns... all in the interest of making a fast buck."[2] As is to be expected, such production values contribute to both form and content of the exploitation repertoire. Rather than offering up-market production values, exploitation substitutes "schematic, minimal narratives, comic-book stereotypes, 'bad' acting, and brief film 'cycles' which disappear as soon as their audience appeal is exhausted."[3] And of course, in order to survive the stronghold of dominant cinema, exploitation relies on large doses of sensationalised sex and/or violence as a competitive edge against safe big-budget features that fail to satisfy prurient audience interest.

Examples of exchange between Hollywood and exploitation are far from difficult to find. As Jonathan Ross points out, both Hollywood and exploitation cinema have historically drawn on similar issues. From the beginning, Hollywood was almost as reliable a source of sleaze as independent exploitation. Filmmakers knew that to avoid prosecution and reach audiences, they had to avoid charges of titillation for its own sake. "To that end, films that played out salacious stories would always adopt a very high moral stance... [since] it was the duty of the filmmakers, as responsible educators and honest men, to use this great tool, cinema, to educate mankind to the evil that lurked all around."[4] An unexpected follower of this method was Cecil B. DeMille. In 1918 he released **Old Wives For New**, whose popularity spurred him to produce: **Don't Change Your Husband, Male And Female** and **Why Change Your Wife**. But eventually bowing to critic pressure, DeMille turned from the free living of the Jazz Age to a source whose stories were just as provocative, but morally impeccable. DeMille's **The Ten Commandments** (1923) quieted the censors without sacrificing thrills. Ross' argument seems to summarise the general consensus among exploitation aficionados. "They just don't make 'em like they used to," he sighs. The traditionally rich well-springs of exploitation: sex, drugs, freaks and violence, found their way into the mainstream[5], since as Ross suggests, exploitation films were just too successful for their own good. Everyone wanted to see what they offered, so Hollywood assimilated and disguised the exploitation ethic of sleaze with big names and stupendous budgets.

More widely disparate than the relationship between Hollywood and exploitation, is the antagonism between exploitation and art. By art, I mean the practices of *avant-garde* cinema which, if one follows Theodor Adorno's argument, descend into hegemonic helplessness at the hands of mass culture. More precisely, Adorno bewails the culture industry for making art commercial. The insertion of art into the culture-industry robs it of its supposed liberatory espousal of bourgeois value. Although Adorno would have us keep art as separate from popular bases and capitalist use-value as possible, in "The Fetish Character Of Music And The Regression In Listening", he realises that the damage is already done. "Films, radio and magazines make up a system which is uniform as a whole in every part"[6] that rapaciously swallows the endeavours of classic music and the revolutionary potential of film. In a fit of honesty, Adorno condemns film as irredeemably bankrupt to the Frankfurt School's liberal political project. I am largely inclined to agree since when examining content and form of exploitation, one finds that it is often difficult to tell them apart from many legitimate cinematic endeavours. In short, some just go for cheap thrills while others offer expensive ones. Unless one relies on authorial intention (which has lately fallen from fashion), only economics and cultural baggage make Pier Pasolini any less an exploitative pornographer than Umberto Lenzi – which for me isn't necessarily a bad thing.[7] For Adorno however, such integrated culture dooms us to the influence of the culture industry since one cannot even depend on the dregs to escape and critique dominant culture.[8] As political representatives of the Italian Left succinctly noted, perhaps "breasts and legs cannot contribute to an analysis of the problems of poverty."[9] This does not however exclude exploitation from jeopardising a practice of film theory which purports to revolutionary impact on the "real world".

THE ROLE OF EXPLOITATION IN POPULAR EUROPEAN CINEMA
Coupling "Europe" and "popular" proves to be an exceedingly complex and slippery matter. "Popular" defies off-hand definition. Does one look to market paradigms and determine a film's popularity according to economic success? Should one instead consider ethnographical indicators such as regional or generational preference? Furthermore, should *folk* be lumped together with *mass* culture or do the two exist as irreconcilably distinct? Second, the difficulties facing the EC project, indicate that except under the Anglo-American gaze[10], the identity of Europe as a homogeneous region is powerfully contested. As Richard Dyer suggests:

*"..even if there is **some** common European identity at the level of high white culture, there is much less beyond it. None the less, European cinemas do have three things in common at the level of their situations; first, the problem of exportability, second, the national standing of high culture, repository of official national identity and the nation's international face; third, not being Hollywood"*[11].

Accordingly, we see that part of the existing map of cinema is coloured quite clearly; there is America, which is Hollywood, which is popular entertainment, and there is Europe, which is art[12]. Since World War I the United States has been a massive part of European cinema, and aesthetic developments in European film such as expressionism and *film noir* have repeatedly found their way into Hollywood productions. Yet one aspect of film which remains stubbornly unacknowledged is popular European cinema. If one relies on general national histories of film, one would be hard-pressed to prove that Europeans have ever produced entertainment cinema, much less gauge its enormous economic and social impact. Far more frequently, popular European cinema is marginalised in favour of little-seen but critically acclaimed art film traditions[13]. To a large extent, one might attribute this arrangement to ideological pressures associated with the term "Europe". As the, excuse my French, *ne plus ultra* of high white culture, Europe seems at odds with the vulgarity of entertainment industry exemplified by Umberto Lenzi's cannibal slaughter-fest, **Make Them Die Slowly** (*aka* **Cannibal Ferox**, 1981).

One need not wonder why most national European governments have been inclined to subsidise art cinema. Such cinemas achieve high cultural prestige by constructing themselves through discourses of European culture, which for socio-historical reasons, are accepted as the dominant national cultures in most European countries[14]. The historical preference for art cinema also operates at an economic level. Since art films are shown at film festivals and on international exhibition circuits, they override the problem of distribution characteristics of many small domestic markets. Finally, art cinema is seen to feed into the "resistance to two filmic 'bad others'; US cultural influence, including television (though Hollywood, particularly the classical era, has occupied an ambiguous place in this constellation), and the despised indigenous low traditions."[15]

Given the above considerations, European exploitation emerges as an intriguing object of analysis. It occupies a position of supplementarity which threatens to topple association of Europe as the *haute couture* of film. Furthermore, popular European industries, which lack the financial power to compete with Hollywood on the level of "quality", rely heavily on the success-in numbers of exploitation. However, before developing these arguments a short account of the development and practices of European exploitation is necessary to highlight the gap that respectable film historians have so desperately tried to efface...

Exploitation filmmaking has played a major role in the popularity, profits and development of film industry from the early days of the Edison kinetoscope[16]. So for current purposes, I have focused on a particularly prolific period in European exploitation: the 1960's and 1970's. During this era, European exploitation reached what many consider its most bizarre forms and powerful socio-economic impact. A new type of cinema emerged which infused previously popular genres such as horror and action with heavy doses of eroticism. In *Immoral Tales*, Tohill and Tombs report that, "this heady fusion was highly successful, causing a tidal wave of celluloid weirdness that was destined to look even more shocking and irrational when it hit countries like England and the USA."[17] Yet sadly, the erotic horror boom lasted only until the mid-'70s. In order to compete with the new-thrills-on-the-block of hardcore classics such as **Deep Throat** and **The Devil In Miss Jones**, European exploitation forged into the skin-flick market. They produced films weirder and wilder than their erotic horror speciality which unfortunately proved too hot-blooded for overseas consumption, too strange and disreputable for Anglo-American censors since unlike earlier erotic European films they could not be marketed as art.

The cinematic roots of this strange phenomenon can be traced back to what the French call the *fantastique*. Erotic, way out and fabulous, linear narrative and logic are always ignored in a *fantastique* film. The pictorial, the excessive and the irrational are exclusively privileged factors. This erotic revolution was also influenced by older cultural movements, "drawing power from surrealism, romanticism and the decadent tradition as well as early 20th century pulp-literature, filmed serials, creaky horror movies and sexy comic strips."[18] Such films defy compliant pigeon-holing and constitute the basis upon which European exploitation breeds hybridity. To fully appreciate the expression and impact of exploitation filmmaking as contemporary *fantastique*, requires close attention to particular examples of filmic production. For a number of reasons, Italian exploitation elucidates the potentialities of such films and ensuing implications to film theory.

THE ITALIAN FILM INDUSTRY

The Italian film industry is one of the oldest and largest in Europe. "From the beginning it has been spectacular, larger than life – a modern day version of the ancient Roman circuses, with blood, passion and spectacle."[19] Since the bridge between art houses and

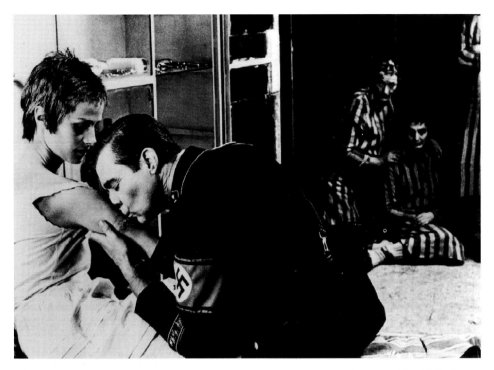

The Night Porter

the Italian cinema fell into disrepair, Rome became a figurative "Hollywood on the Tiber" where the cinema of low-budget productions and high exploitation values thrived. "Whether the glistening bodies and pulchritudinous breasts (both male and female) of the superhero films, or the rape and revenge plots of the westerns, sex and violence were always major components."[20] Consequently, showcasing the mandatory spectacle of Italian cinema highlights several notable "contributions" of exploitation cinema to film studies: namely, a sustained critique of the cinematic cult of originality as well as of the intricate correspondences which engage exploitative and legitimate cinematic practices.

Historically, the pattern of Italian exploitation cinema has been an overlapping succession of genre cycles usually triggered by the domestic popularity either of a specific American film or of a traditional Hollywood genre. During the short lifespan of any individual cycle, a plague of similar films are rushed through production and into distribution before the format wears thin and popularity fades. The period of overlap between cycles often accounts for outlandish hybrids like the horror/peplum and zombie/cannibal trends. Yet regardless of such innovations, Kim Newman insists that:

"..there is a tendency to overlook the way Italian spectacles, horror films, murder mysteries, science fiction pictures, superspy thrillers and jungle adventures do more with the trappings of their Hollywood models than imitate. While many Italian genre films are simply worthless carbon copies with a few baroque trimmings, the best examples of most cycles are surprisingly sophisticated mixes of imitation, pastiche, parody, deconstruction, reinterpretation and operatic inflation."[21]

One particularly bizarre example of this practice is also cited as the most despised product of Euro-exploitation; the Nazi sex camp film. Most notably, Liliana Cavani's **The Night Porter** (1974) opened the floodgates to films like Sergio Garrone's **SS Experiment Camp** (1976) and **SS Camp 5** (1976), Bruno Mattei's **SS Girls** (1976), Cesare Canevari's **Gestapo's Last Orgy** (1976), Luigi Batzella's **The Beast In Heat** (1977), Fabio De Agostini's **Red Nights Of The Gestapo** (1977), and Rino Di Silvestro's **Deported Women Of The SS Special Section** (1977). Although within the context of the Italian movie experience these films make perfect sense[22], general outcry usually condemns them for commercialising and exploiting a "serious" issue. How could anyone stoop so low as to bastardise the terror and tragedy of the Nazi experience for profit? I'll let Adorno answer this question as well. He contends that:

"Overlapping the official models are a number of unofficial ones which supply the attraction yet are intended to be neutralised by the former. In order to capture the consumers and provide them with substitute satisfaction, the unofficial, if you will, heterodox ideology must be depicted in a much broader and juicier fashion than suits the moral of the story."[23]

The culture industry, in effect, subsumes the desire to "make a difference" rendering films from **The Night Porter** to **Schindler's List** (Spielberg, 1993) as politically ineffective – albeit less distasteful – versions of Garrone's films.

FROM FATAL FILM FORM TO FATAL FILM THEORY

Throughout this article I have insisted that exploitation tells us something about film practice in general – especially since such pains are taken to repress and vilify it. If it speaks of film practice, then exploitation necessarily indicates something about the film theory of legitimate film objects. As far as I can presently calculate, the most hostile effect that consideration of exploitation practice has on film theory, is the chewing up and spitting out of value, content and form so dear to cinematic hierarchies. Italian cinema epitomises this characteristic aspect of exploitation filmmaking. Put bluntly, Italy makes the best rip-offs[24]. Such a propensity to "borrow" from other areas (even from itself) is an aspect of exploitation I find particularly intriguing. So although cinema studies clings to auteurial influence in a way that canonises its preferred objects and suppresses the impact of exploitation, Adorno's claim that nothing whatsoever stands immune to mass culture, is piquantly illustrated. Exploitation, the supposed supplement to filmic practice lashes back at the institution which would cast it as Other.

Accordingly, the salvage operation underway in this project involves understanding exploitation's impact on its hosts as analogous to camp culture's relationship to dominant aesthetics. Rather than aspire to art (and the cultural legitimacy this imparts), camp culture thrives on the failure of low culture to become high culture and on the failures of high culture itself[25]. It thus corresponds to Adorno's definition of entertainment as that which fails (or some might say, refuses) the trappings of art. Camp, a culture of consumption rather than production, suggests that parasitical relationships such as that operating between exploitation and legitimate cinema often prove intriguing sites of cultural fecundity. As noted earlier, exploitation's cycles consume and revamp both culture industry and art products. Rather than completely process cultural intake and then expel a waste product, exploitation chews film culture up and offers it for re-consumption.

It remains possible to recognise what has been consumed, while concurrently acknowledging that some digestive juices have been added to the menu and altered the first course. This process can go on and on until all the flavour has been culled and boredom sets in with the current mouthful.

Since exploitation recycles culture industry products from within, it might be construed as a fatal film practice which redoubles the banality of legitimate practice. As a more full than full recycling of film objects, exploitation resembles the holiday boredom which Baudrillard cites as exemplar of day-to-day fatal strategies. "People in their holidays look for a boredom more profound than that experienced from day-to-day – a boredom redoubled, made out of all the elements of happiness and distraction. There is, importantly, a predestination to boredom in holidays, and a bitter premonition that it cannot be avoided."[26] So just as such a fatal theory of leisure forces us to rethink the agency and desire for fun, a fatal theory of film forces us to rethink the relationship of consumption to production and the hierarchies which these express within the dogma of film studies.

Although it might seem incongruous to at this late stage introduce a figure as enigmatic as Baudrillard, I suggest that his theorisations prove a useful tool in drawing together the strands of exploitation, legitimate cinematic practice and film theory. Particularly vital to such a goal is the elaboration of simulation and fatal strategy.

Simulation, or the generation by models of a real without origin or reality, does not imply a misrepresentation of reality. "It is no longer a question of imitation, nor duplication, nor even parody. It is a question of substituting the signs of the real for the real, that is to say of an operation of deterring every real process via its operational double, a programmatic, metastable, perfectly descriptive machine that offers all the signs of the real and short-circuits all its vicissitudes."[27] As such, I understand simulation in much the same way as Saussure, Barthes and Derrida conceptualise the relationship of signifiers to signifieds. In other words, representations refer to other representations just as signifiers rely exclusively on other signifiers to confer meaning. Words avoid meaninglessness even though instead of corresponding to a real, they refer only to other words. Accordingly, simulations are no less concrete than the "real" for exchanging truth values only among the models from which they are derived[28]. One has as much chance of identifying a real beneath the multitudinous codes of simulation as definitively establishing a signified. What Saussure, Barthes and Derrida do for words and meaning, Baudrillard effects for images and referents.

The question now, is how do simulation and fatal strategy relate to film theory and practice? Baudrillard suggest that "we are entering an era of films that in themselves no longer have meaning strictly speaking, an era of great synthesising machines of varying geometry. Is there something of this already in Leone's Westerns ?"[29] That Baudrillard isolates the films of Sergio Leone could not be more fitting. Leone is popularly considered a great exemplar of exploitation film practice. His contributions even spawned a hugely influential sub-genre; the spaghetti western. Thus exploitation, which as previously indicated synthesises culture industry products, can be construed as a fatal film practice. Never paying tribute to the cult of origins, exploitation capitalises on the impossibility of tying images to signifieds, borrowing from even reprehensible images which many agree should be guarded and utilised only to guarantee human well-being (eg. the Nazi atrocity films of Sergio Garrone).

To deal with the proliferation of simulation in the culture industry, Baudrillard pushes Adorno's argument to extremes. To clarify, in response to accusations of resignation by social activists, Adorno's short essay duly entitled "Resignation" asserts that "the uncompromisingly critical thinker, who neither superscribes his conscience nor permits himself to be terrorised into action, is in truth the one who does not give up."[30] Accordingly, Baudrillard hints that theory is the most, if not only, fatal strategy.

"And doubtless the only difference between a banal and a fatal theory is that in one strategy the subject still believes himself to be more cunning than the object, whereas in the other the object is considered more cunning, cynical, talented than the subject... not because they are deeply mysterious, but because they are infinitely ironic."[31]

Thus fatal strategies attempt to deal with cultural implosion, or the continuous recycling of culture that occurs when history and progress no longer have access to continuous expansion. Since the culture-industry renders meaning entirely variable, we must stop wallowing in sorrow for a lost standard of security and work with what we have got. Rather than imply resignation to futility, such advice merely suggests a change of tactics which accommodates the power of cultural objects. In short, the challenge has been extended: explore the implications of a film theory fit to encounter the fatal quality of contemporary film exemplified by exploitation in both its legitimate and outlaw practice.

NOTES

1. Through Roger Corman's Poe cycle, for example, or in the work of those Corman proteges (Scorsese, Dante, Demme, et al) who went on to make big-budget movies.
2. P. Cook (1985), "The Art Of Exploitation, or How To Get Into The Movies," p.367.
3. Ibid., p.368
4. J. Ross (1993), *The Incredibly Strange Film Book*, p.63.
5. Ibid., p.90.
6. T. Adorno & M. Horkheimer (1972), *The Dialectic Of Enlightenment*, p.120.
7. It has been brought to my attention that this claim might inadvertently efface difference, forcing all objects into futility. I would consequently like to stress that rather than levelling objects, this claim merely problematises the hazy appreciation which attributes to objects an irrefutable essence by virtue of their creator. Objects cast off this confusion with passionate indifference (See J. Baudrillard [1990] *Fatal Strategies*).
8. T. Adorno (1991), *The Culture Industry*, p.160.
9. C. Tohill & P. Combs (1994), *Immoral Tales*, p.29.
10. I have chosen to exclude Great Britain from my discussions of Europe since its particularly close linguistic and cultural ties with the United States have rendered it a less foreign package than continental European film products. Although I have retained the term "Europe" to maintain certain worldly connotations, the term "continental" can theoretically replace every instance of it.
11. R. Dyer (1994), *Popular European Cinema*, p.10.
12. Ibid., p.1.
13. An exception to this practice is France whose popular film industry is relatively strong as compared to other European cinema standards. However, when packaged for export popular French films often resurface as art house material.
14. R. Dyer & G. Vincendeau (1992), Op cit., p.8.
15. Ibid., p.8.
16. C. Tohill & P. Combs (1994), Op cit, p.2.
17. Ibid., p.5.
18. Ibid., p.5.
19. K. Newman (1986), "Thirty Years In Another Town: The History Of Italian Exploitation", p.29.

20. C. Tohill & P. Tombs (1994), Op cit., p.30.
21. K. Newman (1988), *Nightmare Movies*, p.188.
22. Ibid., p.34.
23. T. Adorno (1991), Op cit., p.159.
24. K. Newman (1988), Op cit., p.187.
25. Coates (1994), p.3.
26. J. Baudrillard (1990), *Fatal Strategies*.
27. J. Baudrillard (1994), *Simulacra And Simulations*, p.2.
28. Ibid., p.17.
29. J. Baudrillard (1994), Op cit., p.46.
30. T. Adorno (1991), Op cit, p.174.
31. J. Baudrillard (1990), *Fatal Strategies*, p.181.

ANNA WITH A DEVIL INSIDE

Klein, Argento, & "The Stendhal Syndrome"

Julian Hoxter

Dario Argento's films typically play themselves out as hesitant, impeded detective narratives in which the heroes and heroines are marked by an often terminal inability successfully to discriminate between the truth and falsehood of the evidence they encounter. All that should be good in the world reveals itself as corrupt as icons of normality, authority and care turn out rather to represent perversion, impotence and aggression. Social, cultural and, particularly, familial relationships are prone to inversion as the (biblical) universe of moral order – of distinction, hierarchy and what Janine Chasseguet-Smirgel refers to as the Universal Law[1] – gives way to be replaced for the films' protagonists by the killer's perverse universe in which new and perverse relationships, new and perverse hierarchies and new and perverse meanings and interpretations take hold.

Argento's protagonists have to fight for their understanding in a world which is organised specifically for its denial. When they do come towards a resolution, that resolution typically necessitates an immersion into (literally in the case of Jennifer Corvino in **Creepers**, 1985), or incorporation of, the killer's perverse world view. The intimacy of the relationship between detective and killer – particularly in those narratives where their functions directly overlap or in which the one becomes the other such as is the case with Anna Manni in **The Stendhal Syndrome** (1996) – implies a complex, shifting connection between individuals and their particular understanding of the world of objects which they inhabit. This scenario in which identities, relationships and positions shift and blend radically lends itself to interpretation through a model which is designed to account for such personal invasions, expulsions and incorporations. Such a model can be found in "object relations theory" of the sort pioneered in England by the psychoanalyst Melanie Klein[2].

Klein pioneered the development of child analysis initially in Austria and significantly in this country. Her clinical and theoretical insights came out of the interpretation of children's play in the context of analysis (the *play technique*). She viewed phantasies expressed in a child's play as communications of the child's unconscious phantasies in a similar way to Freud's focus on the dreams and free associations of adults in analysis. A Kleinian approach offers the critic a challenging alternative to well-established Freudian and Lacanian approaches to film analysis. Indeed, a critical approach drawing on object relations theory immediately departs from "ego-psychology" in that it requires a fundamental shift in analytical focus from the investigation of what happens within the psyche to what happens with the interaction of inner worlds. In other words, as Elizabeth Wright reminds us, a Kleinian approach would privilege the complex and shifting relationship between artist and medium or critic and text.[3]

Kleinian psychoanalysis is founded in part on the assertion that phantasy is in many ways a *precondition* of any engagement with reality. For Kleinians the process of childhood development is organised around the parallel development of the child's understanding of, and relations with, an ongoing series of encounters with objects (people and things). Unlike the work of Anna Freud and her group, Kleinians interpreted the young child's behaviour and relationship to the analyst as involving transferences or reflections of emotional relationships which the child had to his internal images of his parents. These were termed object relationships as such parental relationships were not just based upon the interaction of the child with its external parents, but such experiences of external parents compounded, distorted or enhanced by the child's feelings towards its parents (loves, hates, desires, fears, gratifications and frustrations) and his phantasies about them; about their powers over him and his (or her) powers over the parents (phantasies of omnipotence etc). Successfully passing through certain stages in the development of early object relations (particularly in the first few months after birth) affects the subject's ability to form successful relationships in later life. Objects are investigated, interpreted, incorporated and otherwise interacted with by the child through "unconscious phantasy". Unconscious phantasy is a term developed by Klein and others to account for what R. D. Hinshelwood describes as: "the mental expression of the instinctual impulses and also of defence mechanisms against instinctual impulses."[4] Furthermore, "unconscious phantasies of relationships with objects constitute the mental activity of the newly born infant. These are the primary experiences from which the rest of life, mind and development starts. They are of fundamental importance."[5]

Importantly, Klein departs from Freud here in rejecting the notion that there is a period in which the infant only relates to itself. As Julia Segal puts it: "One of the baby's first actions is to search for the nipple: the baby is born in some sense aware of the need for something outside itself."[6] In other words, "biological activity comes with pre-formed psychological meaning."[7] Klein proposes the existence of a primitive ego which sets up basic defence mechanisms and transforms initial aggressive instincts, and life preserving instincts, through processes which she called "projection" and "introjection".

Mrs Klein developed the account of projection begun by Freud in 1895 and developed by Karl Abraham (notably in 1924), and its meaning has been continually re-examined by Kleinians and others since her death. At its most simple, in projection the subject identifies parts or aspects of itself – usually hated or violent parts – as existing within an external object (commonly another person). Typically this external object is the mother or father or, in a relatively common scenario, a combined (and often horrific) Mother/Father figure. Incidentally, it is the recurrence of such combined figures in early phantasy which prompted Mrs Klein to argue for the presence of pre-genital Oedipal structures – in other words existing earlier than in the Freudian developmental timetable. "Projection," writes Julia Segal, "can be thought of as *perceiving* someone else as having one's own characteristics..." A more active and even violent version of this activity: "projective identification" "involves ... *getting rid of* something belonging to the self into someone else... In other words, in the child's phantasy, hated parts of the self are forced into the mother who is then identified with these parts of the self and hated violently."[8] These phantasies are experienced as real and often physical and the child believes it has actually performed or is in danger of performing the phantasised actions. In this way Kleinian psychoanalysts and psychotherapists acknowledge a deep and important interlocking between a subject's "biological make-up and psychological experience".[9]

Conversely introjection "is a process whereby qualities that belong to an external object are absorbed and unconsciously regarded as belonging to the self. The infant thus creates an ideal object for itself by getting rid of all bad impulses from itself and taking in all it perceives as good from the object."[10] In this way we can see that the child's development is in many ways about the struggle to understand, and thus to position itself, in relation to external objects. This process of object formation – in which every step is earned through a sort of internal struggle – goes through stages. Specifically, objects are not, at first, "clearly delimited and secure in their separateness as they are for the adult."[11] Thus the child goes through a period where it relates to the world through "part objects".

Part objects are what adults would interpret as elements or aspects of a whole person. The mother's breast, for example, typically becomes a part object for the child. In this way it can be argued that the breast takes on a *metonymic* significance, standing in place of the mother herself. The child invests part objects with phantasies which are both positive and negative. In this way, the child shifts between powerful feelings of love and hate for the part object, splitting its identification (as it does its ego) between, the resulting "good" and "bad" objects – in our example a "good breast" and a "bad breast". The good breast is loved for never failing to provide gratification, comfort and satisfaction; the bad breast is the absent good breast perceived as a present bad breast and hated as an imaginary persecutor.

It is important to emphasise that the Kleinian model foregrounds the shifting nature of identification, and thus of object relations. A major difference between Kleinian and Freudian accounts of childhood development is that for many Kleinians the child experiences aspects of the oral, anal and genital phases as overlapping – even as coterminous. For Freud, these phases were entered into one after another in a rather strict sequence; for Klein, the process is much more fluid. Nowhere is this more apparent in Kleinian theory than in the account of the "paranoid-schizoid" and "depressive positions". Even in their naming we are given a suggestion how they interact. Unlike the bounded Freudian phases, Klein saw the child working through different relationships with objects and was aware that an individual could shift back and forth between these relationships throughout its life.

In terms of the child's development, the first of these two situations is the paranoid-schizoid position in which the child's identification is split between good and bad (part) objects. Unable to appreciate that the mother is a full person and, thus, that she embodies contradictions (good and bad), for example, the child lives in fear of the bad breast and idealises the good breast. As Hinshelwood reminds us, the child's earliest experiences are either wholly good with good objects or wholly bad with bad objects. The early ego splits to protect itself from the wholly bad experiences.

The depressive position occurs later in the first year of life when the child begins to be able to integrate its objects. In this way, the child comes to understand that its objects contain both good and bad elements or aspects. Internalised objects are, in this way, now the focus of more ambivalent responses which prompt feelings of guilt in the child over its previous omnipotent, aggressive fantasies towards the good object. These guilty feelings typically cause the child to want to make amends for its previous actions. Once again, it must not be forgotten that an individual may shift between these positions at different times.

As I have already suggested, a Kleinian approach to aesthetics could help to unravel the complexity of the relationship between the artist and his or her medium and that between the critic and his or her object of analysis. In this way, "the prototype for the aesthetic interaction both as regards the artist to his medium and the audience to the art-object is the (unconsciously) felt encounter between infant and mother. The medium of the artist becomes the mother's body... [and] the creative act repeats the experience of separating from the mother." Depending on the type of representation – specifically if it is in some way either fragmented or integrated – this act can take place in the context of either the paranoid-schizoid or the depressive position.[12]

Of course it is also possible to offer a "Kleinian reading" or "Kleinian interpretation" of the content or narrative of an art-object – and such a reading would, of necessity, be coloured by the implications of the relationship of reader and text as outlined above. As a way of attempting both to explicate the theory outlined thus far and to offer a way of using such an approach for the study of horror film narratives I propose the following account of Dario Argento's **The Stendhal Syndrome**.

Argento's film offers a number of approaches which intersect but begin from somewhat different premises. These might include an investigation of the nature of the problem Anna Manni has with art. Thus the so-called "Stendhal Syndrome" of the film's title requires analysis. The narrative of the interaction between Anna and the killer which results in her taking over his murderous rôle and incorporating elements of his personality offers a clear opportunity for a psychoanalytic reading. Likewise, the playing out of Anna's own encounter with psychoanalysis begs attention. A full reading would also need to take into account the perverse implications of the sadomasochistic interactions of the characters, a narrative thread which, in many ways, links all the previous issues. A Kleinian response to all of these issues could involve asking three fundamental questions of the film, its characters, its makers and its spectators. How do we sort out "good" from "bad" or victim from aggressor when we incorporate both and identify at times with either? How can the integration of objects (such as that required for the move from the paranoid-schizoid to the depressive position) be achieved and at what cost to the self in terms of psychological and emotional pain? Here we are using pain in the sense that Kleinians use the term depression. Finally, and most conventionally, is symbol formation and *sublimation* by artistic creativity one of the means by which we do this work of integration?

In *The Apprehension Of Beauty*,[13] Donald Meltzer writes of the relationship between the infant and the good object in terms of the child idealising and being overwhelmed by its beauty. Indeed so unbearably beautiful is the object – the good breast – that it not only dazzles but frightens. A common response to such an overwhelming sensation is to transform it into a situation of primal envy. Feelings of envy are expressed towards the good object just for being good and beautiful and, furthermore, the infant shows that it resents and is angered by its own state of dependence towards it.[14] These feelings often result in oral sadistic attacks on the object. In this way, the symptoms of the "Stendhal Syndrome" enact in one sense at least Anna's inability to contain this central conflict of identification within herself through dreams, through transference with her analyst or through symbolisation – in this case with beautiful paintings in the Uffizi Gallery.

Envy, in the Kleinian sense of the term, obliterates the distinction between good and bad. In this way it implies a fundamental crisis in discrimination (an uncertainty over what is good and what is bad) which is replicated in Anna's confusion over identification. The idea of a crisis in discrimination typically underpins narrative progression in many *gialli* – as Xavier Mendik has persuasively argued from a broadly Lacanian perspective.[15] Indeed the films of Dario Argento are replete with often unsought and frequently perilous encounters with vengeful and aggressive monstrous maternal and paternal figures. The

The Stendhal Syndrome

narrative positioning of the three mother/witches in **Inferno** (1980); the homicidal psychic mother in **Trauma** (1994); the paradox – as we shall see – of Anna Manni's absent mother and domineering father in **The Stendhal Syndrome** to name but three instances, all embody a problem of recognising good as good and bad as bad. Similar problems occur in the use of gender confusion across a range of films, and the reversal of other types such as bad priests in films like Fulci's **Don't Torture A Duckling** (1972) and Bido's **Bloodstained Shadow** (1978) serve a not dissimilar purpose. They both confuse the detective in the film's narrative and represent manifestations of aggression from cultural good objects. Indeed it is frequently (although not always) the actions or even merely the simple presence of the detective in the past as a child or in the present as a struggling hero/victim which animates the monstrous into aggressive action. In this way it is even possible to argue that *giallo* narratives use envy unconsciously as a central organising principle.

In **The Stendhal Syndrome**, Anna admits to her psychiatrist an ongoing, complex and terrifying relationship with her internal world. Specifically she is convinced that the killer is inside her, continually growing in power and malevolence, and is threatening to take her over. The idea that introjected good and bad objects are believed actually to be present in (and by) the subject and that these internal objects are performing acts which impact directly and forcefully on the subject's sense of self and of

The Stendhal Syndrome

well-being is one of the most important, challenging and controversial interventions of Melanie Klein and her followers. Hinshelwood outlines the curious paradox that lies at its heart:

"It seems like a contradiction – an experience which is unconscious... I cannot go into the contradiction of 'unconscious experiencing', except to state how useful it actually is in psychoanalytic theory and practice, and that the emergence of a patient's insight into such experience is both possible and, ultimately, a healing influence... internal objects are deeply involved in processes which may give identity, or create deep rifts within the personal identity of the individual. Identity is thus deeply bound up with the internalization of objects (introjection), with the degree of hostility towards them in the internalization phantasies and the resulting alienation from, or assimilation to, the internalized object. The term 'introjection' denotes a psychic process; but it is linked with – in fact it operates through – an unconscious phantasy in the patient's mind, the subjective experience of taking something in ('internalizing' or, sometimes, 'incorporating' it)."[16]

When patients introject and identify with a bad internal object, often their hatred of it means that while they resist and, thus, fail to identify with it properly it remains an alien part of them. With the example of Anna and her introjected bad object (the killer) in mind, I am going to work through an example cited by the psychoanalyst Paula Heimann from her own clinical practice in order to illustrate how patients encounter the problem of identification with a bad internal object.

Heimann's account of "The Woman With A Devil Inside" is particularly instructive

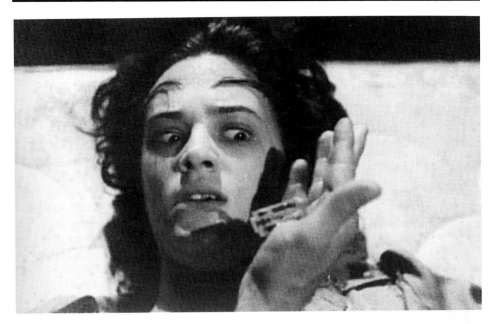

The Stendhal Syndrome

for our current purposes in that the patient (a seriously paranoid woman) was an artist and, for her, the result of introjecting a bad object in anger was for that alien object momentarily to take over the creative part of her and to change the way she expressed that creativity. The woman, on her way to her art school, was angered by a poor driver who nearly made her cause an accident. The patient retaliated through a minor act of what would now be called road rage and challenged the other driver, an older "woman who had a red beery face", for her inconsiderate and dangerous behaviour. When the offending driver shrugged the criticism off, the patient insulted her and drove off. During the art class which followed, the patient felt somehow unhappy about the painting she was doing although she couldn't identify exactly what the problem was. It was only when her teacher noted with surprise that her style had completely changed that the woman realised that she had been painting in the style of a "Victorian family album" – quite different from her normal approach. "Something had literally got into her that turned her off from her own apparent intention and diverted her into following a style of someone fifty years ago – that is a much older woman. The explanation offered [by Heimann] is that the older woman in the car who had turned her off the road she had wanted to go along had actually got into her – an introjection, and then a dominance, by the 'bad' object."[17] The patient was so shocked that she went and had three glasses of sherry. Later, she noticed that she had developed three ulcers in her mouth. Paula Heimann's reading connected the drinking – coinciding with angry thoughts about the woman driver – with the development of guilt and the punishing ulcers:

"She had carried out her impulse to hurt the woman and was consciously pleased with her success. But unconsciously – as the woman stood for [Heimann] and [the patient's]

mother, towards whom she had love impulses as well as hostile ones – she could not bear the injuries she had inflicted on her nor could she remain at a distance from her. She had immediately internalized this mother-figure and she had internalized her in the injured condition for which she felt responsible and guilty, namely as a worn out, fifty-year-old... [18]

The bad object, internalized in hatred, dominated the internal world to the point where the patient became so confused that she experienced a temporary loss of identity. "Capture by this internalized object replicated the hostile aggressive relationship in which the external object had made her helpless." [19] Throughout **The Stendhal Syndrome**, Anna's relationship to the killer – initially her external male object – plays out a similar process. Introjected in hatred, the killer – now as a bad internal object – increasingly causes Anna to behave out of character. Having been attacked, Anna defensively initially projects onto the killer her omnipotent and aggressive desires for power over the receptive object although, of course, she also fears them coming back to her from him. She even tries to play out her phantasies of omnipotence against her insipid boyfriend and later admits to desiring to make love like a man.

In Kleinian terms, Anna's response to the fears of reprisal for her own projected phantasies of omnipotence is to identify through introjection with the male aggressor who is both desired and feared. It is important to remember here that introjection and projection involve a splitting of identification as an ego defence mechanism. It is safer to become the aggressor than to be the victim, and Anna's plot trajectory fluctuates between projective and introjective identifications – between sadistic and masochistic feelings in herself. Incidentally, we see similar instances of victims denying their victimhood by introjecting their aggressors in other films by Dario Argento – perhaps most memorably in **The Bird With The Crystal Plumage** (1970). Returning to the case of **The Stendhal Syndrome**, however, Anna is unable to reconcile her objects, the introjected male object (the killer) grows as a threat – which is experienced as a *physical sensation* of pain – and eventually comes to dominate her internal life. As we have seen, Kleinians often link psychological operations with direct bodily responses. The dynamic internal world of a patient in which his or her introjected internal objects clash and compete in phantasy is frequently experienced in directly physical terms. Arguably, Anna's attempts at painting emphasise this problem with internal objects. The faces she repeatedly paints have huge black (anal) mouths, almost as if they were openings to evacuate (project) the introjected killer which she cannot accomplish in phantasy. The moment when, after breaking into her flat, he covers those mouths with posters of the paintings from the Uffizi, symbolically blocking off the orifices of her own symbolisations, is also the moment after which her attempts to work through her damaged object relations are futile.

Anna's problem is not limited to her interactions with the killer – even if we can be satisfied with a naturalist reading of the film's narrative and accept what happens as "real" or actual in the film's terms rather than as one long extended phantasy. Given the latter possibility, we can ask of the film whether the killer is actually confronting Anna with the unbearable truth and beauty (the Uffizi paintings) of the good object which her phantasies have distorted and which she finds threatening. Is he actually torturing her or is this her paranoid distortion of how the omnipotent part of herself experiences the truth? Anna obviously has a problematic relationship with her past, and specifically with her family. We see her with her father, an austere and judgemental patriarch to whose

The Stendhal Syndrome

house she retreats only with the greatest reluctance. Of her mother we know and see nothing; and it is around Anna's evident ambivalence towards her familial relationships that the film offers another, more radical avenue of interpretation.

The film could be argued to play out the more general conflict between love and longing for the absent mother as evidenced by Anna's ambivalent attempts to internalize symbolizations of the maternal good object on the one hand, and hatred towards the paternal bad object on the other. This latter is expressed through the introjection of her father – specifically of her father's disapproval – as the punishing figure of the killer. Her final submission to the internal bad object signifies in a perverse sense her feelings that "it is now all daddy, mummy has gone". Her paranoid revenge, killing male figures coded as sexualised – her new boyfriend – and authoritative – her psychoanalyst – plays out her inability either to project or to internalize the destruction of the now dominant bad object which she further fragments for apparently easier (although of course ultimately futile) disposal into discreet aspects of maleness.

Such shifting perspectives, such bewilderments and confusions and mental pains are the stuff of the borderline psychotic's existence and at least fleetingly or in dreams – or indeed in films – may be experienced by any one of us. What Argento's films offer us, then – as do most *gialli* – are moments of identification with just such an experiential realm. Whether we identify with victim or aggressor or whether, as is more accurately the case, our identification shifts along with that of the films' psychotic protagonists, our

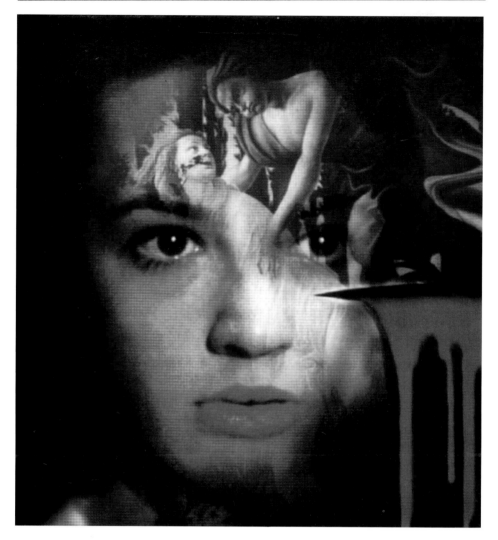

The Stendhal Syndrome

implication in phantasy offers an – albeit transitory – insight into the working of disturbed minds and more importantly (for here we read the significance of Klein's contribution most strongly) of our still powerful capacity as adults for identification with, and at, an *infantile* level of functioning. In saying this, I am not implying that the films are "infantile", rather that in their complex and ambivalent structures – and in our own complex and ambivalent relationship to those structures – they enact, and expose primary processes of phantasy and early object relations and it is from this that they derive much of their power. Indeed, and in final conclusion, Klein herself recognised (although arguably in a Romantic kind of way) the importance of this relationship between the text and its reader in her own attempts at defining the trajectory of creativity in the arts:

"The creative artist makes full use of symbols; and the more they serve to express the conflicts between love and hate, between destructiveness and reparation, between life and death instinct, the more they approach universal form."[20]

NOTES

1. Chasseguet-Smirgel, Janine. *Creativity And Perversion*, London: Free Association Books, 1984.

2. A full exegesis of Kleinian aesthetic theory – let alone of Kleinian and post-Kleinian psychoanalysis as a whole – is clearly beyond the scope of this present paper. Indeed it forms part of an extended research project upon which I am currently engaged. My intention here is simply to present a Kleinian reading of certain features in Argento's films, not to undertake a meta-theoretical mapping of Kleinian thought onto film theory. Such is the function of future publications.

3. Wright, Elizabeth. *Psychoanalytic Criticism: Theory In Practice*, London: Methuen, 1984

4. Hinshelwood, R.D. *A Dictionary Of Kleinian Thought*, London: Free Association Books, 1991, p.32.

5. Hinshelwood, R.D. *Clinical Klein*, London: Free Association Books, 1994, p.28.

6. Segal, Julia. *Melanie Klein*, 1992, p.40–41.

7. Hinshelwood: 1994, p.33.

8. Segal: 1992, p.36–7.

9. Hinshelwood: 1994, p.29.

10. Wright: 1984, p.80.

11. Wright: 1984, p.80.

12. Wright: 1984, p.84.

13. Meltzer, Donald and Harris Williams, Meg. *The Apprehension Of Beauty: The Role Of Aesthetic Conflict In Development, Art And Violence* Perth: Clunie, 1988.

14. The death instinct is deflected by projection into an object which comes to represent the threat of aggression towards the life of the subject.

15. Mendik, Xavier. "Detection And Transgression: The Investigative Drive Of The Giallo" in *Necronomicon: Book One*, ed. Andy Black, London: Creation, 1996.

16. Hinshelwood: 1994, p.58–9.

17. Hinshelwood: 1994, p.76.

18. Heimann cited in Hinshelwood: 1994, p.76.

19. Hinshelwood: 1994, p.76.

20. Klein, Melanie. "Infantile Anxiety-Situations Reflected In A Work Of Art And In The Creative Impulse", *The Selected Melanie Klein*, ed. Juliet Mitchell, London: Penguin, 1986, p.299.

FROM THE MONSTROUS MOTHER TO THE "THIRD SEX"

Female Abjection In The Films Of Dario Argento

Xavier Mendik

"My daughters, together are a mother to me. Without them I would be lost."[1]

INTRODUCTION

Dario Argento is here commenting on the casting of his daughter Asia as the confused heroine Aura, of his 1994 film **Trauma**. The maternal reference in his statement is important as the narrative concentrates on the "headhunter" killer who decapitates the surgeons responsible for the death of her infant son. In this respect, Argento reveals his murderer Adriana, to be a "monstrous" mother whose vengeful actions provoke fear and disgust in the assembled protagonists. The finale depicts the killer presiding over a house which contains the mummified remains of the foetus, and in which the heroine has become incarcerated. The fact that Aura is one of the film's investigators as well as daughter of the "headhunter" killer reiterates the theme of transgressive familial relations at the core of the narrative.

By frequently casting his daughters within the macabre fictional world of the *giallo* as well as depicting violence erupting within and between siblings, Argento has expressed an interest in the destructive and sexual underside of the family. Central to this examination has been a violent and disturbing construction of the mother who threatens to smother the individuality of the offsprings under her charge.

While Argento's interest in the theme of the destructive maternal agent was most famously demonstrated in the figures of the "three mothers" of **Suspiria** (1977) and **Inferno** (1980), it is also present in earlier productions such as **Deep Red** (1975). Here, the effeminate musician Carlo is revealed as part of a murderous duo, assisting in a series of killings in order to protect the identity of his psychotic mother. More recently, films such as **Trauma, Opera** (1987) and **The Stendhal Syndrome** (1996) have indicated Argento's growing interest in the problematic relations between powerful mothers and their daughters. **Opera** for instance, presents the figure of Betty, whose childhood memories are marked by the scenarios of torture and sadistic coitus organised by her mother and her lover Alan Santini.

Although absent from the narrative of **The Stendhal Syndrome**, the mother of Anna Manni still manages to exert a transgressive influence over this central protagonist. The narrative depicts how Manni's repeated encounters with a serial killer result in her becoming psychotic and reproducing his murderous quest. However, Manni's obsession with art which unites her with her male oppressor is revealed as having been instilled in her by her childhood visits to galleries with her mother.

What interests me in the theme of Argento's murderous mothers (and their daughters) is not merely their homicidal intent, but also their physiological construction which often provokes disgust in both the protagonist and spectator. Frequently, these are female figures whose bodies are either forcibly altered through violent interaction or open to supernatural transformation which indicates physiology as unrestrained. By postulating

Trauma

that Argento's films as well (as other forms of Italian horror) are dominated by images of the disgusting, monstrous female body I shall draw on psychoanalytical theories of gender and identity.

In particular, Julia Kristeva's work around abjection and disgust will be employed to indicate how such images draw on the individual's pre-Oedipal and repressed relations to the maternal agent. I shall argue that the figure of the debased, monstrous and yet potent mother which occupies much of her analysis is also central to the themes of Argento's films.

In her attempt to write back the repressed image of the mother into what she defines as male ordered language and historical structures Kristeva is interested in those aspects which disrupt or disturb the sexuality and identity that the symbolic or the speech act gives us.[2] These fissures or gaps in the self refer back to infancy and the repressed relationship with the maternal agent that dominates these early years. According to her analysis, certain types of artistic representation draw upon the attractions and tensions of early infancy and to the period when the child's (lack of) identity was bound up with its relations with the mother.

Although these early, pleasurable encounters are often repressed when the child gains an understanding of its gender identity within the symbolic, they are never fully restrained. These tensions threaten to re-emerge in later life either through mental trauma, nightmares or "poetic" works of art. According to Kristeva, certain aesthetic strategies and modes of art draw upon the primary bond between mother and child. This is seen both through an obsession with excessive, disgusting, infantile acts, as well as an attempt to dislodge and subvert the dominant structures of language which hold our adult, gendered identity in place. In so doing, these artistic works reference not merely the infant's destructive and archaic early tendencies but also the subversive power of the mother during this primary period of development.

I.
IMAGES OF THE MONSTROUS FEMALE BODY IN ITALIAN HORROR.

Upon first appearance, issues of female power would not seem to sit easily with the traditional generic definitions of Argento's work as part of the *giallo* cycle of thrillers that were dominant in Italian cinema during the 1960s and 1970s. This is because films such as **The Bird With The Crystal Plumage** (1970) and **Tenebrae** (1982) were seen by critics as reliant on the voyeuristic depiction of the female body as a site of mutilation. As Mark Le Fanu commented on the release of **Tenebrae**:

*"Argento's preoccupation after **Suspiria** seems to be with devising increasingly nasty ways of killing his characters, especially when they are women. Each murder scene occasions a dazzling assemblage of cinematic effects – the camera tracks its victims who gaze back in erotic appreciation of their own vulnerability."[3]*

Although Argento does dwell on the (sexual) suffering of female victims, it is also noticeable that they can also occupy positions of mastery and aggression within his films. This crucial oscillation can be evidenced through characters such as Monica Ranieri and Anna Manni from **The Bird With The Crystal Plumage** and **The Stendhal Syndrome** respectively. In both films their gender identity is altered as a result of violent male assault which in both cases leads them to adopt a sadistic, murderous male quest. By disclosing the identity of killers whose behaviours eschew gender expectations, the resolutions of both films are shocking.

However, the "female" killers they portray are also rendered "disgusting" by virtue of having their bodies forcibly altered and made offensive because of the male violence which induced their psychosis. In **The Bird With The Crystal Plumage**, Monica's identity crisis is the result of a past genital violation by a male assailant. The repeated violation of Anna Manni at the hands of serial killer Alfredo Grossi results in her having to "reconstruct" her damaged femininity through the aid of artificial cosmetics in order to hide the scars of her ordeal.

Thus, Argento's films use a *giallo* framework to organise narratives around the desire to uncover the identity of a transgressor, while also construct their females as victims of violence or symbolic castration. Paradoxically, they also depict certain female characters who either by adopting the role of the maternal or by virtue of their status as former victims manage to evade this position of oppression. While the existence of these protagonists depicts the construction of aberrant female physiology as a source of disgust, they also indicate these potent characters as being incorporated from other Italian popular genres such as the Peplum (historical adventure film) and the Gothic horror genres of the 1950s.

Traditionally, Italian popular cinema has been seen as a medium marked by a fusion of differing film genres[4] and Carol Jenks has made the link between the *giallo* and other cycles in terms of its depiction of the aberrant female body. Her analysis of the star image of actress Barbara Steele traces her popularity as a Gothic icon in Italian horror films of the 1950s, to a longer tradition depicting fatalistic and monstrous female figures. Steele was frequently cast as a seductive vampire or witch, whose "excessive" desires

Tenebrae

provoked retribution from assembled male characters in films such as Mario Bava's **The Mask Of Satan** (1960).

According to Jenks, these characteristics of the provocative but deadly female figure recall the *Divisimo* films of the silent years. These cast actresses such as Theda Bara in roles which drew on historical and mythical depictions of duplicitous and evil women such as Delilah and Cleopatra. While these historical figures remained popular in a series of 1950s Italian historical dramas, they were complemented by the roles undertaken by Steele, most famously in Bava's film. Here she is cast in the role of the witch Asa, who is executed along with her lover Javutich at the beginning of the film. Before being killed (by having a spiked mask forced onto her face), she swears vengeance on her brother and the Vidor family for her torture and execution. Two hundred years later, her rotting corpse is reanimated by the blood of a Victorian surgeon, Kruvajan, who cuts his arm when examining her tomb. Although Asa carries out her threat to destroy the male lineage of the Vidor family, the narrative reveals her real quest to be to inhabit the body and beauty of her identical descendant Katia (also played by Steele). In so doing the film establishes a pattern where subjectivity and identity between opposing female relations become ambivalent:

"It becomes clear in the course of the film that good and evil have numerous shared traits, an ambivalence that is neatly visualized by the introduction of the heroine. Princess Katia is essentially the antithesis of the witch, yet the separation is not total ...Her duel

role is especially significant; even at this point in her career, Steele was viewed as the ideal dream girl of paranoiacs who imagine hideous menace lurking behind every pretty face."[5]

Asa's attempted fusion with Katia is foregrounded in the finale of **The Mask Of Satan** when the hero (played by John Richardson) is forced to decide which of the pair is the evil witch who must once again be burned for her transgressions. Although the pair look identical (the witch regaining her former facial beauty from the close proximity with her intended victim), Richardson finally identifies Asa by tearing back her gown to reveal her decaying, insect ridden body. The fact that it is her hideous physiology that reveals the witch's true status is important, as it reiterates the construction of the feminine in these cycles as monstrous. This difficulty in locating Asa's body that **The Mask Of Satan** highlights, provided a template for later roles that Steele adopted. In Antonio Margheriti's **The Long Hair Of Death** (1964) Jenks notes that she is also cast as a witch who only reveals her filthy decaying body to her lover after they have engaged in sexual intercourse.

Argento's work has attempted to translate these Gothic concerns around the transformative and monstrous nature of the female body into the investigative framework of the *giallo*. The impact of these two film modes on his work is clearly seen in the film **Demons**, which he produced in 1985. This film was directed by Lamberto Bava (son of Mario), and openly traces the importance of **The Mask Of Satan** on contemporary Italian horror film culture. This set of self-reflexive references is achieved by staging the film's action in a disused cinema, where an invited audience is attacked by possessed patrons while watching an untitled horror film. Among the assembled viewers are a blind man Werner and his female assistant Liz. Their casting refers back to the *giallo*, and to Argento's interest in blind detectives such as Franco Arno in **The Cat O'Nine Tails** (1971). The cinema features other references to Argento's work, with posters for **Four Flies On Grey Velvet** (1971) and George A. Romero's 1978 film **Dawn Of The Dead** (for which Argento wrote the screenplay) being displayed in the theatre foyer.

However, with its emphasis on the visible aspects of the transformative female body, **Demons** also casts clear references to the earlier Italian Gothic horror traditions of the 1950s and 1960s. For instance, the trigger for the chaos that engulfs the theatre is a cursed display mask hanging in the cinema foyer. The mask is identical to the one forced over Barbara Steele's face in **The Mask Of Satan**. Importantly, the first patrons to be infected are two black prostitutes Rosemary and Candy who don the mask before entry to the screening. Their coding as explicit sites of erotic visual display also draws equations with the paradoxes apparent in Barbara Steele's star image. While both the **Demons** characters are depicted as signifiers of sexual attraction, their bodies are marked by a sudden degeneration into decay and death, comparable to that of Asa from Mario Bava's film.

Demons even parodies the duality between Asa and Katia established in **The Mask Of Satan** through its casting of Natasha Hovey as the central female protagonist Cheryl. Although described by Rob Winning as a "symbol of all that is innocent and unblemished in the world"[6], Cheryl unsettles the clarity of this definition. During the film's closing sequence, her body suddenly transforms in to a demon. This act is both horrific (in terms of the intensity of transformation depicted) and unsettling, revealing that the viewer's stable source of identification throughout the narrative has been infected all the time.

While examples from both **The Mask Of Satan** and **Demons** indicate a shared

Four Flies On Grey Velvet

cinematic history, their depiction of an uncontrollable female physiology link them to the processes of disgust and abjection defined by Kristeva. Their bodies reveal defiance of the symbolic's regulation and discipline over physiology, and thus recall an earlier period, prior to the processes of separation between the mother and infant. This imaginary dyad is fragmented as a consequence of the discovery of sexual difference and the threat of castration which defines the child's absorption into the symbolic. It is the child's interpellation into the language system which works to fragment the former ambivalences around its identity and gender.

However, what Argento's narratives do is draw attention to the artificial processes of language itself. By constructing bodies of disgust, paradox and excess the feminine of the *giallo* indicates the ease with which physiology can be dislocated from the terms, polarities and categorisations that discourse constructs. Specifically, Argento's horrific females, by virtue of their impossible construction, foreground the importance of the border in cultural and linguistic systems of classification.

The importance of the "border" as a system of cultural classification has been noted by Mary Douglas's research on ritual communities. Here it is used to initiate common bonds of identification across clan members, legitimising of certain sexual relations, via a capacity to "externalise" outsiders. Such methods, though central to these groups' survival are subject to a series of potential "physiological" disruptions which must be recuperated within the existing system of classification.

Thus, in the Hindu caste system, the position of the privileged Brahmin subset is undercut by waste matter such as excreta, urine, saliva and menstruational blood. These emissions not only undercut the definition of what constitutes the external appearance

Demons

of the body, but are also functions attributable to all castes. This potential for the body's transgression is recouperated in this system by the Coorgs, whose social status as "dirt" is confirmed by their responsibility for the disposal of such waste matter, as well as the preparation of the dead.

It is the symbolic's attempt to resurrect and maintain the self as clean and

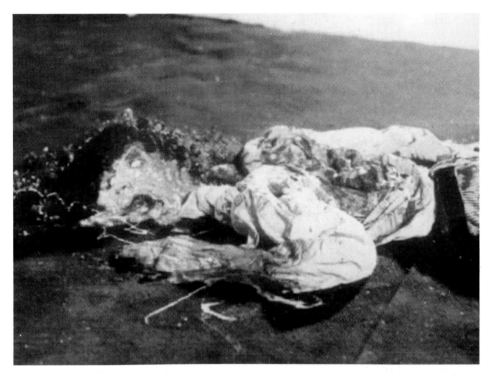

Demons

ordered that is also central to Julia Kristeva's account of abjection. In the book *Powers Of Horror*, she defines abjection as an erosion of the borders of subjectivity which can be explored from a psychoanalytical perspective. The child's identity is formed through its absorption into a system of language which is itself dependant on the polarization of self, sexuality and external body image into a series of discrete binaries and categories. These terms:

"...need to be oppositionally coded in order for the child's body to be constituted as a unified whole and for its subjectivity to be defined and tied to the body's limits. They are conditions under which the child may claim the body as its own, and thus also the conditions under which it gains a place as a speaking subject."[7]

Central to the functioning of this system of subjectivity is the repression of the infant's pre-linguistic fascination with its own body and its associated waste products. Here, Kristeva draws on Douglas's definition of the body's waste products as a troubling type of "dirt", marked by matter such as faeces, urine, vomit, spittle and menstrual blood. These body products are seen as "taboo" because they operate and intersect at the space between the interior of the self and its external image. As a result, they deny crucial borders through which the symbolic attempts to construct "the clean and proper body."[8]

Although Kristeva argues that despite the symbolic attempts to banish these forms of primary pleasure, they recur in later life either through psychological disorders

Demons

or unconventional works of art. Kristeva draws similar conclusions to Lacan's work on psychosis, highlighting the ability of such disorders to rob the subject of the security which surrounds the perception of an established body image. Equally, her conclusion that the abject occurs through certain unconventional works of art is replicated by both the content and form of Argento's cinema.

Central to many of his films is the displacement of the border and the mechanisms of symbolic clarification that they represent. For instance, bodily matter such as blood and mucus proves central to the source of infection that marks the Metropol cinema in **Demons**. Here, it is Candy's blood that initiates infection when she is scratched by the cursed display mask in the theatre. As a result, her external body image displays a lack of integrity and control by erupting in to a series of facial lesions, which eventually burst, sending a shower of blood and green pus cascading down her neck.

As with the construction of waste matter in Kristeva's analysis, the eruption of these bodies in **Demons** provokes disgust because it undercuts the established boundaries of external appearance. In the case of Candy, this corporeal "corruption" is marked by the "shedding" of her established form: her fingernails and teeth being replaced by claws and a phallic shaped tongue. According to Barbara Creed's book *The Monstrous Feminine* it is the corruption of established body and identity boundaries which remains at the core of the horror film's paradoxical appeal through disgust. Adapting what she identifies as key borders transgressed in horror cinema, it can be argued that Argento's work is also concerned with the elision of the boundary between the human and unhuman (as in **Demons, Inferno, Suspiria** and **Creepers** [1985]), as well as the boundary separating established gender distinctions (**The Bird With The Crystal Plumage** and **Deep Red**).

II.
FILTH, FOOD, SEXUALITY AND THE MOTHER: CATEGORIES OF THE ABJECT

Despite the difference in the above type or category of abjection, in each case Argento concentrates on the female body as a signifier of disgust and chaotic transformation. Although **Demons** details a process of physical possession afflicting both sexes, it is interesting to note that the narrative does not visualize the male body undergoing the same excessive transmutations afflicting depicted female characters. One reason behind this preoccupation links these images back to infancy and in particular the young child's initial relations with its mother.

Prior to the discovery of its own autonomy the infant's dependence on the mother is indicated in her primary role in the training, coordinating and controlling of its body. Her role is particularly marked through the supervised expulsion and disposal of waste matter such as urine and excreta. Kristeva defines this process of maternal control over the infant's body as a process of "primary mapping". This includes activities such as sphincteral training which allows the child to discover the contours of his own developing body, while retaining the gratification of contact with the mother's form (through activities such as breast feeding).

As a result of her close proximity to these sources of waste matter, the mother becomes viewed as "abject by association" by the child when it enters the symbolic. Although her influence in this primary period of physical development is repressed, it returns as a sight of horror and disgust in the unpalatable representations of the female body in Italian horror cinema. These figures display an inability to control bodily hygiene, an association with images of mucus and filth that confirms bodily matter as a key form of abjection.

This capacity for waste matter to invoke this primary maternal bond is indicated in Kristeva's example of "A". This case study detailed the actions of a four-year-old child whose recurrent nightmare focused on his attempted expulsion of faeces.[9] When the substance was emitted, it refused to be detached from "A"'s body, and in fact transformed into a monster, which the child defined as a cross between a frog and a crocodile. The threat that the monster offers, is as a disruption to the unity of the external body image, and its links to symbolic regulation. Whereas the established image of the self offers the individual a guarantor of distinct identity, faecal matter is marked by "the mixtures, alterations and decay"[10] that run counter to such modes of classification. Importantly, the nightmare that plagued the child coincided with his emerging understanding of the rules that govern modes of verbal communication. The dream thus reveals a slippage between two developmental registers: the past realm of the mother, the body and its waste products and the symbolic with its attempted repression of these former contacts and modes of gratification.

The fact that "A"'s nightmare evokes a period prior to his construction as a subject is intimated by the entrance of the father into the narrative; the dream ending when he "sees the animal and threatens punishment."[11] Indeed, given that the monster which attached itself to "A"'s anus possessed a transparent membrane, it is worth remembering that in **Demons**, during her transformation, Candy's face is transformed by a network of blood vessels rising from the interior of her body to corrupt its external appearance.

While waste matter remains one of the key types of abjection that Kristeva identifies, other variants such as food loathing and the obliteration of the signs of sexual

Suspiria

difference are also furnished by Argento's works. According to Kristeva, food loathing is "perhaps the most elementary and archaic form of abjection"[12]. As she notes in *Powers Of Horror*, such loathing is of particular importance in the renunciation of this maternal bond. Not only does it evoke the primary "oral" period of infantile dependence, but it also undercuts the role of distinction cultural categorization. Kristeva exemplifies the notion of food loathing and the cultural borders it disturbs with the example of the skin that forms on fetid milk. This provokes disgust not only because of its smell, but also as it conflates the distinction of the food matter as *either* solid or liquid, eroding the border "between two distinct entities or territories"[13]. Evidence of food loathing is provided in Argento films such as **Suspiria**. Here, meat is rendered unfit for human consumption through an infestation by maggots. It is also linked to a plague of rats in the film's sequel **Inferno**.[14]

What is important about both **Suspiria** and **Inferno** is that abject waste matter is clearly equated with the maternal through the narrative concentration on a trio of witches called "the three mothers". These destructive figures are revealed to dominate the world and spread pestilence via a series of cursed locations in Rome, New York and Freiburg. **Suspiria** explores this destructive maternal presence by concentrating on the activities of Mater Suspiriorum, who hides under the guise of Helena Marcos, the head of a dance school in Germany.

Suspiria

The film shows that this witch and her female assistants work to infantilise those in close proximity with them. **Suspiria** depicts the school as dominated by a series of destructive female figures, in particular Miss Tanner, a dance instructor, and Madame Blanc, the key principal of the institution. Importantly, Argento makes these two figures the focus for a series of masculine figures who are dependant on them as maternal substitutes. For instance, Madame Blanc is constantly accompanied by her nephew Albert, a young child upon whom she directs all her affection.[15] This relationship is in turn mirrored by Miss Tanner's fondness for a young (and destitute) male dancer whom she allows to stay on at the academy despite his inability to pay the fees. Even the academy pianist is rendered dependant on these female agents (as guides) by virtue of his being blind.

What **Suspiria** points to is an absence of controlling male figures, allowing these maternal figures to limit the autonomy of the individuals under their charge. The film reveals that they violently dispatch those who discover their true identity. The inspiration for **Suspiria** can be partly traced to the experiences of Argento's former partner and long term collaborator Dario Nicolodi at a ballet school during her youth. Although Nicolodi moulded rumours that the institution was ruled by witches into a screen play for the film, it was Argento who constructed these figures as destructive maternal agents. As he stated:

"...in an early draft I even planned to have the action take place in a school where the witches were teachers who tortured the children."[16]

According to Leon Hunt's article "A (Sadistic) Night At The Opera", further sources of inspiration for **Suspiria** and **Inferno** are Thomas De Quincy's essay *Levana And Our Ladies Of Sorrow*[17], as well as earlier Italian Gothic narratives popularised by the 1960s works of Mario Bava and Antonio Margheriti. As a result, they appear to differ from the *giallo* framework that characterises other Argento texts. However, despite the supernatural emphasis to both films, they retain the investigative quest that defines other Argento works. In **Suspiria**, the lead female protagonist Susy Bannion assumes the role of investigator in order to discover the truth behind the disappearance of her friends at the school. In the film's sequel, **Inferno**, the role of detective is taken be Mark Elliot, whose sister Rose discovers one of the witches living in a New York apartment. Rose is subsequently killed for gaining this knowledge about the mothers, resulting in Mark's journey to the hotel to investigate her disappearance.

Both films (reiterating Argento's statement) construct the three mothers as cruel, duplicitous and threatening. These traits can be once more be linked to Kristeva's theory of abjection. She argues that upon entry into the symbolic, the infant renounces the mother as a figure of erotic attraction. While the functioning of the symbolic relies the clean, ordered and categorised body, the repressed dyad points back "to that time when the mother-child relationship was marked by an untrammelled pleasure in 'playing' with the body and its wastes."[18] However, this process of repression is frequently disturbed by mothers who refuse to allow their children independence.

In such cases, the infant becomes trapped between the two developmental registers: the initial mode of maternal dependence (which she terms the semiotic) and the later stage of identity and language acquisition implicit in the symbolic. As a result of this split, the mother becomes recast from a nurturing to a threatening figure, who works to limit the autonomy of her offspring. In *The Monstrous Feminine*, Creed pinpoints the long tradition that the horror genre has of constructing such destructive maternal figures. For instance, she pinpoints the characters of Mrs Bates from Hitchcock's **Psycho** (1960) and Mrs White from De Palma's **Carrie** (1977) as two examples of maternal agents who restrain the autonomy of their children. In these works:

"...the maternal figure is constructed as the monstrous feminine. By refusing to relinquish her hold on her child, she prevents it from taking up its proper place in relation to the symbolic. Partly consumed by the desire to remain locked in a blissful relationship with the mother and partly terrified of separation, the child finds it easy to succumb to the comforting pleasure of the dyadic relationship."[19]

It is this threatening construction of the maternal which frames Argento's **Inferno**. Here, the status of the three mothers as an abject and threatening presence is established in the pre-credit sequence, when a voice over (revealed to be that of an architect named Varelli) narrates how he designed three dwelling places for the witches. His reference that these locations have become the "repository of all their *filthy* secrets" establishes an equation between the maternal and abject waste matter in the narrative.

Inferno reveals a New York hotel to be the home of another of the trio: Mater Tenebrarum. As well as being plagued by rats, the location is also revealed as having a

Inferno

Inferno

sickening stench which disgusts those inhabitants in close proximity to the site. Indeed, Varelli's voice over which opens the film comments that the deathly "reek" of the mother's dwelling place acts as a "primary key" to their foul presence. This reference locates the maternal realm at the level of physiology and corporeal mapping, and (as the narrative reveals), beyond the limits of discourse. The film's opening sequence depicts the film's ill-fated heroine Rose Elliot exploring the caverns of the New York hotel after reading Varelli's writings. These underground locations, which remain submerged in water instantly connote the maternal through a womb-like structure. However, the film instantly introduces a tension into the traditional equation of the maternal with the fertile by having Rose's exploration disturbed by her discovery of skeletons and abject body bits in the underground location. This recasting of the womb as a site of death rather than the source of creation confirms Varelli's initial statement of the witches as barren mothers who are "incapable of creating life"[20].

Importantly, the significance of a hidden chamber or secret room which contains a site of death and decay is central to several key Argento texts. While **Inferno**'s submerged cellar holds the key to Mater Tenebrarum's identity, her counterpart from **Suspiria** is concealed in a secret room whose passages are lined with the dead bodies of her victims from the dance academy. In these locations the monstrous mother "commits dreadful acts in a location which resembles the womb. These inter-uterine settings consist of dark, narrow winding passages leading to a central room, cellar or symbolic place of birth."[21] The fact that these locations are so often the sites of death and decay in Argento's works can also be linked to Kristeva's analysis of waste matter, abjection and the dissolution of identity. In *Powers Of Horror*, she identifies key examples of waste matter as menstruational and excremental. Not only do these fragment the border dividing interior and exterior divisions of the body, but they also refer to the womb and the mother's reproductive abilities. While the mother's fertility is referenced by the menstruational cycle, the actual birth act is also connoted through the (often violent) expulsion of excremental and decaying substance.

It is these images of blood and violent birth that Argento's film's and the earlier Italian horror cycles play upon. For instance, evidence of the abject construction of the womb in Gothic horror works such as **The Mask Of Satan**. Here, the witch Asa assumes the role of "barren" mother by resurrecting her dead lover Javutich from a deserted graveyard. This sequence appears as if a parody of birth, with the male figure emerging from "the erupting earth, his hands covered with a web of mucus"[22]. A similar equation of the womb as a site of death and decaying bodily waste is evidenced in **Demons**, (once more demonstrating Argento's wish to comment on the importance of Mario Bava's film). Here, one of the film's key protagonists Cathy, experiences a bizarre version of the birth act when a demon literally *tears* through the surface of her skin following a process of unnoticed internal incubation. According to Kristeva, in such images the:

"...evocation of the maternal body and childbirth induces the image of birth as a violent act of expulsion through which the nascent body tears itself away from the maternal insides."[23]

While depictions of the grotesque female body and the birth act provide a clear link between **Demons** and Bava's work, a direct comparison can also be found between **The Mask Of Satan** and **Inferno**. This is seen in the fact that Mario Bava worked on the

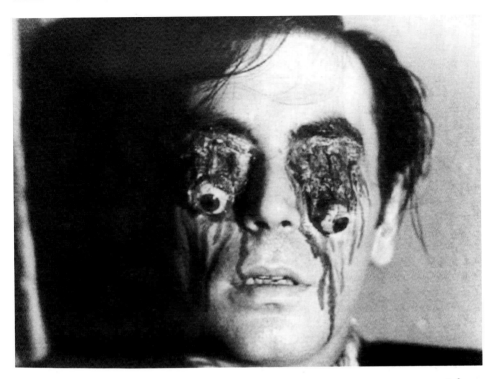

Inferno

latter in the capacity of special effects designer (his son Lamberto also featured as an assistant director on the production). Bava's role in **Inferno** included the creation of the underwater cavern that Rose Elliot discovers prior to her disappearance.

Importantly, the only represented reference to the mothers during this sequence, is a painting of Mater Tenebrarum which hangs in the underground cavern that Rose Elliot explores. However, confirming Kristeva's conclusion that the female form cannot fully be represented by a male ordered language, it appears pertinent that only the *name* rather than the image of the mother is presented in the painting. This feature is itself important as it points to another type of abjection that Argento's mothers share: the ability to upset or transcend an established body image and the signs of sexual difference.

The mothers prove to be female characters whose presence undercuts external and internal categorisations of the body, once more reflecting the primary ambivalence that surrounds the infant's sense of self. For instance, Mater Suspiriorum exists in **Suspiria** as a force without either shape or distinction[24], only being locatable by her breathing (which, in sounding like a death rattle reiterates her body as a site of decay). Importantly, the film's heroine Suzy manages to destroy the witch by identifying the shadow of her outline in a thunderstorm. When in death Suspiriorum does materialise (revealing herself to be an aged hag) her body is once more coded as a site of "dead" flesh.

This ability to defy symbolic codes of physiological representation is also present in the closing sequence of **Inferno**. Here, the hero Mark Elliot discovers the lair of one of the witches after investigating the disappearance of his sister Rose at Mater

Suspiria

Tenebrarum's New York apartment block. His actions set in motion a blaze at the building, in which he discovers tha' Mater Tenebrarum is actually a nurse who tends for the (now mute and disabled) architect Varelli. While recapitulating the reduction of the male to infantile status initiated in **Suspiria**, Tenebrarum's unholy power is also indicated in her sudden transformation from human into skeletal form as she chases Elliot through the blazing building[25]. This apparent ability to defy the stability of categorical representation fits well with the conception of the mother as a dominant and feared figure whom (the infant often fantasizes) is able to transcend the borders of her own form. The trauma that this imagined ability for transformation provokes in the subject's sense of self seems recapitulated in the film's ending via the fear induced in Elliot when Tenebrarum states his own body will undergo a series of changes under her power.

Mater Tenebrarum's transformation in **Inferno**'s finale indicates the transience of the barrier between the ordered exterior of the body and its underlying physiology. More important, by appearing as a figure of death she draws attention to Kristeva's definition of the corpse as "the ultimate abjection". Her conclusion that death ejects the self from the body shell is echoed by Douglas who finds the corpse as governed by a duel process of decay, initially retaining the external features which defined its former identity, before this "pseudo identity" is itself replaced by a drive towards ultimate decay.

Suspiria

III.
FROM THE MONSTROUS MOTHER TO THE "THIRD SEX".

What is also evidenced by the corpse is the displacement of the centrality of the symbolic's drive towards sexual definition. Here, in the absence of distinct identity, any concept of biological difference is replaced with the notion of the body as "flesh". Beyond **Suspiria** and **Inferno**, several other key Argento's films figure the human form reduced to as series of body "bits" under the influence of the abject and monstrous mother. For instance, this construction is clearly marked in **Creepers**, in a narrative which deals with a cannibalistic serial killer whom stalks a Swiss border town community. The only clues that the police have to trace the murderer are the series of pieces of discarded flesh left at the scene of each crime. As with **Suspiria**, the key to the identity of the assassin is revealed to be contained in a dance school once more populated with aggressive female teachers.

The film's heroine Jennifer Corvino discovers the killer to be the deformed child harboured by her school headmistress Mrs Bruckner. The film depicts the dyad between Bruckner and her child as a mutual preoccupation with the flesh. This is indicated in the closing sequence of the film. Jennifer, trapped in the secret caverns of Bruckner's home (again reflecting an abject depiction of the womb) falls into a vat containing the decaying limbs of the victims that the killer has been collecting. In his review of the film, John

Creepers

Martin has noted the film's preoccupation with abjection, commenting that:

"...the killer is inextricably bound up in the world of the flesh, to the extent of surrounding himself/herself with human remains, and is eventually revealed as a cleft-headed mutant... Conceived in an act of brutal rape and itself a necrophile, the monster testifies to an overpowering disgust with the whole process of procreation..."[26]

As Martin notes, the gender of the monstrous child remains ambivalent, a feature which once again recalls the elision of the boundaries of sexuality through abjection. Importantly, this denial of difference is replicated by Bruckner's own body which is revealed to have been mutilated in the rape that impregnated her. This attack occurred when a mental patient under her charge pulled her through the bars of his cell, disfiguring her breasts in the process. As a result, Bruckner is left with a "damaged" body that can no longer fully be classified as feminine. This concentration on the damaged female body that denies biological classifications can be seen as consistent trope in Argento's films.

Thus, Bruckner's deformity is matched by Monica Ranieri's genital violation in **The Bird With The Crystal Plumage**. Here, the painting that leads amateur detective Sam Dalmas to uncover the killer's identity (depicting a woman being genitally penetrated by an assailant's knife), is revealed to a representation of the attack Ranieri suffered and then used as a psychotic template to assault other young women.[27] This act of "feminine" mutilation itself prefigures the fate of Adriana Petrescu, the psychic "headhunter" killer from Argento's later film **Trauma**. Here, her vagina is penetrated with a surgeon's knife while she is giving birth. This act not only alters her own genital appearance but decapitates her baby, resulting in her quest to exact vengeance on the malpractice which aborted her pregnancy.[28]

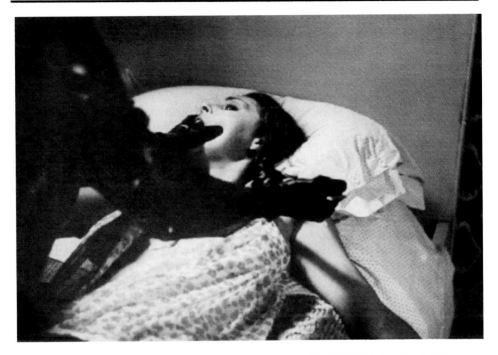

The Bird With The Crystal Plumage

As with **Creepers, Trauma** provides a point of comparison to the narrative of the "three mothers" by constructing the maternal as a mutilated deviation from symbolic boundaries of categorisation. A comparison with the "dead" womb of Mater Tenebrarum's hotel basement is replicated by Petrescu's damaged reproductive organs, while Adriana is also cast as the powerful pre-Oedipal mother who threatens to smother her daughter Aura's autonomy.[29] As a result, Aura comes to attain a complex position in relation to the investigative processes of the film. Believing her mother's powers as a medium have resulted in her assassination by a killer fearful of exposure, Aura teams up with David Parson, a typical example of Argento's amateur male detectives. As with other masculine investigators from the cycle, Parson is shown to lack the symbolic mandate needed to resolve the enigma of the killer's identity. His close proximity to the case is revealed through his role as a design artist in the television studio covering the head hunter killings.[30] Parson is separated from an appropriate position of knowledge needed to resolve the crime. This is indicated through his inability to make accurate visual deductions about the killer's identity (whom he believes is Aura's male psychiatrist Dr Judd).

An indication of this visual inability to read a scene for "evidence" is provided not only through Parson's misguided belief that the killer is male, but that Aura, like her mother is a passive potential victim. This belief is marked in the opening sequence when David manages to save Aura from drowning, agreeing to help her through a belief that she is unbalanced. Later in the film, Parson discovers that Aura is anorexic after she confesses that she is unable to have intercourse with him.[31] Soon after this revelation he receives a note from her stating that she has "gone to join her mother", leading him to presume that she has committed suicide while in an unbalanced frame of mind.

As a result, he falls into a state of a psychosis and begins to wander the streets, endlessly mistaking other women for his lost love object. It is only in the closing stages of the film when Parson finds Aura alive and living with her aggressive murderous mother that his perceptions equating passivity and femininity are unhinged.

Indeed, Aura's anorexia, the disorder which confirmed Parson's view of her passivity can in fact be re-read as a sign of her resisting a stable form of sexual identity.[32] As a result of this disorder, Aura's relation with the abject is doubly coded. Firstly, her mother's transgressions take the form of decapitating and then dissecting the bodies of her victims. Equally, her own anorexia recalls food loathing as a fundamental form of abjection related to the infant's primary period of development under the mother.

Louise J. Kaplan has linked disorders such as anorexia nervosa to the concept of "maternal perversity"[33], arguing that the complaint is actually the extension of the dyad that marked the infant's relation to its mother. In the book *Female Perversions* she notes the disorder to be marked in patients who feel unable to transcend the control of the pre-Oedipal mother despite being caught up in the symbolic's mode of sexual classification. The girl's response to this contradictory situation is (through a denial of food) to attempt to refuse any external signs of sexual difference. She thus attempts a return to a primary state of semiotic fusion which discards gender difference.[34] In this respect, it is important that Kaplan has found the disease to be marked in those girls who recall having powerful, maternal figures in their lives.

Kaplan has noted the historical emergence of the disorder in relation to 19th century medical and aesthetic discourses around femininity. However, rather than see it as a sign of female passivity, she argues anorexia represents a form of physiological resistance to the symbolic. As a result, the anorexic can be seen as another instance of the diseased female that provoked disgust in Freud's dream. Their diseased body provokes offence in those males who are in close proximity to them. What the sufferer attempts to do in this condition is return to an arena which denies the notion of sexual difference and the mother's body as lacking. (As Kaplan noted in *Female Perversions,* it is important that the disorder only emerges in a girl's teenage years when her mature sexual identity is becoming marked).[35]

Although the anorexic appears to be defined as a passive, genderless child, Kaplan argues that this desire to become the "third sex" demonstrates the female's possession of aggressive pre-Oedipal instincts. As one sufferer indicated, the desired effect for physiological transformation was only deemed successful in the advanced stages of the disorder. Here, she was no longer able to menstruate, and hormonal imbalances had produced the growth of facial hair:

"I got my wish to be a third sex, both girl and boy. Standing in front of the mirror. I saw a lovely attractive woman. My other self, the body outside the mirror, was a lusting young man preparing to seduce the girl in the mirror. I was having a love affair with myself."[36]

The anorexic's ultimate aim is the regression to a realm where sexual difference and the law of the father are denied. It is this wish that is reciprocated in the ending of **Trauma**. Here, Aura is revealed to have literally returned to a primary arena of the maternal. Parson discovers her (in an advanced anorexic state) and Adriana living in a house which contains the mummified remains of the aborted infant that initiated the mother's quest. Although Adriana the monstrous mother of the text is destroyed in the film's finale, the questions over her daughter's ambivalent sexuality remain unresolved. The film ends with her having to be helped from the scene by Parson.

Indeed, during the end credit sequence, the camera shifts away from the couple, pans across the street and comes to rest on a young girl who is dancing in a window. Although this action has no apparent diegetic motivation, the young girl's body is as asexual and prepubescent as Aura's. As with Argento's other films, this seems to confirm that the text's "troublesome" construction of the female body exceeds simplistic generic definitions as a victimised, mutilated form. Rather, it represents a disturbing, potent and unclassifiable body that resists ideological recouperation even in the closing stages of his films.

I would like to thank Martin Stollery for his helpful comments on earlier drafts of this article. I am also indebted to Julian Hoxter for discussions of his recent work on Dario Argento and Melanie Klein.

NOTES

1. Dario Argento, quoted in David E. Williams' article "Argento's Enigma", *Film Threat* #8, Volume 2, February 1993, p.44.

2. Kristeva's interests in language, ideology and the representation of the feminine are split along a number of important publications which chart the formation of her ideas on the repression of the maternal in patriarchal society. Texts such as *Revolution In Poetic Language* (New York: Columbia University Press, 1984) provide an examination of the strict, rule bound systems of language that govern the symbolic, while contrasting them to the fluid forms of communication which exist between the mother and child. Both this volume and *Powers Of Horror* (New York: Columbia University Press, 1982) indicate how subversive forms of discourse used between the pair reappear in certain forms of modernist literature. Although cinema remains largely absent from her analysis, it is the examination of the mother as a sign of symbolic disgust and loathing within these texts that resulted in critics such as Barbara Creed applying Kristeva's work to the horror film. More recently, volumes such as *Tales Of Love* (New York: Columbia University Press, 1987) have shown Kristeva attempting to write accounts of the history of motherhood using unconventional and subversive written techniques. These methods are present in chapters such as "Stabat Mater" in order to show how an "infantile" use of discourse can be used to represent the feminine in language.

3. Mark Le Fanu, "Tenebrae" in *Films And Filming* #348, September 1983, p.36.

4. See Christopher Wagstaff's "A Forkful Of Westerns", in Richard Dyer & Ginette Vincendeau (eds) *Popular European Cinema*, London: Routledge, 1992. Here, Wagstaff has sought to give historical reasons for the dominance of the generic hybrid in post-war Italian popular film. He linked the phenomenon to an attempt to appeal to regionally distinct audiences on the part of producers and filmmakers. Drawing on the geographical distinction between the industrial, "sophisticated" North and the rural South Wagstaff has argued that these distinct locations are marked by differing audience tastes in terms of narrative type and generic mode of engagement. While one specific film cycle may be popular in the sophisticated areas of the country, this appeal may not be matched in rural locations. Thus, by fusing a number of different generic concerns into a single narrative format, producers ensure a market for the film in all areas of the country. Another important account in this area is Leon Hunt's influential article "A Sadistic Night At The Opera: Notes On The Italian Horror Film" (*The Velvet Light Trap* #30, 1992). Here, Hunt situates the Italian horror film between other Italian cycles dominant in post-war years. As a result, he argues that critics often fail to recognise that the curious construction of these narratives does not necessarily represent deficiencies on the part of the director and their knowledge of plotting and film technique. Rather these texts are very

self-conscious attempts to appeal to the *specific* interests of these different Italian viewing groups.

5. David J. Hogan, *Dark Romance*, Northampton: Equation, 1988, p.168.

6. Rob Winning, "Demons" in *Cinefantastique* Volume 17 #2, March 1987, p.44.

7. Elizabeth Grosz, "The Body Of Signification" in John Fletcher & Andrew Benjamin (eds) *Abjection Melancholia And Love: The Work Of Julia Kristeva*, London: Routledge, 1996, p.86.

8. Barbara Creed, *The Monstrous Feminine*, London: Routledge, 1994, p.11.

9. In her article "Ellipses On Dread And The Specular Seduction" in *Wide Angle* Volume 3 #2, 1979.

10. Kristeva, *Powers Of Horror*, p.108.

11. Kristeva, "Ellipses On Dread And The Specular Seduction", p.45. It seems pertinent that the narrative does not specify to whom the punishment will be directed: the monster for its sudden appearance, or the infant for creating such a figure from its own "filth".

12. Kristeva, *Powers Of Horror*, p.2.

13. Ibid., p.9. The basis of food loathing is also indicated in Douglas's book *Purity And Danger*, London: Routledge, 1991. This book analysed the rationale behind the construction of certain animals as taboo in religious or ritual practice. In orthodox Judaism only animals whose characteristics equate with the category of their appropriate environment are seen as fit for consumption. Thus, the snake is seen as taboo from this schema because it can inhabit both land and water despite possessing neither gills nor legs and as such defies the distinguishing categories between land animals and fish.

14. This connection is made by Creed in *The Monstrous Feminine* (p.76–77). Her analysis of both Argento's films is tied to the cultural history of representing the female witch as a filthy, unclean presence.

15. Importantly, the boy (aged around seven or eight years old) is clothed in mock Victorian dress more suited to a much younger child. This factor, along with Albert's apparent inability (or refusal) to enter into conversation in the film, redoubles the relationship of the mother to the Pre-Oedipal and pre-articulate child.

16. Maitland McDonagh, *Broken Mirrors Broken Minds: The Dark Dreams Of Dario Argento*, London: Sun Tavern Fields, 1991, p.129.

17. His essay itself privileges uncontrollable physiology, linking the mother's presence as "functions pointing to the flesh". Cited in McDonagh, p.136.

18. Creed, p.13.

19. Ibid., p.12.

20. Ibid., p.77.

21. Ibid., p.53.

22. Jenks, in Richard Dyer & Ginette Vincendeau (eds) *Popular European Cinema*, p.157.

23. Kristeva, *Powers Of Horror*, p.101.

24. Comparisons with Creed's analysis of Mrs Bates from **Psycho** are important here. As she notes this maternal figure operates through the power of the semiotic: she is literally the disembodied "voice", who can only be represented in terms of the "flesh" of a dead corpse. Equally, the body that is revealed as belonging to Mrs Bates in the film's conclusion is marked by a collapse of external image onto "internal" features such as bone structure.

25. Her transformation from the guise of nurse to a "genderless" skeleton reiterates the division of the interior and exterior modes of physiology that abjection attacks.

26. John Martin, in Pierre Jouis (ed) *Fantasy Film Memory: Directed By Dario Argento*, Paris: Gothic Press, 1991, p.42.

27. It is possible to argue that the theme of the "damaged" female body as a trigger for violent psychosis represents a trait in Italian horror beyond Argento's productions. For instance, in his review of Sergio Pastore's **The Crimes Of The Black Cat** (1972), Mark Ashworth links a series of savage murders occurring at a fashion house to an earlier accident suffered by the killer Francoise Balli. See his review of the film in Stephen Thrower (ed) *Eye Ball: The European Sex And Horror Review #1*, Autumn 1989. In Pastore's film, after her breasts and abdomen are disfigured in a car crash, Balli begins to mutilate other females in order to avenge the loss of her own feminine figure. Another

example can be found in Aldo Lado's 1975 film **Late Night Trains**. This features Macha Meril as a sadistic businesswomen who goads a pair of thugs into raping and killing two young girls on a trans-European train. Following Monica Ranieri's example Meril kills one of the victims by penetrating her vagina with a knife, to the disgust of her two male assistants. When pressed by them as to the motivation behind these extreme actions, Meril replies that her own body was similarly deformed by a surgeon's knife during puberty.

28. The construction of the "mutilated" female heroine as a repeated Argento trait is confirmed in the figure Anna Manni from **The Stendhal Syndrome**. Following the repeated wounding on her body by Alfredo Grossi, she experiences a "psychotic" loss of gender identity. As a result she attempts to remodify her image by cutting off her hair and practising body building in order to achieve a more masculine appearance. The dislocation of her body from dominant notions of sexual difference is evidenced in an alteration of Anna's sexual habits. She confesses a hatred of being penetrated during intercourse, even gesturing towards the anal rape of her boyfriend Marco during a lovemaking scene.

29. The casting of Piper Laurie for this role is pertinent. She is most famous for playing the sadistic Mrs White who denies her daughter autonomy in Brian De Palma's **Carrie** (1977). However, as Martin Coxhead has noted, Adriana's construction (both her hair colouring and death at the hand of her own decapitating machine) link her to previous Argento mothers such as Martha from **Deep Red**. See Coxhead's article "Traumatised" in Allan Bryce (ed) The Dark Side, April 1994.

30. This redoubles the obsession with replaying visual scenarios of death that marked the similarity between investigator Sam Dalmas and Monica Ranieri in **The Bird With The Crystal Plumage**.

31. Aura's inability to fully adopt a feminine role for the purposes of intercourse mirror the behaviour of Betty in **Opera**. Her access to her mother's past crimes prevents her from developing a mature sexuality, indicated in her inability to engage in intercourse with a young stage hand.

32. Argento consistently retards his heroines' sexuality in the same way that Aura's disorder prevents her taking up a fully feminine position. Indeed, when asked about his ideal of "female" beauty by Phillip Nutman Argento explained his choice through the figure of Jennifer Corvino from **Creepers**. Here, Argento stated, "In my opinion she is an angelic vision of womanhood... Her face and form are really powerful, and she's almost sexless." See Nutman's review of **Creepers** in Anthony Timpone (ed) Fangoria #49, November 1985, p.54.

33. In the book Female Perversions, p.410.

34. From a Kristevan perspective it can be argued that the anorexic's body can be viewed as a site of abjection on a number of levels. The body becomes a shapeless body shell, thus undercutting existing categorisations of what constitutes established body image. Equally, the ingestion of food becomes impossible: the patient is forced to expel the substances reiterating the inability to control one's own physiology that marked the fate of victims in **Demons**. Recalling Creed's definition of the abject in horror cinema as a site of grotesque spectacle and display, Kaplan notes that through the excessive remoulding of her body, the anorexic holds sway over an audience both fascinated by the extent of physical change as well as repulsed via their proximity to the body without form.

35. As Kaplan notes, the sexual nature of the disorder's manifestation is implicit in the German term for anorexia: "Pubertatsmangersucht".

36. Hilde Bruch, The Golden Cage: The Enigma Of Anorexia Nervosa, Cambridge: Harvard University Press, 1978. Cited Kaplan p.461.

ROPE OF FLESH

Culture And Identity In Russ Meyer's "Mudhoney"

Stephanie Watson & Jack Sargeant

American "exploitation" *auteur* Russ Meyer began his career with a string of films which included **The Immoral Mr Teas** (1959), **Erotica** (1961), and **Europe In The Raw** (1963), amongst others. Dubbed "nudie-cuties", the films were characterised by their combination of dead-pan, almost unintentionally funny, narration, and images of – frequently large breasted – semi-clad, or naked, women. Then, in 1964, Russ Meyer's stylistic approach transformed as he directed a cycle of stark black and white features in which the bawdy voyeurism of his previous nudie-cuties was replaced by a more downbeat, sinister, and narrative-driven aesthetic. Beginning with **Lorna** (1964), this short cycle of films took in **Mudhoney** (*aka* **Rope Of Flesh**, 1965), **Motorpsycho** (1965), and – possibly Meyer's most famous movie – **Faster, Pussycat! Kill! Kill!** (1966)[1]. Part of the change in direction for Meyer was undoubtedly the decline of the audience's interest in the nudie-cuties, a wane of enthusiasm he combated with the introduction of grim violence and sex, no doubt ever aware of the audience's salacious interests; however this does not fully explain the sheer black cynicism of these films, with their trajectory of sexual and social transgression, violence, and narrative focus on the criminal, or marginalised, outsider.

Whilst **Faster, Pussycat! Kill! Kill!** has received most acclaim, it is possibly **Mudhoney** which represents the most interesting film in this cycle of "nudie-noir", with its depictions of: a "bad" guy in a white cowboy hat, an impotent overweight sheriff, a gun-toting woman, a sadistic hypocritical clergyman, a deaf-mute girl, a good man called Calif (think California), plus drinking, raping, lynching, whoring, small town bigotry, murder, madness, and manslaughter – a colourful list which testifies to **Mudhoney's** deeply patriotic yet cynical vision of Depression America.

Based on the novel *Streets Paved With Gold*, by Friday Locke, **Mudhoney** ("...leaves a taste of Evil!" stated the publicity) is set during the Depression, at the peak of prohibition, in the small, rural community of Spooner, Missouri. A cross country traveller Calif McKinny arrives in town, and is soon employed as a farmhand on the Wade farm, where he works for the good-natured, but weak-hearted, Uncle Luke, and his niece Hannah, both of whom are dominated by her drunken husband Sydney, who is waiting until Luke dies and he can get his hands on the property and the money. Sydney spends most of his time at the local whore-house, run by Maggie Marie – who also distils illegal peel liquor – and her two blonde daughters: Clarabelle (played by Lorna Maitland, star of **Lorna**), the sassy and sharp sex bomb, and Eula (Rena Horton), a deaf-mute, and, judging by her vacant stares, possibly retarded, woman-child. When he's not whoring, or drinking, Sydney is beating his wife, or brawling, whilst Calif looks helplessly on, unable to interfere due to his fear of killing Sydney. As the narrative progresses it becomes apparent that Calif has recently been released from prison, having completed a five year manslaughter conviction for the accidental killing of a strike breaker. As the weeks pass Calif and Hannah fall in love, much to Luke's satisfaction, who changes his will leaving Calif as his trustee, and Hannah's guardian. Following a brief fight with Calif, Sydney is befriended by Preacher Hanson, who declares that Calif is the "Child of Satan". Preacher Hanson decides to set the townfolk against Calif, Hannah, and Luke, who dies of a heart attack

Faster, Pussycat! Kill! Kill!

shortly afterwards, having warned Calif against the townspeople. A drunk, and increasingly insane, Sydney disturbs the old man's funeral – having discovered the change in his will – and is chased away by the small congregation. Sydney retaliates by burning down the farm house, hoping the blame will be placed on Calif. Sheriff Abel takes Calif and Hannah into protective custody, whilst sending his men out to look for Sydney. Sydney, now completely insane and believing that Preacher Hanson's wife is Hannah, assaults and kills her, before being caught by an enraged mob led by the Preacher. As the mob prepare to lynch Sydney, Calif, Hannah, and Sheriff Abel arrive and try to stop the hanging. They fail and, in the process, Calif shoots the Preacher. As the crowd watch the deaf-mute Eula runs forward to clutch Sydney's corpse, sobbing and screaming, she has – at last – found her voice.

Characterised – like many of this cycle of films – by an atmosphere of palpable sexual tension, **Mudhoney** repeatedly emphasizes the dysfunctional nature of all of its protagonists via *mis-en-scène*: the villainous one-time-success Sydney – frequently shot from a low angle to emphasize his menacing drunken weight, the Preacher who is blind to the anything except dogmatic doctrine and whose appearance is marked by crazed organ music, and toothless Maggie Marie who is shot repeatedly in distorted close-up, all devices which echo the gothic tone of disorientation and fragmentation. The film also exudes a visual, and diagetic, pleasure in assertive big-breasted women. However, unlike Meyer's previous films, it both resonates with, and examines the construction of, the American Dream, in a way which goes beyond kitsch parody.

Mudhoney has a didactic storyline which aspires to moral teaching as it charts the victory of good over bad. It focuses on the Depression years of 1930's America and has political and sociological overtones. It tells of the downfall of the American Dream of prosperity, the slip into American Nightmare and the rebirth of the Dream by the "little" man who comes from nothing and becomes a success. The film specifically locates its story within a historical milieu of change, and within the geographical location of the small town, traditionally viewed as the store-house of American values.

The American Dream has always been clothed in religious metaphors – a new Eden, the Promised Land – a land of freedom and opportunity, where victims of religious, political, and ethnic persecution can find themselves, can "grow", or become born again. A land full of new and equal Adams whose individual rights and desire to succeed are held sacred. This new Adam has of necessity always been seen as a traveller, an explorer, a shape-shifter. An anti-hero or victim of circumstances beyond his control, who once had all the odds stacked against him, often resulting in criminal behaviour, but who can now reverse his fortunes and become a "good" guy.

Cutting through American culture – from Westerns to sci-fi movies, from "body" and "growth" cultures, to the self-confessional chat show and even Andy Warhol's "15 minutes of fame" – is the mythic figure of the self-made man who can become anything he wants to be if he works hard enough. The American Dream is often represented in the journey West, particularly during the 1880's gold rush fever. The Dream has a nightmare twin who raises its monstrous head when the self-made man loses his successful status. The American Nightmare has been powerfully evoked in the literature of writers such as Nathaniel Hawthorne, Edgar Allan Poe, William Faulkner, and Flannery O'Conner, and in the classic B-movie genres of film noir, thrillers, melodrama, and horror films.

In a society where appearance is all, where there is no truth of experience the fear begins to grow that if a man can become "good" he can also become "bad" – the white Stetson might hide a black heart. Identity is not fixed, therefore the appearance might not be what it seems, it can become "slippery" and ambiguous – the labels become interchangeable/meaningless and cannot be relied upon to reflect the product. In many B-movies, and certainly in **Mudhoney**, the angst regarding deceptive appearances becomes – at least in part – transformed into a pleasure, which is faced, and banished through a narrative driven cathartic process. The other, even the other-at-home, is faced and confronted. Similarly **Mudhoney** presents clichéd social stereotypes and draws on religious archetypes. Spooner is a mixed-up town where appearances have been reversed – Luke Wade (an atheist martyr), states "This whole town has been cheated, cheated by the times", and "This town has got to hate something, or somebody". The town folk are unable to admit that the community's decline has come from within, from the economic collapse of the American Dream, and thus the protagonists hang on to the symbols of success rather than acknowledge the reality of failure, and the rot from within. Thus, for example, Sydney is constantly demanding to be treated with respect for the man he used to be, a wealthy employer of twenty people in pre-Depression Kansas City where he enjoyed the "good times". He represents a dead incarnation of the American Dream – the individualistic cowboy – who must now give way to the union man, Calif. Sydney taunts Calif , saying "California is a place not a name". Sydney does not understand the belief in the American Dream as being a state of mind as well as material possibility. Sydney also accuses Calif of not being "a real man". Images of male impotency abound in Spooner – Sheriff Abel (the Biblical victim of Cain), is a good man but unable to exercise any law enforcement within the town. His option for Hannah and Calif, when faced with persecution from the misguided community, is one of escape rather than confrontation, which both Hannah and Calif reject. Hannah will not abandon Sydney in

Mudhoney

his hour of need, not because she's masochistic, but because she's not a quitter; she has a sense of righteousness which is not strictly Christian or moral in terms of social appearances. Rather, Hannah still clings to the vestiges of her dreams.

The gender balance in Spooner is also out of patriarchal control – Luke Wade tells Calif that Hannah is the best shot for miles around, including the men folk. Although Hannah is Sydney's victim she will not be broken, whereas, as the narrative progresses, Sydney cracks under the pressure of having no money or status. Eula, the deaf-mute who masochistically accepts Sydney's abuse, only regains her voice through his death of Sydney – in other words Sydney the fake cowboy and his equally deceptive religious friends and moral tongue-waggers, have created a climate where women have filled male "roles" and/or lost their own "roles". Calif restores this balance for Hannah; he will build her a new Eden in California with her Uncle's money over which he is trustee, in possession.

Perhaps this is not the ideal scenario of equality for an American Eve – yet Russ Meyer does give his female characters some respect. As sexual figures they often have a strength, independence, and morality which exceeds social institutions, they are shown to be trapped by unfair laws, male greed and aggression, but remain fair in their treatment of others. They are not wicked temptresses/whores or deliberately passive Madonna figures, they are merely trying to survive and have a good time in a man's world.

Mudhoney is a melodrama which shows what happens when a good thing turns bad, yet it has a deep-rooted respect for the power of the "little" man and woman to overcome the chaotic wilderness of poverty, exploitation, and emotional despair. The success of the American Dream is shown to be dependent on the ability to change, travel, and take risks. The rural hometown nostalgia seen in American television programmes such as "The Little House On The Prairie", or "The Waltons", is redundant for Meyer, because these texts treat the American Dream as static, rooted in the past. **Mudhoney**, through its B-movie credentials and exaggerated characters, functioning as fantasy, is able to explore the myth of the American Dream within the locus of the small towns in which it was first realized, and both examines and contributes to mythology and, through the character of Calif, suggests the American Dream is still an active process which can never be constrained.

NOTES
1. All available in the UK through Troma video.

IMPROPER BURIALS, UNBURIED MEMORIES

"Night Of The Living Dead"

Mikita Brottman

The premise of **Night Of The Living Dead**, George A. Romero's classic 1968 zombie epic, is that atomic radiation from a space satellite has the power to animate the recently deceased, and these mindless ghouls thereupon prey indiscriminately upon the living, eating their warm bodies. The zombies can be stopped only when their warped brains are completely destroyed.

Night... has been analysed in a variety of different ways by a range of different critics, who have generally paid attention to the film's ideological content. Richard Dyer in *Screen*, for example, is particularly interested in the racial elements of the film and the specifically white dimension of the relationship between these zombies and the American society that has created them. He writes:

"If whiteness and death are equated, both are further associated with the USA. That the film can be taken as a metaphor for the United States is established right at the start of the film.

It opens on a car driving through apparently unpopulated back roads suggesting the road tradition of 1950s American movies... with its idea of the 'search for America'. When the car reaches the graveyard (the U.S?), a stars-and-stripes flag flutters in the foreground".[1]

In a similarly ideological vein, Jane Caputi in *The Journal Of Popular Film And Television* takes a look at **Night...** with reference to the nihilism of much post-1950s U.S. cinema, which Caputi speculates tends to reflect the anxiety of the nuclear age. She studies the film's imagery for its nuclear elements, relating the psychic experience of zombiedom to the partial shutdown of mental facilities and emotional responses experienced by the survivors of nuclear war. According to Caputi:

*"**Night Of The Living Dead** offers not only a symbolic description of the landscape of a post-nuclear world: it provides a powerful metaphor for the psychic numbing that characterises general consciousness in the Nuclear Age."*[2]

Others, including Steve Beard, are more interested in the role of the zombie as surplus human capacity processed through the system as grotesque human waste, and conscious fears about mass unemployment in the recessionary climate of the time. In other words, the heterogeneity of Romero's zombies contains the implication – and one that has become more transparent since 1968 – that "nobody is immune from the social restructuring of post-Fordism ...Everybody's job is potentially at risk"[3].

Romero himself helped to back up this ideological interpretation of the living dead. "Zombies are the real lower-class citizens of the monster world, and that's why I like

them", he says. Individually, as Beard has pointed out, they are slow, stumbling and weak. Collectively, they are a rampaging mob of clawing hands and gnashing teeth[4]. What is special about Romero's zombies, however, is their cannibalistic appetite. Romero is almost entirely responsible for the familiar incarnation of the zombie as ghoulish cannibal, as blood-thirsty anthropophage who adds to his numbers by feeding on living human flesh.

Taking the cultural taboo of cannibalism as a starting point, it seems evident that there are a number of psychoanalytic issues in **Night Of The Living Dead** which have not been widely discussed, which seems unusual for a film which has managed to earn such an established critical reputation. In this brief article, I want to take a look at what traditional psychoanalysis can bring to our understanding of Romero's zombie epic.

Both psychoanalysis and anthropology have a lot to say, for example, about western cultural taboos surrounding the burial of the dead. In Romero's film, John and Barbara have come to Maryland to lay a wreath on their mother's grave. John is impatient and irritated that Barbara spends so long kneeling by the grave. "C'mon Barbara, praying's for church", he tells her on a couple of occasions. He also complains that it's a waste of money to buy a new wreath every year, and they'd be better off recycling the old ones. Later on, while the survivors are watching television, a medical authority warns of the dangers of any delay to the destruction of corpses:

"No, you're right, it doesn't give them time to make funeral arrangements. The bodies must be carried to the street and... and... and burned. They must be burned immediately.

Soak them with gasoline and burn them. The bereaved will have to forego the dubious comforts that a funeral service will give... They're just dead flesh, and dangerous."

High levels of radiation from a malfunctioning space probe have led to the revival of recently-deceased corpses. This is a film about the dead returning to life, and our collective cultural fears surrounding improper funeral rituals and inadequate bereavement. Images of the unburied dead fill the screen repeatedly, seemingly bent on avenging a culture that has casually broken this most sacred of western taboos. According to traditional anthropology, anxieties surrounding burial neglect relate to a society's fear of the ancestors' jealousy of the living, and their need to avenge that jealousy on their surviving ancestors. In psychoanalytic terms, however, the dread of improper burial is quite clearly connected to our fears surrounding the notion of repression – the dread that whatever terrifying anxieties and taboos lie hidden in the unconscious have been inadequately buried, and may revive at any moment, breaking through into the conscious world of logic and reason. And as anthropology has established, that which fails to fit into traditional cultural categories – such as the living, walking dead – is always regarded by a culture as abject and contaminating.

The pathological dimensions of this incomplete repression are symbolically embodied in the architectonics of the house, with its front facade (under attack by the unburied dead), its upstairs (where the dead body of the previous tenant lies half-eaten), and the cellar (representing the dark nether regions of the human body, sexuality and repression). In **Night Of The Living Dead**, much of the final section of the film is taken up with an angry debate between Ben and Mr. Cooper about whether they are safer staying upstairs, confronting the marauding zombies head-on, or else barricading themselves in the cellar. Mr. Cooper wants to get together everything they might need and hole up in the cellar. The cellar, he claims, has only one door, which can be locked from the inside, but upstairs there are too many doors and windows. Cooper argues that the cellar is the safest place to hide; Ben thinks it's a death-trap. "If you've locked yourself in the cellar and those things get in the house, you've had it", he claims. "At least up here, you've got a fighting chance". Unknown to the survivors, however, the cellar is already inhabited by a zombie of its own. Karen, Mr. Cooper's young daughter, has been bitten by one of the ghouls and is about to revive in the form of a zombie. In an added irony, it is only Ben who survives the night – and only then by barricading himself up in the cellar.

The psychological dimensions of this analogy are obvious. Like the besieged survivors in Hitchcock's **The Birds** (1963)[5], another film about inadequate repression, the characters in **Night Of The Living Dead** try to barricade themselves into the house whilst the menace proliferates outside. As in **The Birds**, attacks occur at moments of mounting social tension in the narrative. Surplus repression reveals itself in the form of the gathering undead, and social traumas and conflicts manifest themselves in the form of inexplicable paranormal mayhem. The temporary makeshift barricades constructed by Ben represent the barriers of repression we build to separate conscious from unconscious neurosis, to defend our unstable egos against the return of the repressed. The breaking down of these barriers by the inexplicable threat is a symbolic re-interpretation of that which we, as human beings, fear the most: mental breakdown, neurotic collapse, or the process of becoming caught, like Barbara, in that liminal, terminal no-man's land between the conscious of logic and stability and the unconscious of unreason, repression and neurosis.

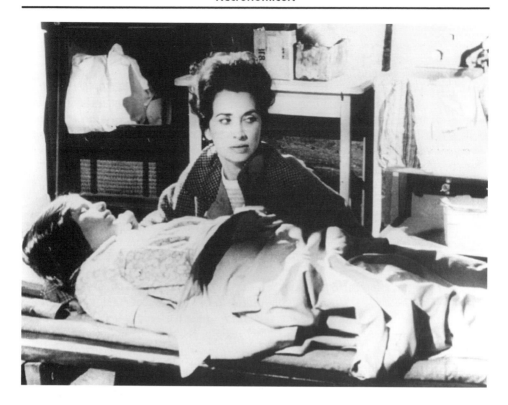

It seems somehow right, then, that the zombies can be killed only by aiming a gun or other implement at the physical embodiment of their minds. As the radio announcer says, "kill the brain and you kill the ghoul". But one question remains. What terrifying trauma lying buried somewhere in the unconscious does this inexorable assault represent?

Night Of The Living Dead is the story of a night when the whole world turns upside-down. Much is made, in the opening sequence, of the fact that this is the first day of winter, the day the clocks go back, giving an extra hour of daylight, before night falls with shocking suddenness. John and Barbara have somehow accidentally driven into a topsy-turvy world, a world in which the dead reanimate mysteriously, roam the earth, and seek to devour living human flesh. This is a world of the lucid detailing of human taboos.

The first taboo to be broken is that of bodily control. The zombies stumble and drool in their clumsy quest for flesh, often with intestines spilling out or severed limbs dangling. Brains splatter against the wall; zombies collapse groaning to the ground. The human body – even your own body – is out of control, and you are no longer able to understand or relate to it.

The second broken taboo is that of incest. Barbara's obsession with her brother's death leads her to remain in a catatonic state throughout the remainder of the movie, but the psychic numbing she so obviously manifests is a version of the psychic state that is more subtly and powerfully represented by the ghouls themselves, including her beloved brother John, who returns from the dead at last to claim her for his own.

The third and most significant broken taboo is that of cannibalism, especially

intra-familial cannibalism (endophagy). The inversion of traditional feeding behaviour is first made manifest when Ben and Barbara take refuge in the kitchen whose table is laid out neatly for a meal. Ben gathers together the plates and crockery in the tablecloth, pushes it all to one side, upends the dining table and dismantles it to make boards for the windows while Barbara takes the lace tablecloth, folds it and cradles it, hanging on uselessly to this symbol of traditional eating behaviour. Ben, who tells Barbara that he was first attacked in a nearby diner, kills the intruding zombies one by one then throws the bodies outside to appease the hunger of the others, at least temporarily, while Barbara listens transfixed to the radio broadcast which is emphasising, over and over again, the predatory nature of these cannibalistic ghouls, and their unsavoury appetite for human flesh:

"...consistent reports from witnesses of people who acted as though they were in a kind of trance who were killing and eating their victims prompted authorities to examine the bodies of some of their victims. Medical authorities in Cumberland have concluded that in all cases the killers are eating the flesh of the people they murder... Civil defense authorities have told newsmen that murder victims show evidence of being partially devoured by their murderers. Medical examinations of the victims' bodies show conclusively that the killers are eating the flesh of the people they kill..."

Barbara sits stunned, staring at the radio in utter incomprehension and disbelief, trying to make some sense of what she has heard. Meanwhile, the zombies move in, stumbling slowly and clumsily towards the house, motivated solely by the desire to find and devour

living human flesh.

The film ends in a nightmare of chaos. The lovers, Tom and Judy, are roasted to death when their truck blows up, and they are graphically consumed by the ghouls who move in on them like a pack of hyenas. The explosive nuclear family ends up eating itself – Mr. and Mrs. Cooper bicker and snipe constantly until their dead daughter Karen, kept down in the dark recesses of the cellar, revives only to destroy and eat her parents. Barbara's brother John, who teased and tormented her while she was living, and whose death caused her to revert to a state of catatonic stupor, returns from the dead to break down the kitchen door, seek out his traumatised sister and eat her alive. And the heroic Ben, who alone survives the terrible night, is mistaken for a ghoul by a roving posse, shot in the head and dumped carelessly on a pile of dead bodies. When the improperly buried return from their makeshift graves into the realms of the living, there can be no survivors. No-one remains to greet the morning.

NOTES

1. Dyer, Richard, "Whites In Film", *Screen* XXIX 14: Autumn 1988, p60–61.
2. Caputi, Jane, "Nuclear Issues In The Cinema", *Journal Of Popular Film And Television* XVI.3: Fall 1988, p103.
3. Steven Beard, "No Particular Place To Go", *Sight And Sound* iii/4: April 1993:30.
4. See ibid.
5. See Brottman, Mikita, "Psycho/The Birds" in *Necronomicon Book One*, Creation Books 1996.

NOUVEAU NOIR

The Nietzschean Nihilism Of "Seven"

Andy Black

*"I'm always interested in movies that scar. The thing I love about **Jaws** is the fact that I've never gone swimming in the ocean again."*

—David Fincher, director of **Seven**

ONE

"Long is the way and hard that out of Hell leads up to the light."
(Milton)

"Scar" is nowhere near the word. This caustic film doesn't simply scar the soul or lacerate the mind – it systematically devours all decent, rational thought, consumes any trace of compassion before spitting out the remnants of humanity into an unholy heap.

Just as Fincher bravely/foolishly (choose your own viewpoint) took the conventions of the **Alien** series and turned them inside out – the futuristic trappings of the first and the gung-ho militarism of the second supplanted by arcane, monolithic surroundings and murderous convicts in his unique **Alien 3** (1992) vision, together with Ripley's "make-over" from resourceful and feminine into embittered and (almost) asexual – so too does Fincher reinvent the somewhat stale serial killer genre, infusing **Seven** (1996) with an unremitting stench of pure human evil – the nebulous world he renders before us barely touched by the solitary tendril of light, of hope even, suggested by the disaffected Somerset's (Morgan Freeman) final words.

It's like the cloying, claustrophobic atmosphere and unsavoury characters in **Alien 3** – Fincher's "dry run" for **Seven** – as these elements are expanded upon to an almost unbearable degree. I mean, this guy Fincher is the ultimate control freak, playing with our minds from the word go as the disembodied credits roll, accompanied by a cacophony of abstract, industrial nerve "music" which clearly establishes that there is a disturbed and diseased intelligence at work here – big time!

Fincher's absolute control and ability to manipulate the viewer's emotions within the cadre of his intricately-drawn characters – and yes, I do mean characters (a long-forgotten element in the majority of contemporary horror/thriller films today) – is clearly his own *modus operandi* to augment the shredding of our nerves and raping of our minds.

As he himself commented on **Seven**'s climax: "From the time he opens the box and Morgan's running to Brad (Pitt) and the killer, it's like you realise that the end of this movie's been written in stone and you don't have any choice. All of a sudden it became a horror movie and it's like how do you deal with circumstances way beyond your control."

TWO

"He's preaching. These murders are a sermon to us."
(Lt. William Somerset)

GLUTTONY • GREED • SLOTH • PRIDE • LUST • ENVY • WRATH

In the killer John Doe's (Kevin Spacey) mind, there is a perfect symmetry to his cycle of murders, culminating in his own at the hands of Detective Mills (Brad Pitt). In the first murder, "Gluttony", an obese man is found in an almost Boschian scene – face down in a plate of spaghetti, the subsequent autopsy revealing he had been force-fed for two days and then beaten in order to burst his stomach walls. A return visit by Somerset to the cockroach-infested apartment reveals a further clue, the word "Gluttony" etched appropriately in grease on the back of the fridge.

The second victim is a lawyer forced at gunpoint to remove a pound of flesh from his own body à la *The Merchant Of Venice*, with the word "Greed" being daubed in blood on the floor of his office.

Most horrifying of all is the detectives' discovery of the drug-pushing "Sloth" victim – his atrophying body tied to a bed, surmised to be dead before a gut-wrenching cry from his skeletal face provides a macabre shock.

"Pride" is represented by the model who literally has her nose cut off to spite her face, "Lust" the unfortunate prostitute fucked to death by a deadly metal dildo – a punishment vicariously enjoyed by Doe via the victim's "client", who is forced at gunpoint to wear the grotesque appendage.

"Envy" is the fate befalling Mills' wife Tracy (Gwyneth Paltrow) and her unborn child at the hands of Doe – who is envious of Mills – with "Wrath" symbolised by Mills' summary execution of the monstrous Doe.

Misguidedly, Doe sees himself as some kind of moral visionary – justifying his callous deeds as punishing the "guilty" for their "sins" – yet his wanton acts of atrocity condemn him to the level of butcher rather than messiah. His attempts at addressing the transgressions of the seven deadly sins merely serve to underline the flaws and futility of his actions – after all, how will the removal of a handful of supposed "sinners" improve the quality of the world? And what of such religious values as mercy, compassion, tolerance and understanding – all singularly lacking in Doe's diseased mind.

THREE

"Ernest Hemingway once wrote 'The world is a fine place and worth fighting for'.
I agree with the second part."
(Lt. Somerset).

You can kind of glean what message Somerset is transmitting here when contemplating the bleak, depressing urban *milieu* which underpins **Seven** – most definitely not a "fine place" to live or to consider raising children, as Tracy confides to Somerset before her untimely end.

Both visually and stylistically the film's environment signposts the moral decay of the characters, only expressed in blatantly physical terms. So, just as the arch vampire

Seven

Barlow in Tobe Hooper's **Salem's Lot** (1979) inhabits a squalid lair which was once an opulent mansion house, in **Seven** there is the relentless downpouring of rain – the "devil's rain" in effect – which permeates the dark alleys and grime-filled pavements of this chiaroscuro, charnel-house metropolis.

It's symbolic that even this veritable deluge of rain cannot even begin to wash the scum from the streets – this apocalyptic tone reinforced by the subtle strands of sickly yellow light which infuse many scenes, impregnating our skin like the noxious nicotine-stained walls in an old house.

The presence of Arthur Max as production designer and of Darius Khondji – both previous veterans of Jeunet and Caro's surrealistic movies **Delicatessen** (1991) and **The City Of The Lost Children** (1995) – is notable in giving **Seven** the hellish, muted colours which fully visualise its tortured fever dreams as they insinuate our soul and mind.

The final irony/contrast is provided however, by Fincher in the taut climax as the inveigling bright light of the desert finale may sporadically punctuate the hitherto all-enveloping gloom, and yet only serves to be the ultimate false dawn (to counterpoint Doe's false prophet perhaps?) as the full magnitude of the horror unfolds before us, reaching the very darkest pit of human revulsion and then burrowing beyond it.

FOUR

"Apathy is a solution" ... "Love costs."
(Lt. Somerset)

So just why is **Seven** such a stunning *tour de force*? Just what makes it so special when judged with the "ten-a-penny" serial killer chillers which clutter up the cinema screens before invading the video stores?

Perhaps, just one simple reason... characters. Or, to be precise, real, *believable* characters who can actually invoke a genuine feeling of pathos and empathy in the audience. Mills may not be quite at the beginning of his police career but he retains enough enthusiasm, naivety if you will, to provide a glaring contrast to Somerset's retiring, world-weary figure.

When Somerset perceptively announces that the first killing is "the beginning", that many more murders will follow, he strives to "save" Mills from what he knows will be a harrowing, endless nightmare.

Somerset's defeatist admission concerning the case that Mills "wanted it" is met with an equally optimistic confession from Mills: "I'm all over it!".

It is Mills' instinctive behaviour – his heart ruling his head – which leads to Tracy confiding in Somerset and not her husband that she is pregnant. She realises that Somerset's more considered approach, exhibiting a cool and reasoned head, will elicit a more thoughtful response.

In fact, it is this self-same reason which Somerset uses to persuade Mills not to break open Doe's apartment door before they have obtained a search warrant and so not prejudice any eventual trial – yet Mills' emotions (having nearly been shot dead by Doe) lead him to break down the door anyway.

This is the impulsive behaviour which the deranged Doe requires to complete the murderous circle of events at the conclusion.

But whilst we can berate Mills for his impulsiveness, perhaps this is what is lacking in Somerset during the climactic scenes as Doe sneers a number of subtle hints regarding Mills specifically and his wife – almost signposting the horrors to come – and yet the usually astute Somerset appears unaware, or frozen, by these remarks, only intervening when it is already patently too late.

Yet Somerset's pivotal comment to Mills earlier in a bar that "You know this isn't going to have a happy ending" appears to render both men impotent when it comes to countering Doe's calculated mind games.

The notion that "apathy is a solution" becomes almost real for Somerset, who on repeated occasions appears ready to turn his back on humanity and retire to "a farm somewhere". His own self-doubt forces him to confront the sick elements of society and to stand up and be counted. It may be the clicking of a metronome which helps him to sleep but it's the heartbeat of humanity which does the most to awaken Somerset – in one library scene he is literally glimpsed as a solitary beacon of goodness/light, and so he concludes via Hemingway that the world is "worth fighting for" after all, the one glimmer of hope in an otherwise supremely nihilistic film.

And what of the broken Mills? Now reduced to the same level almost as the "scum" he seeks to extinguish by his inevitable slaying of Doe. Whilst the killer dies quickly and so ends his mental anguish, Mills' forlorn, ghostly face as he is driven away

Seven

signals that it is only the beginning for his own personal nightmare – hell has only just begun for him.

Perhaps Doe sees "death" as a merciful release – far better than being doomed to a life of mental suffering as will happen to both the unfortunate prostitute's client and Mills, who now seem condemned to no life as such, merely existing within the confines of a virtual living death.

FIVE

"You're no messiah. You're a movie of the week, a fuckin' t-shirt."
(Mills to Doe)

When Mills and Somerset search Doe's lair they discover a huge neon cross hung above his bed, juxtaposed with the discovery of numerous polaroids of his victims. There are no such cliché'd, trite comments handed down like "God told me to do it", because although Doe pursues his perverse course with religious zeal and devotion and considerable attention to detail, his motivations are strictly from within his own twisted psyche. The 2,000 notebooks which litter his apartment contain the handwritten thoughts and moods and ramblings of a deluded mind, and yet Doe's conviction is that it is *he* who is pure, *he* who is the moral crusader and *he* who is cleaning up the garbage of human society and depositing it in the "sin bin".

Doe appears very much as an intelligent but sad, lone figure, desperately needing to make his mark on civilisation in some way – the "will to power" as Nietzsche's "ubermensch" or "superman" ideal would have it – concluding that: "Intellectually superior individuals have the right to dispose of inferior ordinary people for the good of mankind."

And so Doe's delusions are thus based, lecturing Mills that "You should be thanking me for this... you're going to be remembered for this", and commenting upon his victims' "dubious" character – drug pusher, prostitute and so forth – that "Only in a world this shitty could you try and call these people innocent."

In fact, the problem with Doe is not that he is a believer in god or that he is a non-believer, but that he has delusions of grandeur in aspiring to take god's place in deciding all of our fates.

As Nietzsche pinpointed, modern man's prayers are now offered to nihilism – the new god – and Doe is adrift in an increasingly complex society where god is perceived to be at the very least dying, if not already dead.

The ultimate futility and pathetic symbolisation of Doe's miserable existence is brazenly obvious when he feels compelled to give himself up to the two detectives – tired of awaiting his capture. He chooses a supposedly dramatic entrance, covered in blood – (Tracy's, unknown then to us or Mills) – as he surrenders, but he is forced to shout out repeatedly before he can attract anyone's attention, let alone disturb Somerset and Mills. He is literally an insignificant figure who blends unnervingly into modern society, and who resorts to violence to create an impression upon humanity.

It is this very seamless integration into society however, which provides the greatest horror of all. There are no colossal monsters or fantastical aliens here to pore over in escapist delight. Here *man* is the ultimate instrument of destruction and evil – a monster/alien on the inside but with the physical, outward appearance of one of the sane masses. This is the true horror of **Seven**.

SIX

"A hell of a film... much more powerful, disturbing and memorable than 'Silence Of The Lambs'."
(Daily Telegraph)

The only serial killer film to receive more attention than **Seven** subsequently received was one of its high-profile and critically acclaimed predecessors, Jonathan Demme's **Silence Of The Lambs** (1991).

Whilst Demme's film features equally well-drawn characters, exceptional acting and some authentic *frissons*, it also very much plays as Hollywood aiming to tackle a controversial, taboo subject matter and yet always conscious of the jangle of box office tills in the background.

As such, Jodie Foster as FBI agent Clarice Starling is a watchable heroine – a young woman vulnerable enough to invoke empathy and yet resourceful enough to tackle a serial killer. Where **Silence Of The Lambs** perhaps lacks the courage of its convictions (by way of Thomas Harris' source novel), is in its relegation of serial killer Jamie Gumb to almost peripheral status in order to elevate Hannibal Lecter (Anthony Hopkins) to the role of anti-hero supreme.

Lecter is intelligent, apparently urbane, charming even, almost likeable in a roguish way – even down to his telegraphed killing of the tiresome prison governor

Silence Of The Lambs

Chiltern before walking away free into a tropical township.

Lecter's "likeability" is that film's escape valve. It lets the film and its audience off the hook. Having spent much of its running time creating tension and a sense of nausea at the gruesome subject matter, the horror is then dissipated in the black humour of what is, in all honesty, a somewhat vapid denouement.

Seven offers no such safety valve. The scale of unremitting horror and suspense is continually built up throughout the film and is scarcely punctured by Somerset's final words of hope. The killings are far more gruesome and bizarre in **Seven** and remain undiluted by Doe's palpably abhorrent figure.

There is no way you can like or sympathise with this creature. He offers no glamour, no humour, no personality. Sadistic torture is the only "pastime" to animate his otherwise lifeless soul. As Doe so rightly and perceptively observes to Mills: "It's more comfortable for you to live with the notion that I'm insane." The ominous significance of this statement is left hanging like an axe poised to drop and split asunder all our (pre)conceptions of what constitutes a "civilised" society. It poses the nightmare scenario that perhaps Doe *is* sane and it is the rest of us who are out of kilter with life.

SEVEN

"You know this isn't going to have a happy ending."
(Somerset to Mills)

Seven is simply *the* most nihilistic, valedictory piece of cinema you are ever likely to encounter, and yet to Fincher's considerable credit, he has drawn us all into a coterie of very believable, likeable characters in Mills, Somerset and Tracy. Sure, they've all got their various foibles and frailties but they are rendered all the more human for that. The fact that we care so much for them is also intrinsic to the considerable shock we experience at the climax.

Despite the overwhelming horror of the final scenes in particular, it's a miracle that out of this cesspool of grotesque killings, decaying civilisation and demented minds, we can still reach out a hand to claw back some vestige of humanity and hope, no matter how small, how tenuous, with which to hearten the soul and propagate the future of the human race.

Seven

MAINSTREAM SICKNESS

The True Horror Of "Copycat"

Andy Black

"A fictional Count Dracula's power to terrify is greatly diminished when a real-life Ted Bundy is prowling the highways. We need to know our monsters, particularly if they are human... ...violent films and publicity given to serial killers can provide a blueprint for nascent criminals."
—Poppy Z. Brite, from "The Poetry Of Violence" in *Screen Violence*, edited by Karl French (Bloomsbury, 1996)

Horror novelist Poppy Z Brite's above assertions that we need to explore and investigate that 20th century phenomenon, the "human" predator or serial killer in order to "understand" the weird workings of their mind is central to explaining the considerable success of such films as **Silence Of The Lambs** (1991), **Seven** (1996), and the less celebrated but equally compelling (for different reasons) **Copycat** (1995).

Brite rightly draws attention to the declining influence and shock value of such staple horror creatures as the vampire, Frankenstein's monster, the zombie and the plethora of rubber-suited monsters and aliens. Such figures are now held by audiences with an almost romantic affection in the face of the unfathomable atrocities perpetrated by the real-life serial killer. Horror really has come home to roost, with the veneer of respectability and normality associated with such "human monsters" generally disguising an inner soul rotten to the core and so masking a multitude of evils.

It is our desire as a race to pursue psychological profiling, amassing data and empirical evidence which drives the need to peel back the layers of normality and step into the mind of an obsessive killer, so begetting such complex films as Jon Amiel's **Copycat** where a range of emotions and ideas are portrayed, analysed and discussed – as much by the audience as the characters in the film.

As such, this is a problematic film in many aspects, yet all the more challenging because of it, as certain taboo areas are visited – though with often inconclusive results. The basic premise in **Copycat** has Sigourney Weaver essaying the role of a criminal psychologist, Helen Hudson, whose near death at the hands of a psychopath, Daryll Lee Cullum (Harry Connick Jnr.), reduces her to an apartment-bound, paranoid agoraphobic whose only contact with the outside world is via that other contagion (as some would have us believe) of the 20th century – the Internet.

When a series of killings are perpetrated, Hudson is contacted via the "world wide web" (as it proves to be for her) by the killer – who also corresponds with the now incarcerated Cullum. Her hand forced, as her own life is now in danger, Hudson, aided by Holly Hunter's ambitious, feisty police detective Monahan and her partner Goetz (Dermot Mulroney), sets about catching the "copycat" killer Peter Foley (William McNamara) – so named for his propensity for literally restaging infamous serial crimes as committed by such heinous creatures as De Salvo, Berkowitz, Bundy and Dahmer.

One of the most intriguing aspects of all of this is the almost "technophobic" treatment meted out by Amiel as modern technology ie. the Net, plays a major (negative) role in this entry. Despite her own traumatised condition it's still indicative of a dysfunctional society that the Net has become Hudson's "best friend", her main contact with the outside world (save for her rather perfunctory gay flatmate, whose sole purpose seems to be as convenient victim for Foley when he turns to Dahmer for "inspiration").

Hudson makes a poignant comment at one stage on the existence of serial killers: "These guys are like viruses, there's always some new mutation". The use of the word "virus" is germane, since Foley communicates his crimes to Hudson via the Net. As Hudson (again) reinforces her isolated existence by playing against her computer's "Chess Demon", her "mail" icon flashes and here we go – she finds herself locked onto the killer's web page as we glimpse the downloaded image of a previous victim lying prone in her bath, before the image mutates into a picture of a peace-loving festival girl who will become the next victim. Her face is manipulated into a skeletal face mask before a cluster of worms wriggle out of her chest – a bizarre but very effective use of shock tactics by Amiel.

The killer's misappropriated ingenuity doesn't end there though, as all attempts to save the file flounder as it self-destructs on the PC screen before their eyes. Hudson's total sense of frustration is accentuated by her helplessness at not being able to identify the next victim: "She looked like a girl. She looked like a million other girls," she opines. It is the classic reverse of the expected serial killer conundrum. Instead of just trying to identify who the miscreant is from the teeming masses in society, Hudson also has to pinpoint the next intended victim. By announcing his murderous intent, Foley increases the tension and sense of desperation we feel.

Hudson's (understandable) knee-jerk reaction to this invasion of her privacy through her PC is: "I'm unplugging it. It's an open window he can crawl into. What am I – the lamb tied to the stake? This is the only 'space' I have." So, not only is Hudson's physical space and body threatened, even her mental and technological (virtual) space is too, doubling the torment.

This dual assault raises the stakes as well as the tension; previously we have seen Hudson's already fragile mental state disturbed as on one occasion she showers, only to return to her bedroom to see the red dress she was wearing when nearly killed by Cullum, displayed on her bed as if mocking her. Later, even more harrowingly, she discovers a book left on her bed with a macabre book marker inserted – a severed finger, closely followed by an infestation of ants which proceed to swarm over her bed. The fact that the book is Cullum's self-styled confession, *My Life With A Knife*, only serves to heighten the terror.

It's also highly symbolic that all these disquieting incidents are concentrated upon Hudson's bed – the killer is not only invading her living space but also her sleeping space, her own comfort zone, whilst also indicating that her sexual imperilment is also high on the killer's warped agenda.

This cold, calculating manipulation, together with the visible undercurrent of sexual tension, is also accentuated as Foley is shown outside videoing a potential victim – a runner – and then magnifying the images back at home on his PC monitor, especially the gaping open mouth which is perversely formed into a hideous scream.

Given the cowardly, non-confrontational nature of the killer's approach it is of no surprise that Hudson's professional opinion in profiling Foley concludes that he is a relatively weak and insignificant individual whose own inadequacies (and implied impotence) are embodied in his attempts to gain control and therefore power over others. His highly organised approach and modus operandi is explained by Hudson through her

Copycat

study of his victims: "He strangles them face to face so they can see his power and he can watch their terror – that's what gets him off."

Having examined photographs of a previous murder victim (not Foley's), Hudson accurately extrapolates that these deaths were not the work of a serial killer; one victim's face had later been covered by the murderer, showing remorse and that sex had been a significant motive – unlike a serial killer. Thus clear lines of demarcation are drawn by Hudson.

The need for control and power and self-gratification to boost the fragile ego is perfectly captured, as we enter the killer's lair. Here we see Foley being subservient to his wife, before then descending into his private cellar where he clinically dons a white coat and with surgical precision, injects the writhing victim he has tied to an impromptu operating table. Once again, he shows his need to be in total control, the surrounding walls acting as an eerie shrine in displaying a macabre gallery of pictures he has taken of his victims.

As Hudson observes: "These men are robotic. The murder is like a ritual. They don't change their routine," but then the growing realisation intrudes her thought pattern as the "copycat" killings proliferate: "Consistency is the hobgoblin of small minds," she points out, continuing that: "He wants to dazzle us... 'look out, I'm just getting started'."

Foley may well be trying to "dazzle" us, but it's the plagiarism, the misdirected worship of previous crimes which renders the "copycat" scenario to be a direct product of a media circus spiralling out of control, plumbing the depths of a sick cesspool of human debauchery – which by implication, we are all culpable of "reading and watching it", and therefore "wallowing" in that which we purport to condemn.

Isn't it so that every major serial killer now captured is instantly guaranteed fame and fortune – if not freedom? We can note how those such as Gein and Manson have been elevated to almost god-messiah-like status, so they are not even considered infamous or notorious any more.

It is just such a backdrop of ill-judged publicity which fuels Brite's opening verbal attack in the aforementioned "blueprint for nascent criminals" claim.

In **Copycat**'s case, Foley uses the name of a child-killer, Kurten[1], in (sick) homage when corresponding with another of his hero figures, Cullum; whilst by resolutely imitating previous killers, Foley somehow becomes, accumulatively, an even greater personification of evil than any other murderer.

There are no highly-charged emotions here, no crimes of passion. This is the point. Everything, absolutely everything down to the most minute detail is meticulously planned and then carried out with military precision. The killings are so cold-blooded, so emotionally uninvolving for the killer – this is the true sickness of the acts. That the victims are almost always arbitrarily chosen also reinforces that these atrocities form the very nadir of the human psyche in their randomness – a vacuous emotional response far removed from the genuine warmth, feeling and altruism we look for individually and collectively in a civilised society.

It is only the fact that in no way is Foley portrayed as a sympathetic or attractive character that has saved **Copycat** from any greater controversy for "glamorising" serial killers or trivialising the grotesque aspects to these crimes.

One must also congratulate Amiel for not succumbing to the requisite "woman-in-peril" script and characterisations so often embodied in films of this genre. Instead, he is prepared to transcend such cliché'd notions in search of a rather more engaging and challenging approach to the contentious subject matter.

Hudson's opening scenes are pivotal in firmly establishing her as a three-dimensional character – lecturing perceptively to a university audience to convey her intellectual credentials, vitally important when considering the emotional mess she later turns into.

"What turns on a serial killer is the suffering and death. Serial killers are not a 20th century invention, but we seem to be spawning them in ever-increasing numbers". She continues pointedly: "We spent $8 million on executing Ted Bundy. Wouldn't it have

Copycat

been better to spend the money on studying him scientifically?"

It may be a mite clinical (Hudson after all, is also a lady who not only wipes but covers the toilet seat with tissue paper!), but it suggests that perhaps our extirpation of such killers merely serves as a convenient collective catharsis – the executions in no way increase our understanding of such monsters or aid our attempts to detect future crimes, they are simply a way of gaining our "revenge", our justice for such heinous acts, which in no way progresses our research.

Hudson is later held captive in the university toilets by Cullum and forced to watch the psychopath killing a cop in a harrowing ordeal. It is no surprise then to find Hudson 13 months later encountering such mental anguish – even the simple act of retrieving her morning paper from the hall becomes an act of bravery before hurriedly retreating back into her circular glass apartment.

This too is of symbolic importance as Hudson has written books on serial killers and is recognised as an authority on them, so it should be of no surprise that they are likewise fascinated by her: "I'm their damn pin-up girl," she retorts at one stage and her *quid pro quo* arrangement with Cullum to help capture Foley involves his information/ insight in return for a (used) pair of her panties! It's almost a case of those in glass houses... The circular apartment signals that there will be no corners, no recesses, no hiding places for Hudson, she must confront her inner demons, something she rises to in the circuitous denouement as she this time faces Foley back in the university cubicles – a complete case of *déjà vu* as he, true to form, dispenses with two cops in Cullum fashion.

Whether driven by fear, self-preservation, personal and professional pride or, in fact, all of these, Hudson manages to wound Foley both verbally and physically, allowing sufficient time for her to momentarily escape and force a rooftop confrontation which she survives to Foley's ultimate cost.

So, having cured her agoraphobia in no uncertain terms and dispatched the ghosts which have haunted her, Hudson can move her life forward, though the film's valediction sees Cullum in prison now receiving correspondence from a "new" disciple, who wants to continue the violent line of serial killers – reinforcing the infinite danger which continues unabated. This then, remains the admonitory legacy of **Copycat**.

NOTES
1. Peter Kurten, the "Monster of Düsseldorf", whose murderous career began in 1929, with the stabbing of nine-year-old Rosa Ohliger. His case inspired Fritz Lang's classic **M** (1930).

PROGRESSIVE HORROR

Transcending Genre Boundaries:
"Nightwatch" And "Mute Witness"

Andy Black

"I don't know why the hell they put a key in here."

—**Nightwatch**

"It makes you sick to watch it... and you never forget the look of sheer terror and panic in the victims' eyes as they are about to die."

—**Mute Witness**

Bob Rusk (Barry Foster) is the infamous necktie murderer who is terrorising London. He puts the body of his latest victim in a sack and dumps it in the back of a potato truck, but later realises that his monogrammed tie pin is missing. He returns to the truck where he discovers that the pin is grasped in the victim's fingers. Due to the effects of rigor mortis, he has to break the victim's fingers to free the pin causing a nauseous crack.

—**Frenzy**, Alfred Hitchcock

In the morgue Jens (Kim Bodnia) hacks off his thumb in order to escape the handcuffs restraining him and save his friends from a serial killer.

—**Nightwatch**, Ole Bornedal

The terrified actress Alicia (Barbara Cupisti) stares across from behind the shower curtain at her adjacent friend Laurel (Mary Sellers) as the killer stabs her repeatedly – the victim momentarily mouthing to her friend for help before her body slumps to the cubicle floor and the killer departs.

Stagefright, Michele Soavi

The mute Billy (Marina Sudina) watches in helpless horror as the girl is stabbed to death on a bed – her mouth forming an "o" to scream but is silent as her life ebbs away – staring in sheer terror at Billy who remains in her hiding place.

Mute Witness, Anthony Waller

Forlorn, exposed, vulnerable, impotent – helplessness. Call it what you will but it's that basic, primal feeling of desperately trying to cope with outside influences seemingly beyond your control. It's that struggle for survival, to reach *terra firma* whilst the enveloping quicksands of deceit and subterfuge are tearing at your ankles in order to suck you into the maelstrom of despair.

These are authentic feelings all too readily trampled upon and later discarded in that most problematic of sub-genres, the modern horror thriller.

The majority of trashy and insipid offerings either mistake gore for authentic *frissons*, prefer violence to tension, or substitute special effects for genuine thrills.

Fortunately, within the last four years, there have been isolated, audacious attempts to evoke the cogent atmosphere of what could be termed the "persecution" or

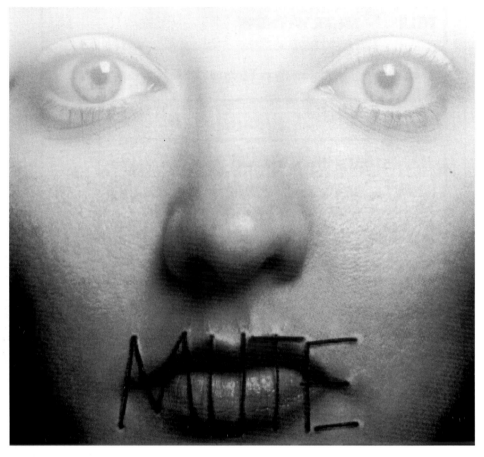

Mute Witness

"victim" thriller, embodying the above-mentioned feelings of helplessness so successfully realised in Alfred Hitchcock's canon.

With Danish director Ole Bornedal's **Nightwatch** (1994) and British director Anthony Waller's **Mute Witness** (1995), we see a welcome reprise of the tension, imaginative plot and character-driven development which Hitchcock made his own, together with a natural sense of affinity for the characters – the situations they find themselves in may be somewhat bizarre but they are all the more captivating for that, and their subsequent flirtation with death makes the scenarios all the more believable.

For Bornedal, the main location is that most unnerving and remote of places, the morgue – and yet it taps into a subconscious fear in all of us, not just the fear of dying but the realisation that this solitary place is one we are all pre-destined to visit in our final journey.

We also see a likeable young law student, Martin (Nikolaj Waldau), inexorably drawn into a web of murder and intrigue as his nightwatchman duties in the morgue link him into an extraordinary chain of serial killings.

Mute Witness

In **Mute Witness** there is a similarly original and taut premise revolving around a mute American make-up artist, Billy (Marina Sudina), who is working on a low-budget horror film in Russia and who finds herself the silent witness to a "real-life" snuff movie in which an unknown girl is brutally killed by two of her male colleagues on the set.

Immediately, both films create an all-pervasive feeling of disquiet and genuine despair, as Martin is faced with mounting circumstantial evidence to implicate him in the heinous crimes and must somehow prove his innocence, whilst Billy must make her other colleagues and police aware that there are two murderers in their midst – and one dead body.

There's an incredible amount of tension and atmosphere created in both films by their respective director's attention to detail, mounting a brace of forceful thrillers filled with escalating suspense.

In **Nightwatch** we see Martin given an ironic "greeting" to his macabre night job by the wily old stager he replaces: "Welcome to Mars," the curt pronouncement. With great relish the octogenarian gives Martin the "tour", explaining how he needs to visit every "key-point" hourly, located in the various chambers in order to reset the alarm system. Martin is instantly perplexed by the ritual – I mean, it's not as if the corpses can get up and leave, is it?

During his first night alone on duty he gets increasingly spooked as he listens intently for any strange noises, watches the alarm on the wall and alternates between this

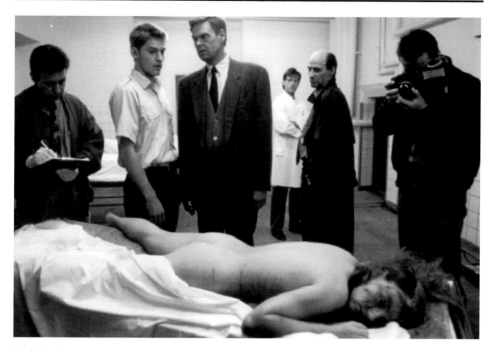

Nightwatch

"silent" study and the raucous rock music which belts out of his ghettoblaster – only forced to turn it off again so he can listen for any slight noise. The ultimate dilemma!

There are also priceless moments from Bornedal as we see Martin totally phased by his timer clock alarm sounding – signalling the start of his "key" rounds and culminating with his careful navigation between the rows of corpses either side to reach the keypoint. His trepidation is perfectly captured here with the "screw" being further tightened after his audible sigh of relief in leaving the corpses – only then forced to return to the morgue in order to turn out the light he has forgotten about.

Each subsequent night on duty becomes a test of nerve for Martin – the morgue alarm sounding (unheard of) only for his investigations to reveal a toe-tag on one corpse reading "Hey Martin", the white shroud rising slowly to reveal... Jens (Kim Bodnia), his practical-joking friend. The next night Martin discovers a gruesome trail of blood leading through the clinical, white corridors to a mutilated cadaver – only for it to have then disappeared by the time he coerces the duty doctor to come and see it.

The *pièce de resistance* however, occurs when having mined the "death" seam, Bornedal then goes for the "sex" accompaniment as Martin and his girlfriend Kalinka (Sofie Graaboel) make love against the morgue wall – an act Martin lives to regret during the next night when a female cadaver is found violated, legs apart and with traces of Martin's semen lying nearby.

In **Mute Witness** Waller goes straight for the jugular with an (apparently) tense scene as a stocking-masked killer stabs his "victim" before her convoluted, theatrical "death" is revealed to be the film-within-a-film being made by Andy (Evan Richards) as a brat American director, aided by Billy's sister Karen (Fay Ripley). "This is not Chekhov

Nightwatch

– you're not the star, you're just another victim," being the frustrated director's riposte.

Waller increases the tension considerably as the day's shooting wraps and as everyone is leaving, Billy has to return alone to retrieve a mask which is required for the next day. Unfortunately, this proves to be a conscientious but unwise move as Billy finds herself locked in the old warehouse building that is the film's set.

The creepy, deserted set's long expansive corridors echo with noises as doors bang in the distance before Billy then hears voices. Having secreted herself onto the set, Billy then witnesses the "snuff" film – the victim's bulbous eyes literally piercing Billy's gaze with sheer terror, blood spraying from the numerous knife wounds inflicted and the victim's mouth forming a "scream" and yet unable to shout it, a mirror of Billy's own helplessness at being unable to fully articulate the horror she has witnessed via words.

As Billy attempts to escape she is heard by the two murderers who then pursue her in an almost unbearable cat and mouse "game" which lasts for over 20 minutes of screen time. So, we see the killers pouncing on a shoe protruding from beneath a curtain, only it's a set prop and not Billy, then we see Billy hang precariously on a ledge over the warehouse store before finally falling into the rubbish bags and murky waters below to try and retrieve the key to open the locked set door.

At one stage, Billy comes face to face with the bloodied victim, who has been thrown into the store – Billy's silent scream counterpointing the victim's similar reaction upon her grisly death. There's also a moment when Waller phases in three rapidly advancing close-ups on Billy's eyes – mirroring an identical camera move which hones in on the victim's wildly terrorised eyes at the point of death.

As Karen and Andy then arrive to save her, they immediately (and unknowingly)

Mute Witness

leave Billy alone with one of the murderers and although she survives, her frustrations only increase when the police arrive and she tries to implicate the killers. Firstly, the bloodied knife she points to isn't the real murder weapon but a substituted stage knife and then, having identified the roll of "snuff" film, it is replayed by the police only to be the day's normal rushes (the killers having also switched rolls).

Mute Witness doesn't have a monopoly on frustration in the face of murder however, as Martin in **Nightwatch** finds himself implicated in the serial killings, partly by the eccentric games of his best friend Jens. Their "challenge" game involves the "loser" forfeiting his freedom by getting married and settling down, but this "innocent" game is corrupted when it is subsequently linked to the sexually-motivated murders. "So we'll play with destiny," is Jens' flippant but later prophetic remark. Jens then screws around with a local prostitute Joyce (Rikke Loise Anderssen) – only he tells her his name is Martin! With friends like this...!

When Joyce causes a scene with Kalinka, her eventual murder implicates the innocent Martin. This whole murder scene is agonisingly played out as – unknown to the killer – Kalinka witnesses the graphic slaying. The killer's white attire and gloves are soon bathed in red as he lifts Joyce's body into the air using his knife, before writing Martin's name in blood to further implicate the beleaguered student.

This is a pivotal moment in the film as we, the audience, discover the killer's identity – the investigating detective on the case, Inspector Wormer (Ulf Pilgaard) – but Kalinka (who doesn't see his face) and Martin remain unaware.

All of which sets up a taut denouement as searching in the morgue records,

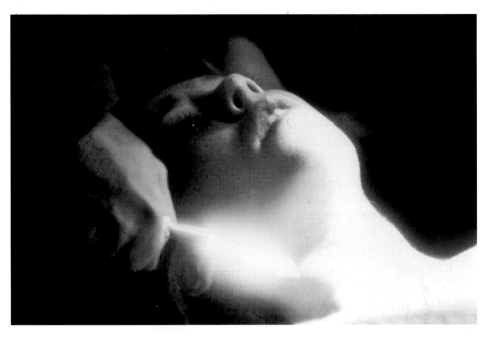

Nightwatch

Martin stumbles across details of Wormer's psychiatric treatment, resulting from his previously documented acts of necrophilia. When Wormer and Kalinka then enter the morgue Wormer convinces Kalinka of her boyfriend's "guilt", only to later give himself away by whistling the song playing on the radio when he murdered Joyce.

Having been tied up by Wormer, Kalinka tries to escape and get help by crawling over the morgue floor – now littered with broken glass – managing to set off the alarm and alert Jens, whose entrance is curtailed by Wormer's baseball bat blow to the head; he awakens later to find himself handcuffed.

The squirm-inducing moment as Jens hacks off his thumb with a saw in order to escape is highly effective for the viewer, and even more so for his friends as he appears just in time to shoot Wormer – now hovering menacingly over Martin and Kalinka with a bone-saw revving for action.

It's a highly-charged climax to a gripping film with the suspense generated by the audience knowing the killer's identity, unlike Martin and Kalinka until it is almost too late. Indeed, Kalinka's realisation of the killer's identity at the precise moment that she is locked in a room with him is superbly handled and milked for maximum shock value.

There's also the perplexing question of identity/mistaken identity as Jens plays his name games with Joyce with disastrous results, and Wormer's own calculated attempts to conceal his crimes by using Martin as a decoy/scapegoat enable him to finish his killings and yet satisfy the public demand for a killer to be brought to "justice".

Bornedal even concludes **Nightwatch** with some ironic identity humour as Martin and Kalinka, Jens and Lotte (Lotte Anderson) take part in a joint wedding ceremony, only for the vicar to mix up the identities of the couples marrying! (It will be interesting to see how this year's British remake starring Ewan McGregor of **Trainspotting** notoriety is received).

There is no such black humour residing in **Mute Witness** as Billy is forced to shoulder her terrible burden and literally "suffer in silence"; though the tension is in some way dissipated by the sub-plot which although adding intrigue, detracts from Billy's personal trauma as Alex Guiness' "Reaper" figure appears from the shadows to add an organised crime, KGB and police corruption involvement to the proceedings.

Guiness as the Russian ganglord is revealed to be the master behind an international trade in snuff and porn films with illegal immigrants providing the unfortunate participants.

The climactic chase scenes involve the police executing the two killers to conceal their crimes whilst an undercover policeman, Larsen (Oleg Jankowskij), materialises to help Billy to escape the Reaper's clutches. In a fraught sequence Billy is "gunned" down, only to later reveal the bullet-proof jacket and blood squabs as she escapes unharmed – unlike the unfortunate Larsen who, whilst forcing a gagged criminal into his car, fails to notice Billy's concern at the terror in the man's eyes, all too appropriate as seconds later an incendiary device blows Larsen and the car to smithereens.

It's an explosive finale for sure and it contrasts vividly with the almost "restrained" tone which has preceded it – all "silent" suffering and subterfuge, an intriguing variant on 1967's **Wait Until Dark** where on that occasion a blind Audrey Hepburn is terrorised in her apartment by a killer gang searching for a doll containing heroin.

In the case of both **Nightwatch** and **Mute Witness**, it is the convincing communication of helplessness, of being unable to control one's destiny, which captures the raw emotion and shredded nerves which constitute the authentic horror thriller.

FEMALE VAMPIRES

Girl Power From The Crypt

Bev Zalcock

INTRODUCTION

Although horror is not an obvious genre for locating positive representations of women, the very marked presence of the female vampire in the ranks of the monster movie makes it a rich vein to tap when searching for examples of cinematic "girl power".

Rampant females in the exploitation picture generally seem to denote an overt castration threat rather than a positive image, and the vampire picture is no different in this respect. As with other genres, such as juvenile delinquent, biker and prison movies, females on the rampage are intended to feed directly into the male fantasy. Hence the skimpy attire, the fetish gear and the sex and violence scenarios that characterise such films. And the inevitable denouement which guarantees the containment of the transgressive female, be it by way of marriage, imprisonment or a stake through the heart.

In a sense, horror more than any of the other exploitation genres, with its monsters of the imagination, feeds fantasy and configures fear in a very direct way. With its linking of sex and death, horror taps into the unconscious and is associated with surrealism and the fantastic in both literature and cinema. Desire becomes the primary *mise-en-scène* within the realm of the supernatural and, as David Pirie observes in his excellent book *The Vampire Cinema*[1], there is a strong cultural connection between our perception of sex and the supernatural. Pirie cites an article by Susan Sontag written in 1967 entitled "The Pornographic Imagination"[2] in which she locates the fantastical realm of the human imagination as the site in which the two are classically connected.

Sontag's article is instructive, occupying as it does a historical position between the libertarian impulse of the swinging '60s (sex and drugs and rock 'n' roll) and the impending critique of patriarchy (with its colonising of the female) by the Women's Movement in the '70s. In this influential article, Sontag locates pornography as endemic to the unconscious and discusses its articulation in literature, using the writings of Sade, Bataille and Réage to illustrate her points. Sontag's arguments connect with the cinema, as when she refers to Luis Bunuel's **L'Age D'Or** (1930), which like the writing of Bataille "charts the journey of estrangement of the self from the self".[3] As such, her article provides a useful starting point for a consideration of what is at stake in the vampire-sex film of the '70s. In fact her description of the nineteenth century 'libertine pot-boilers' coming out of France invokes many of the films produced by the Hammer Studio throughout the '60s: "...typically situated in a fantasy England, populated by brutal aristocrats with enormous sexual equipment and violent tastes along the axis of sado-masochism".[4] Subsequently her account of *The Story Of O* is vividly evocative of the *mise-en-scène* of the vampire films made by French director Jean Rollin: "...that conveniently isolated château, luxuriously furnished and lavishly staffed with servants, where a clique of rich men congregate and to which women are brought as virtual slaves, to be objects, shared in common of men's brutal and inventive lust. There are whips and chains, masks worn by the men when the women are admitted to their presence, great fires burning in the hearth..."[5]

Although quite distinctive in style the vampire films of the Hammer studio and those of *auteur* Jean Rollin do both connect with the pornographic imagination that Sontag is describing. As we shall see there are a number of differently orientated vampire films, from surrealist to gothic, from soft core to gore. What they all share is an interest in sado-masochism; a lust for power and desire for sex.

With the demise of The Hays Code throughout the '60s and the social changes which led to a decline in the Church's authority in the west, the issue of censorship became the focus of debates around morality. In popular culture sex and violence were increasingly graphic and explicit. To circumvent film censorship, Hammer marketed lurid images of female nudity and blood lust as supernatural rather than realist. As we've seen, exploitation became sexploitation, and horror was fast becoming a favoured genre. The potential for the vampire picture to supply sexy images was being realised. The fascination for the vampire that had been revived in the literature on nineteenth century Europe found a visual counterpart in twentieth century cinema. The connection between extreme erotic experience and death, what Bataille describes as "living through excess" was the very staple of the vampire picture. In Bataille's words: "People who want to be receptive to pleasure but keep horror at bay are misguided. Horror excites desire."[6]

SOURCES OF THE VAMPIRE

Alfred, Lord Byron, the personification of the gothic romantic hero, had in 1816 written an outline for a story called *The Vampyre*. His former companion, John Polidori, completed it three years later. The story features a glowering vampire who is irresistibly attractive named Lord Ruthven, obviously based on Byron. It is believed to have influenced Bram Stoker. Stoker's *Dracula* (1897) was a key source for early vampire films and remains hugely influential. Another seminal literary source was J Sheridan Le Fanu's novella *Carmilla* (1871) which one hundred years later was to provide the inspiration for the lesbian vampire film.

Vampire legend is based to some extent in historical fact. Two blood-swilling serial killers, one male and one female, whose acts of sadistic torture are shrouded in the mists of fifteenth and sixteenth century Europe, give credence to the vampire novels. The fictional Dracula is based on Vlad Dracul, known as Vlad the Impaler, ruler of the Rumanian province of Wallachia in the latter half of the fifteenth century. Supposedly he had a penchant for impaling his enemies alive and watching them die. Apart from perfecting the art of murder and mutilation, he frequently drank the blood of his victims. The second real-life vampire was The Countess Elisabeth Bathory, born in 1560. She tortured and murdered over six hundred girls during her regime and drank their blood in the belief that it would keep her young and beautiful. Finally she was sentenced to death and bricked up in her castle.[7]

A number of female vampire films use Bathory as their model, including Hammer's **Countess Dracula** (1971), Harry Kumel's **Daughters of Darkness** (1970), Rollin's **Requiem Pour Un Vampire** (1971), Jorge Grau's **Ceremonia Sangrienta** (1972), and the major segment of Walerian Borowczyk's **Immoral Tales** (1974). The Countess' exploits hook into the notion of the castrating female and her particular proclivities, the torture and draining of the blood of young virgins, suggest sexual perversion. In cinematic terms she's a great ghoul.

A much more sympathetic female vampire is provided by Le Fanu's *Carmilla*. Carmilla the central character is, like Bathory, a Countess – the Countess Millarca

Immoral Tales

Karnstein, who reappears a hundred and fifty years after her death. Unlike Elisabeth Bathory who is a hardline sadist, Carmilla is a soft and seductive lesbian, who is erotically drawn to her victims (young girls by choice) and who whispers sweet nothings as she bites their breasts. The character of Carmilla Karnstein is the key source for the early '70s Hammer trilogy **The Vampire Lovers** (1970), **Lust For A Vampire** (1971) and **Twins Of Evil** (1971). It is to Hammer's long vampire cycle that I now want to turn.

FROM COSTUME MELODRAMA TO HAMMER HORROR

Costume melodrama was a staple of the British filmgoers' diet throughout the war and afterwards. The Gainsborough Studio produced a popular costume cycle aimed at the women's audience, beginning in the early '40s. Titles included **Fanny By Gaslight** (1944), **Madonna Of The Seven Moons** (1944) and **The Wicked Lady** (1945). In her examination of Gainsborough's output Sue Harper observes: "The films have a rich visual texture and evince a preoccupation with the sexual mores and lifestyle of the upper reaches of the landed classes; they all contain female protagonists ... who actively seek sexual pleasure".[8] The preoccupations with the landed gentry, which drew on populist notions of rural Britain was also a feature of melodramas coming out of other British studios; Powell and Pressburger's Archer's production **Gone To Earth** (1950) is typical.[9] Shot in evocative technicolor in the Shropshire countryside, the film is based on a novel by Mary Webb and tells of the love-hate relationship between a young wild country lass and a brutal good-looking lord of the manor. With its hunt scenes and heaving cleavage, it prefigures the scenarios of the Hammer studio, which combined elements of the costume melodrama with a much darker tradition.

DRACULA'S DAUGHTER

The *frisson* of the lesbian sub-text was already present in Universal Studio's **Dracula's Daughter** (1936), the official sequel to Tod Browning's **Dracula** (1931) which had starred Bela Lugosi five years earlier. Based on Stoker's *Dracula*, Lugosi played the Count as charming but with a sadistic edge. Less popular than **Frankenstein**, another Universal horror title released a year later, it took a while for the follow-up to arrive. There were few precedents for the female vampire film. A silent American film in 1912 called **The Reincarnation Of Karma** had Rosemary Thebe playing an Indian dancing girl who is metamorphosed into a ten-foot serpent when she is cursed by the high priest of The Temple of Innocent Manhood. In a similar vein, an early British short **The Vampire** (1913) has another Indian girl turned into a snake and sink her fangs into the man who shoots her. Two years later in **Heba The Snake Woman** the pattern is repeated, except the woman-turned-snake is in this instance an Aztec. These films set the trend for the female vampire as foreign and exotic.

In **Dracula's Daughter**, Gloria Holden plays a Hungarian Countess, Marya Zaleska, who wrestles with her nature as a vampire. As David Pirie observes: "This notion of the schizoid female vampire was later utilised to exemplify and caricature the male polarisation of woman into goddess and animal."[10] The Countess in desperation turns to a stiff upper-lipped English psychiatrist to cure her of her blood lust. He fails, however, and she is reduced to picking up young girls in Chelsea with the help of her manservant.

One young street girl is bribed to leave her night time haunts to pose as a model for the Countess in her Curzon Street studio. There she is hastily plied with refreshment and instructed to remove her blouse. As her gaze locks with the female vampire she asks in a panicky voice: "Why are you looking at me like that?". But it's too late to retreat and she's duly hypnotised, ravished and dispatched by the hungry Countess.

Shot in Expressionist style with low key lights and strange angles, **Dracula's Daughter** bears all the hallmarks of the vampire films of the period. The evocative black and white photography of **Dracula** and **Dracula's Daughter**, and the imaginative direction of Siodmak's **Son Of Dracula** (1943) with Lon Chaney Jnr, make the vampire offerings of Universal classics. But the days of vampires as monsters were numbered and as the '40s progressed, the Hollywood vampire cycle tailed off, making way for a new clutch of cold war mutants. Hammer, as we have seen, revived the vampire film in the late '50s.

HAMMER'S HORROR

Hammer studio began its popular horror cycle in 1957 with **The Curse Of Frankenstein** and followed up one year later with **The Horror Of Dracula**; both features starring tall, dark and handsome Christopher Lee. The Stoker-influenced vampire films did well at the box office throughout the sixties with titles like **The Brides Of Dracula** (Terence Fisher, 1960), **Kiss Of The Vampire** (Don Sharpe, 1963), **Dracula, Prince Of Darkness** (Terence Fisher, 1966), **Dracula Has Risen From The Grave** (Freddie Francis, 1969), **Taste The Blood Of Dracula** (Peter Sasdy, 1970) and **The Scars Of Dracula** (Roy Ward Baker, 1970). All the films dealt with the struggle between good and evil with archetypical good, tight-lipped vampire hunter Van Helsing (absent only from **Kiss Of The Vampire**), portrayed by Peter Cushing, often up against the charmingly wicked vampire Dracula played to perfection by Christopher Lee, proving that the devil has much more fun.

This cycle was typically costume drama edged with horror and set in lavish baronial halls, village taverns and moonlit woods. For a decade the formula was a winning one but it began to pall and needed a new ingredient to spice it up. Although '60s vampire films featured the decadent lord of the manor and the virginal village girl as well as having its share of female vampires, what was missing was explicit sexual content. By the early '70s the sex vampire was installed. This added a *frisson* to the already luridly realised melodramas and suggested more obvious deviance and desire. Vampirism as sado-masochism was mooted in **The Satanic Rites Of Dracula** (Alan Gibson, 1973), where in an early scene we have a bevy of female vampires chained to the walls in a cellar. These strumpets hiss and show their fangs in a thoroughly wanton manner. When an innocent gentleman tries to help them he is warned off with the words: "Don't touch them, they are vampires!", implying of course that they are unspeakable perverts, or vectors of venereal disease. The tradition of the female vampire as sexually perverted is as enduring as vampire cinema itself.

THE CARMILLA TRILOGY

Cashing in on the titillating and transgressive female vampire, Hammer revived its by then flagging genre with a '70s trilogy in which deviant women were centre-frame. Based on Le Fanu's novella *Carmilla*, the films offered female nudity and lesbian sex. A low-budget British horror film made in 1969, **Incense For The Damned** (aka **The Bloodsuckers**), which dealt tangentially with vampirism had made an overt connection between male impotence and the female vampire. In the film, Richard, a young English academic is seduced by Chriseis, a Greek vampire and initiated into psychedelically induced sex orgies. His impotence is shown as the root cause of his vulnerability to the predatory female and throughout the film it is female sexuality that is foregrounded.

In the subsequent Hammer female vampire cycle, it is obvious that it is women who possess sexual energy and drive. Male characters are simply either vulnerable or punitive – intent on closing down the threat. In Le Fanu's novel it is the fathers, the keepers of the law who are cast in the role of vampire hunters. Hammer's first film in the cycle **The Vampire Lovers** (directed by Roy Ward Baker) is fairly faithful to the book. As in the novella, the action takes place in Styria, near a small village, perched beneath the shadow of the ruined castle of the Karnstein family. The pre-title sequence, like so many Hammer horrors, is lurid and ghoulish, involving the decapitation of a female vampire.

Throughout the sequence we hear a male voice-over narration of events leading up to the beheading. We learn that the small group of vampire hunters are men. They seek to destroy the polymorphously perverse, sexually active female vampires. In her discussion of **Daughters Of Darkness** Carol Jenks has remarked that in **The Vampire Lovers** (and in fact it is true of all three films in the trilogy) there lurks a dark cloaked man, most plausibly the Count Karnstein, an archetypical Dracula character who stands on the sidelines watching and by implication controlling events.[11] The piercing red-eyed gaze of this somewhat extraneous character serves to guarantee the ultimate power of the male. Ironically the presence of this character with his black cape and slicked back hair is the most reassuring element of these films, at least for male audiences, in that he ensures that the carnivalesque disarray and sexual anarchy of the female vampires – in which the real horror of the film resides – is kept in check.

The female on female desire that characterises **The Vampire Lovers** is conveyed early on at the ball when Laura, a young innocent (Bertha in the novel), is informed by her beau Karl that the newly arrived beauty Marcilla, is eyeing her and not him. Soon

The Vampire Lovers

enough, Marcilla is seducing Laura in her bedroom, stroking her hair and kissing her breasts, sending Laura into an erotic monochrome fantasy which recalls Roger Vadim's surrealistic, Carmilla-inspired film **Blood And Roses** (1960). Vadim's film is narrated from Carmilla's point of view and there is a moment too in **The Vampire Lovers** where the camera, in a subjective shot, constructs Carmilla's point of view for the audience. Throughout the episode, Carmilla's approach to Laura is seductive rather that violent. "I shall never leave you my dearest Laura," she whispers tenderly as she sucks the life blood from her.

In the second part of the film Carmilla is installed into a new household where Emma (Laura in the book), a naïve young girl with a periodically absent English father, becomes Carmilla's next object of desire. We see the girls flirting together in the bedroom, swapping gowns and slipping in and out of negligées, followed by more monochrome erotic dreams – desire laced with danger – and much nuzzling of necks. Breakfasts are a languorous affair with no one really hungry – until the governess gets suspicious. Inevitably she is initiated into the nocturnal romps and a lesbian triangle is formed with much bodice ripping and meaningful looks.

Carmilla is a hypnotic influence on the household. She declares her love for Emma – "You'll always be safe as long as you're with me" – mocks heterosexual romance, laughing hysterically at Emma's reading matter, and shrinks from passing funerals. Apart from an occasional nocturnal bloodletting in the village, everything seems

The Vampire Lovers

perfect. Perfect that is until the fathers intervene. At one point there is a cut away to the watching male vampire and soon enough men start arriving with stakes. Patriarchal law appears to be the sole impediment to the lesbian arcadia. In the end the absent father and intermittent boyfriend return to close it all down. In the novel the young girl Laura sounds somewhat dazed and disappointed that it's all come to an end and, as she embarks on a historical trip around Europe with her father, we can understand why.

The lesbian erotic focus is somewhat blurred in the second film of the trilogy, **Lust For A Vampire** (directed by Jimmy Sangster). By way of a compromise it posits a heterosexual romance at the centre of the narrative between Carmilla and a writer turned schoolmaster called LeStrange (a fictional representation of Le Fanu himself). The shift from the female on female desire of the novella actually jars, although it lacks the bare-faced bad faith of Jesus Franco's 1973 porn film **The Barebreasted Countess** (aka **Female Vampire**) in which a fetishised female vampire *fellates* her male victims to death.

In **Lust For A Vampire** Carmilla makes love to the schoolmaster to prove she is not a vampire. At various intervals during this explicit scene, we see the vampire resisting the temptation to puncture the man's neck. Back in his room the besotted LeStrange falls into a reverie where he pictures his beloved Mircalla (for thus she is now named) in washes of acid colour and slow motion, going down on him to the strains of an awful early '70s ditty entitled "Strange Love".

While **Lust For A Vampire** has strayed some way from the original novel, it does reference *Carmilla* (1688–1710) and a good deal of the action is set at the Karnstein castle. The pre-title sequence is a lurid affair in which Carmilla is resurrected by sacrificial

female blood and arises from her coffin naked and bloody. Like **The Vampire Lovers** it's set in Styria but the surrounding countryside suggests a location closer to home. On the plus side most of the action takes place in a finishing school for young ladies which coincidentally is situated adjacent to the Karnstein castle. The girls' school, in narrative terms, provides rich pickings for young Mircalla and this includes fun and frolics at the graeco-roman dance class (swirling taffeta and a harp accompaniment), moonlit skinny-dipping, and nocturnal activities in the bedrooms. It's all divinely decadent but the body count begins to get out of hand and the villagers – plus a handy cardinal – march on the castle and burn it down.

Last of the Hammer trilogy, **Twins Of Evil** (directed by John Hough) departs even further than **Lust For A Vampire** from the 'Carmilla' source but retains the female interest. The pre-title sequence shows the Karnstein castle, in whose shadows a group of witch hunters gallop to a sub-Ennio Morricone soundtrack. As its central premise the film takes the internal struggle between good and evil and personifies these qualities in the twins Maria and Freda. These unfortunate girls are the nieces and wards of Gustav Weill (Peter Cushing) puritan and witch hunter extraordinaire. On their arrival, Cushing berates the girls for their low-cut green velvet costumes and ostentatiously plumed hats. Though it's months since their parents died, he insists they wear black. Life is a stark affair at the Weill household and it's no wonder that Freda, the good-time girl of the two, seeks richer pastures at the castle Karnstein. Meanwhile the present-day Count, a libertine who seeks more and more sexual excitement, is wearying of the S/M charades being staged for his after dinner entertainment. One evening, angry and frustrated, he offers one of his village girls up as a blood sacrifice to Satan. In so doing he awakes the spirit of Carmilla, the family heirloom, and succumbs to her seductive sucking. Excited at joining the ranks of the undead and having no mirror reflection, the Count proceeds to initiate Freda, the bad twin, into the ways of the vampire.

Freda relishes the opportunity of some wicked action and gleefully she and the Count torment another young village girl before Freda stabs her to death. The implication of kinky sex in this *tableau à trois* is unmistakable and the film explores a number of issues relating to both sexual repression (represented by Gustav Weill) and sexual excess (represented by the Count). Weill and the black garbed brotherhood persecute and kill young independent women – those who live alone or will not marry – as witches. In the film their self-righteousness and misogyny are clearly a result of their repressed lives. Freda who rejects the role imposed on her by family and church alike seeks liberation through sexual gratification, leaving the house nightly to hang out with the decadent aristocrat. But she goes too far and sells her soul. Maria the good and obedient twin, clearly does not go far enough and clutches her rosary in a panic at night, while Freda is out gratifying her blood lust.

Throughout the film there's plenty of swashbuckling from the Count and tight-lipped moralising from Gustav Weill. The middle ground is occupied by Antoine, the schoolmaster who falls under Freda's spell but finally realises – almost too late as Maria is about to be burnt at the stake – that it's better to be good than to submit to the delicious pleasures of evil. Antoine rescues Maria in the nick of time and swiftly substitutes her as his object of desire, although he can actually only tell them apart by their reaction to a raised cross.

The film concludes with the proposition that the devil has all the best tunes. There's much more cleavage and even some brief full-frontal shots at the castle Karnstein

and, although Freda has been summarily dispatched, the Countess Carmilla still lurks about in the vault. Lurking too is the black cloaked Dracula figure who has appeared in all three of the films. His role has been to oversee the action as a kind of omnipotent master of ceremonies. Surplus to plot requirements one can only assume he is either – as Carol Jenks has suggested – the personification of the controlling male gaze; or a kind of Hammer trademark, the vampire as logo. At all events it is the female vampire that proves to be the most active and inspirational in the 'Carmilla' trilogy and particularly in **The Vampire Lovers** (and with diminishing returns in **Lust For A Vampire** and **Twins Of Evil**) there is a strong sense of a females-only 'no go' zone, the wild zone, which as we have seen elsewhere no man may enter.[12]

THE FEMALE VAMPIRE AS SADIST

There is a spate of films in the '70s that use as their model for the female vampire, the bloody Countess, Elisabeth Bathory. Hammer's one offering, **Countess Dracula** (Peter Sasdy, 1970), stars Ingrid Pitt as the Countess Nadasdy; Pitt also played Carmilla in **The Vampire Lovers**. **Countess Dracula** includes (literally) a blood bath and plenty of blood letting – as when the serving maid is accidentally cut and her blood spurts out, spattering the Countess' face – but there is no actual vampire action. As with the 'Carmilla' cycle there's plenty of heaving cleavage, exotic female flesh (this film features a belly dancer) and a cut away full-frontal shot now and again to relieve the somewhat tedious narrative. The film is more a Jekyll and Hyde than vampire film; the Countess Elisabeth transforms into a nubile girl after she's bathed in the blood of a virgin but when the spell wears off she's more raddled and gruesome than ever.

Countess Dracula is notable for its construction of period detail. The title sequence consists of a series of medieval woodcuts, providing a sense of historical authenticity to the story that follows. Music, dance and street theatre richly costumed and choreographed make for an atmospheric backdrop but the female characters lack the polymorphous perversity that gives the Carmilla films their frisson. The Countess in **Countess Dracula** desires young virgins solely for their blood, to enable her to once again assume the mantle of youth and marry a handsome young army officer. As such the film is crucially about female menstruation (fertility) linked to heterosexual desirability. Unlike Carmilla with her freewheeling sexual energy, the Countess Nadasdy is constrained by the strict requirements of heteropatriarchy – stay young and beautiful if you want to be loved.

Other versions of the Elisabeth Bathory story are much more transgressive, casting the Countess as either a bisexual or a lesbian. In Harry Kumel's **Daughters Of Darkness** she is fundamentally hostile to men. In **the Hunger** (Tony Scott, 1983) she's a power-hungry woman who can swing both ways, using sex among her repertoire of charms to get what she needs. In both films the figure of Elisabeth Bathory becomes the objective correlative for sadism, lesbian chic, sado-masochism and death. As such the Bathory films are much more identifiable with the pornographic imagination that Sontag has defined in her article, than is the lesbian-liberational 'Carmilla' cycle.

In Jean Rollin's **Requiem Pour Un Vampire** (France, 1971) for example, the chamber of horrors in the castle dungeon where two young innocents stray is set up for a bondage scene. The female vampire, who at first sight appears to be in charge, is dressed in a man's suit and cloak and oversees the action which is not the perverse pleasure and pain the film has promised but a standard soft core sex scene, inserted it would seem against Rollin's will by his producer.[13]

Countess Dracula

The legend of Elisabeth Bathory spans a range of cinemas. On the low-budget end Rollin's surrealist, soft core independently made features are the most bizarre, on the other end of the spectrum the star-studded Hollywood production **The Hunger** is so mainstream that it resembles an expanded music video. Somewhere in between is **Daughters Of Darkness**, basically a European art house movie made by Belgian film theorist Harry Kumel. Both his film and **The Hunger** use a famous continental actress in the role of the Countess. In **Daughters Of Darkness** it is Delphine Seyrig, in **The Hunger**, Catherine Deneuve.

As we have already seen, the tradition of casting the female vampire as foreign and hence exotic can be traced back to silent cinema at the beginning of the century. In **Dracula's Daughter** the female vampire is an erotic *émigrée*, and Carmilla in the Hammer films is played by Ingrid Pitt and Yutte Stensgaard respectively. In **Daughters Of Darkness** the central heterosexual couple are under threat both from within and without. Stephan is a rich old man's toy boy, a fact he conceals from his new young bride Valerie. Deceived and betrayed by Stephan, Valerie ultimately succumbs to the hypnotic charms of The Countess Elisabeth Bathory. Set in a modern-day Ostend, bleak and forbidding under the grey winter skies, the film is atmospheric and plotted like a tarantella. Colour is crucial and the characters change clothes from red, to black, to white (silver) as formally as they change partners. The action is set against the backdrop of an almost deserted gothic-style hotel, which has the fading elegance of a nineteenth century costume ball.

The Countess, and her servant/lover Ilona mingle with Stephan and Valerie, the

Daughters Of Darkness

only other couple, indeed the only other guests, in the hotel. Tripping the light fantastic, Elisabeth begins to weave her spell around the newly-weds. She seduces Stephan with ease, picking up on his sadistic bent – he is, it seems, turned on by ideas of the torture and death of young girls – but it is actually Valerie who she is most interested in. Valerie is a much more sympathetic character and appears unimpressed by stories of sadism. She is finally seduced by the Countess but she puts up a strong resistance. The Countess is totally controlling and impossible to resist. Her piercing gaze fixes her prey and she radiates a 'frozen sparkle'.[14] Seyrig's cool and enigmatic beauty captures to perfection the power and fascination of a truly ruthless woman. She steals the show – but she's supposed to; characters, camera and audience alike have eyes only for her.

Catherine Deneuve as the aristocratic Miriam in **The Hunger** has a similar impact. Based on a novel by Whitley Streiber and directed by Tony Scott (who had made his name as a director of commercials – and it shows), the film is set in contemporary New York City and is in part a showcase for early '80s urban chic. The title sequence is set in a nightclub where a new wave band (Bauhaus), pale and thin with burning eyes, clad in bondage gear, sing a punk anthem to the undead. Back in their huge uptown apartment Miriam and her husband John (David Bowie) play with their respective victims and the sex games take on a lethal edge as they rip their jugulars with the sharpened

The Hunger

Egyptian oules they both wear around their necks.

Smart clothes, stylish interiors and low-key lighting set the mark on the film's visual style. It's a cool, unruffled and aesthetic lifestyle for the vampires. They play chamber music with the neighbours' teenage girl and an aura of elegance cushions them from the real world. That is until John starts into an accelerated aging process and no amount of fresh human blood can save him. When he is almost dead, Deneuve dispatches him to the attic which is littered with the coffins of all her former, now moribund, lovers.

Deneuve, by now clearly a Bathory style character, proves to be a smooth operator, and cool as ice she lures Sara Roberts (Susan Sarandon) into the bedroom, after one glass of dubious sherry and four or five chords on the piano. Sarandon, ready to play sex slave to Deneuve's dominatrix, writhes on silk sheets while the blood is drained from her body. The scene in which Miriam vamps Sara is a celebrated one. All swirling drapes and operetta, it has attained a lesbian cult following. But perhaps the most dramatic scene in the film is where the undead in the attic rise up out of their coffins with (more) drapes and doves flying about, in a fright-night style orgy of death. As in **Daughters Of Darkness**, there is a coda. We see Sara taking over the role of the rich Countess in a strikingly similar way to that in which Valerie has appropriated the position of Elisabeth Bathory. What this all goes to show is that evil can never be destroyed, it is simply transferred. Elisabeth Bathory lives!

EUROPEAN VAMPIRES
Jean Rollin, master of erotic horror, resides at the artistic end of the European soft-core spectrum by virtue of his visual flair and an *avant-garde* approach to narrative which gives

Female Vampire

his films a dreamlike, surrealistic feel. At the sleazier end of the market are the female vampire films of Italian director Jesus Franco, including **Vampyros Lesbos** (1970), **La Fille De Dracula** (1971), and the aforementioned **Female Vampire**. Franco, whose films are aimed at a Euro-porn market, attempted to make a serious vampire film and persuaded Christopher Lee and Klaus Kinski to appear in his version of Bram Stoker's *Dracula*, called **Count Dracula** (1971), but it was not a critical success. Between Rollin's films and Franco's we can place Spanish director Joseph Larraz's **Vampyres** (1975) which was filmed in England and inadvertently turns into something of a parody of the Hammer vampire movies. In the film a nice young couple set up their holiday caravan in the grounds of a deserted mansion where all variety of sexual orgy are taking place. In both Franco's and Larraz's films the function of the female vampires is to provide titillating lesbian sex for straight male audiences. Jean Rollin, on the other hand, has a different agenda, in spite of the fact that he is frequently – and inappropriately – compared with Franco. In an interview he explains his approach to film making and his motives for using the female vampire as central to all his films: "Maybe it's (also) got something to do with my nature and the nature of my films. A vampire is like an animal, a predator – wild, emotional, naïve, primitive, sensual, not too concerned with logic, driven by emotions, but also very aesthetic and beautiful, and these are terms also often used when my films are being described...."[15]

Hailed by many critics as an *auteur*, Rollin's films are a bizarre mix of Expressionist, surrealist and pulp influences. His takes are long, his plots are barely coherent but the power of his imagery – his angles, his composition and his use of colour – conveys an atmosphere of the uncanny. Daniel Bird, in an appreciation of Rollin's work,

Vampyres

makes the following observations: "The trilogy **La Vampire Nue** (1969), **Le Frisson Des Vampires** (1970) and **Requiem Pour Un Vampire** (1971) have the look of a comic strip, their interiors drowned in colourful spotlights, integrating them into his flat mosaic of cobalt blue and scarlet ..."[16] Bird also cites the 'chaotic collages' of Max Ernst as an influence and describes Rollin's *oeuvre* as 'pulp gothic'. Since Rollin was making his female vampire trilogy at approximately the same time that Hammer produced theirs, it's worth discussing his films in some detail.

In **La Vampire Nue** the paraphernalia of erotic bondage predominates, with female vampires sporting long gold fingernails, and dressed in chains and leather. Outside in the night time city, men in tuxedos, wearing animal masks, pursue a lone woman through deserted streets. The plot, which is loose and meandering, is always subservient to the ritualistic *mise-en-scène* (this is ostensibly a science fiction fantasy) with a richly textured iconography of velvets, candelabra and taboo *objets d'art*. Oscillating between an Expressionist mood of high seriousness and seedy schlock, the female vampires in fetish gear and the serving wenches in diaphanous drapes pose and posture for the camera. In one sequence a tormented artist fondles his naked model between brush strokes, providing a perfect image for the film's uncomfortable quandary.

Le Frisson Des Vampires is more accomplished, and celebrated by some as Rollin's best and most atmospheric film. There are plenty of powerful female characters, vampires and servants alike, who conspire to undermine the relationship of the newly-wed couple in peril, Isabelle and Anthony. With an erratic narrative development, there are some moving, scary and erotic scenes, among them the appearance of the female vampire Isolte from out of the grandfather clock. Isolte's quest is to seduce Isabelle and she

returns the next night, emerging from out of the chimney. Again while the serving maids make love on a fur-lined bed, Isolte, dressed as a dominatrix in chain mail tunic and leather boots, appears in the graveyard at the gates of the castle. Isabelle is seduced by the apparition and has sex in the moonlight with the female vampire, while Anthony languishes in his bed on his wedding night. The film accumulates its fantastic moods using elemental effects, smoke, wind and fire, a languorous pace and a musical score of drug induced rock'n'roll. Isolte as the focal female vampire is tall and thin, pale and wan and completely erotic. Rollin's female vampires, particularly the dominatrix, are invariably impressive. The visual highlight of his first vampire feature **Le Viol Du Vampire** (1967), filmed in black and white, is the vampire queen who emerges from the sea clad in leather with cloak, belts, buckles, straps and fringes. Unlike the pale snake-like Isolte, the vampire queen is stocky and black. She licks blood off the blade of her great dagger with relish and clearly enjoys the attentions of her entourage of young female vampires.

In all Rollin's films, the vampires are doomed and there is an elegiac quality even in the midst of sex and violence. Isolte, near the end of **Le Frisson Des Vampires**, pulls Isabelle to her breasts out of which protrude sharp spikes. And desperate for blood in the final moments of the film she is reduced to drinking the blood from a vein in her own wrist. It is a sight more sad than horrible and is one of the most powerful images that vampire cinema has to offer.

Requiem Pour Un Vampire, the third film in the trilogy, is by far the most surreal, with a plot that meanders like automatic writing. Rollin describes the process by which he wrote the film as follows: "I had some ideas and put them down in the screenplay for no special reason. First the clowns, then the motorcycle and the ideas of the girls playing the piano in the cemetery. The first vision I had was two clowns playing piano in a cemetery. I have never seen that in a film before and I *wanted* to see it, so I just wrote it in. Afterwards I re-used the image of the clown in other films as some sort of quotation. I like that; I often make references to my earlier films. It connects dreams and stories like a construction system and the audience can make their own thing out of it."[17] In the pre-title sequence of **Requiem** we see two female clowns, one dressed as Harlequin, the other as Coco, firing guns out of the back window of an escaping car. The sequence is composed of a number of long takes and the camera is set up at a distance. The car crashes, the girls bail out and there follows some spectacular shots of the car exploding in flames. The reason for the shoot out is never explained and thereafter we see the girls wandering, seemingly aimlessly, around the French countryside. During this time various strange incidents occur; they steal a motorbike and rest up in a graveyard, where one of them is accidentally almost buried alive in an open grave. They stare, in big close-up, at a colony of vampire bats and then they arrive at a castle. Hardly a word has been spoken. It is as though the two young women are wandering in a dream. The beauty of the landscape and the slow pace of the film helps to construct this sense of unreality.

In the castle a female vampire called Erica and her attendant Louise, with three ragamuffin men in tow, lead the clowns down into the basement. The dungeon is a site of sadism, bondage and depravity and the three roughs proceed to sexually assault the various women who are chained to the prison walls. This pornographic episode was, according to Rollin, not of his choosing. He blames the scene on his producer: "Lionel (Wallman) obliged me to put some sex scenes in **Requiem** ...during the dungeon sequence. I told him I wasn't too fond of that kind of thing."[18]

It emerges that the young women, though lovers, are technically virgins and their services are required by the head vampire, a male Dracula-style figure with a red lined cloak. He is the leader of the vampire commune which, through lack of blood, is declining. The two young women attempt to escape but, as in a nightmare, every path they take from the castle leads them back again. The sense of doom, theirs and the vampirism is powerfully expressed, for ultimately, as Rollin conveys, the image of the vampire is the image of death.

The films of Rollin's female vampire trilogy work together as a kind of rolling text. If the unconscious is structured like a language as Lacan suggests, then the films of Jean Rollin are its cinematic articulation. Apart from the influences of the Surrealists, the work of fantasy writer Gaston Leroux has made an impact on Rollin; he even wrote an extended essay on Leroux, famous for his *Phantom Of The Opera*. In terms of visual style the paintings of Max Ernst have been cited. It's interesting to note that Ernst's own short film **A Collage Of Nightmares**, which he made for Hans Richter's surrealist compilation piece **Dreams That Money Can Buy** (1944–46) and is based on his series of five books within a book *La Semaine De La Bonté*, is very close in mood and pace to Rollin's work. On the film front, Rollin shared the Surrealist's appreciation of the films of early French director Louis Feuillade, whose crime series **Fantômas** (1913–14) in which the hero is a master criminal skilled in the art of disguise, and series called **Les Vampires** (1915), are obviously influential. Roy Armes, writing about **Les Vampires**, could be describing a Rollin film: "Made to rival the imported American serials, this series reflects the chaotic wartime state of French production in its improvised stories refusing all logic, its bewildering changes of casting... its economic use of real locations and dazzling moments of total incongruity."[19]

Although it would be unfair to compare Hammer's vampire trilogy with that of Jean Rollin's – because one is the product of a commercially-driven national studio system and the other the creation of an independently financed *auteur* – there are conclusions that can be drawn about the nature of their respective representations. If there is any author behind the Hammer films it is J Sheridan Le Fanu himself, upon whose book the films are based. Each of the Hammer films has a different director but in all three cases Tudor Gates was the screenwriter and the small studio itself guarantees a specific house style. While for Hammer plot and character are crucial, for Rollin the narrative continuity is secondary and the characters are the visual mark of the imagination. In the final analysis therefore, the *mise-en-scène* of Rollin's films is the expression of his personal mindset. The female vampires are the figures of his fantasy; they are constructed out of his desire for them. In the Hammer films the vampires are separate from their creator (by a different medium and by over a century). The collaborative aspect of the studio production further distances the character from a single mind and provides them with a modicum of autonomy. In spite of the odds, the female vampires in **The Vampire Lovers** do desire each other, in a way that Rollin's vampires can never do. This is why, for all the beauty and bizarreness of Rollin's films, his female vampires can never be inspirational to a female audience precisely because they are *his*. He is the master of their universe and they exist vis-à-vis him as subjects to their god; a relationship that is patriarchal and controlling.

VAMPIRES IN L.A.

In the clutch of low budget vampire films that were made in North America in the '70s, only Stephanie Rothman's **The Velvet Vampire** (1971) displays any real interest in the female of the species[20]. Rothman was the first woman ever to direct a vampire picture. She was first hired by Roger Corman at American International to complete a project started by Jack Hill, a film called **Blood Bath** (1966). Hill and Rothman share the directorial credit for both the film and the TV version released the same year, **Track Of The Vampire**.

Discussing her own project **The Velvet Vampire**, Stephanie Rothman observed: "I wanted to make a vampire film that dealt explicitly with the sexuality implicit in the vampire legend."[21] Her film is both knowing and comic – her characters visit an exhibition at The Stoker Gallery, and her female vampire who has a liking for velvet is named Diana Le Fanu. The story features the classic heterosexual couple in peril, Susan and Lee, and the action revolves around a love triangle. The three central characters meet in the Mojave desert, Diana appearing out of nowhere driving a yellow dune buggy and inviting Susan and Lee (a reference to Christopher Lee perhaps) to her desert home. Rothman uses the iconography of classic horror, but the characters behave like regular young people in the '70s. Diana seduces Lee and Susan gets interested watching. As the two women begin to bond around their shared interest in voyeurism, the man starts to sulk and wants to go home. The anticipated seduction of Susan by Diana is interrupted when Lee falls out of Diana's cupboard. The film ends with Susan being pursued by Diana in spectacular style around Los Angeles, and Rothman's visuals capture the psychedelic flavour of the time and place. Rothman's film is ahead of its time, anticipating the impending women's movement and portraying the vampire as a liberated young woman. It is interesting that **The Velvet Vampire**, the only film in this discussion to have been directed by a woman, is the most politicised. In fact Stephanie Rothman has shown, in her reworking of the Women In Prison genre **Terminal Island** (1974), that she is adept at (skilfully and comically) turning the sexist value system of the exploitation movie on its head.

Although none of the films above discussed have presented a cohesive vampire sisterhood, they have illustrated the potential of the female vampire. Powerful, sexually active and fearless, the representations provide plenty of scope and suggest strong possibilities for the vampire girl gang. We await with interest the realisation of this great potential.

NOTES

1. Pirie, David, *The Vampire Cinema*. Quarto Publishing: London, 1977.
2. In Sontag, Susan, *Styles Of Radical Will*. Dell Publishing Co Inc: New York, 1966.
3. In **L'Age D'Or**, Bunuel depicts de Sade leaving Château Selliny in the image of Christ.
4. Op cit. Susan Sontag, p50.
5. Ibid.
6. Op Cit. Susan Sontag.
7. For the complete story of Elisabeth Bathory, see *The Bloody Countess* by Valentine Penrose (Creation Books 1996).
8. In Gledhill, Christine (ed), *Home Is Where The Heart Is: Studies In Melodrama And The Woman's Film*. BFI: London, 1987, p167.
9. Powell and Pressburger were often criticised for the visual and emotional excess of their films by the more staid ranks of British cinema. Powell's career was virtually ruined by the release of his controversial **Peeping Tom** (1959).
10. Op Cit. David Pirie, p57.
11. In Black, Andy (ed), *Necronomicon, Book One*. Creation Books: London, 1996. "Daughters Of Darkness: A Lesbian Vampire Art Film" by Carol Jenks.

12. The idea of a wild zone, a conceptual and emotional space closed off to the men, is based on an idea elaborated by Linda Williams in her essay "A Jury Of Their Peers".

13. See the interview with Peter Blumenstock in *Video Watchdog: The Perfectionists Guide To Fantastic Video*, #31.

14. The phrase is coined in *The Lavender Screen* by Boze Hadleigh.

15. In *Video Watchdog*. Op cit. p45.

16. In *Necronomicon*. Op cit. "Fascination: Jean Rollin: Cinematic Poet" by Daniel Bird, p69.

17. In *Video Watchdog*. Op cit. p48.

18. Ibid. p49.

19. Lyon, Christopher (ed), *The International Dictionary Of Films And Filmmakers: Directors*. Macmillan Publishers Ltd: London, 1984, p178.

20. Although in Robert Kelljan's L.A.-based **Count Yorga, Vampire** (1970) and its sequel **The Return Of Count Yorga** (1971) there is a fair amount of screen time devoted to the female vampire slaves of the eponymous Count, the girls themselves are slow and haggard, more like zombies than sensual predators.

21. "Stephanie Rothman: R-Rated Feminist" by Dannis Peary in Karyn, K and Peary, Gerard (eds), *Women And Cinema: A Critical Anthology*. E P Dutton, 1977.

INDEX OF FILMS

Page number in bold indicates an illustration

Creation Books International: http://www.pussycat.demon.co.uk
UK office/mail order sales:
83, Clerkenwell Road, London EC1R 5AR
Tel: 0171-430-9878 Fax: 0171-242-5527 E-mail: creation@pussycat.demon.co.uk
US office/mail order sales:
PO Box 13512, Berkeley, CA 94712 Tel: 510-540-7937
Creation products should be available in all proper bookstores; please ask your local retailer to order from:
UK & Europe: Turnaround Distribution, Unit 3 Olympia Trading Estate,
Coburg Road, Wood Green, London N22 6TZ Tel: 0181-829-3000 Fax: 0181-881-5088
Benelux: Fringecore, Meibloemstraat 30, 2600 Berchem, Belgium
Tel: 03-239-6770 Fax: 03-281-3389 E-mail: dee@fringecore.com
Italy: Apeiron Editoria & Distribuzione, Piazza Orazio Moroni 4, 00060
Sant'Oresta (Roma) Tel: 0761-579670 Fax: 0761-579737
USA: Subterranean Company, Box 160, 265 South 5th Street, Monroe, OR 97456.
Tel: 541-847-5274 Fax: 541-847-6018
US Non-Book Trade: Last Gasp, 777 Florida Street, San Francisco, CA
94110-0682. Tel: 415-824-6636 Fax: 415-824-1836
Canada: Marginal, Unit 102, 277 George Street, N. Peterborough, Ontario
K9J 3G9. Tel/Fax: 705-745-2326
Australia & NZ: Peribo Pty Ltd, 58 Beaumont Road, Mount Kuring-gai, NSW
2080. Tel: 02-457-0011 Fax: 02-457-0022
Japan: Tuttle-Shokai, 21-13 Seki 1-Chome, Tama-ku, Kawasaki, Kanagawa 214
Tel: 44-833-1924 Fax: 44-833-7559